Farmland, Food and the Future

The Soil Conservation Society of America, founded in 1945, is a nonprofit scientific and educational association dedicated to advancing the science and art of good land use. Its 15,000 members worldwide include researchers, administrators, educators, planners, technicians, legislators, farmers and ranchers, and others with a profound interest in the wise use of land and related natural resources. Most academic disciplines concerned with the management of land and related natural resources are represented.

This book was prepared in cooperation with a seven-member project advisory committee. The members of that committee included Pierre Crosson, Resources for the Future, Inc.; R. I. Dideriksen, Soil Conservation Service; Robert G. Healy, The Conservation Foundation; Walter E. Jeske, Soil Conservation Service; Charles E. Little, American Land Forum; Dallas Miner, Office of Coastal Zone Management; and R. Neil Sampson, National Association of Conservation Districts.

Contributors

NORMAN A. BERG, Administrator
Soil Conservation Service, Washington, D.C.

DAVID L. BROWN, Sociologist
Economics, Statistics, and Cooperatives Service, Washington, D.C.

MARTIN CHORICH, Staff Member
External Relations, Office of Coastal Zone Management, Washington, D.C.

MARION CLAWSON, Consultant in Residence
Resources for the Future, Inc., Washington, D.C.

RICHARD C. COLLINS, Chairman
Division of Urban and Environmental Planning, School of Architecture, University of Virginia, Charlottesville

ROBERT E. COUGHLIN, Vice President
Regional Science Research Institute, Philadelphia, Pennsylvania

PIERRE CROSSON, Senior Fellow
Resources for the Future, Inc., Washington, D.C.

R. I. DIDERIKSEN, Director
Inventory and Monitoring Division, Soil Conservation Service, Washington, D.C.

J. DIXON ESSEKS, Associate Professor
Department of Political Science, Northern Illinois University, DeKalb

W. WENDELL FLETCHER, Vice President
American Land Forum, Washington, D.C.

ROBERT G. HEALY, Senior Associate
The Conservation Foundation, Washington, D.C.

A. R. HIDLEBAUGH, Assistant Director
Inventory and Monitoring Division, Soil Conservation Service, Washington, D.C.

CHARLES E. LITTLE, President
American Land Forum, Washington, D.C.

HECTOR MACPHERSON, Farmer
Albany, Oregon

DALLAS MINER, Chief
External Relations, Office of Coastal Zone Management, Washington, D.C.

R. NEIL SAMPSON, Executive Vice President
National Association of Conservation Districts, Washington, D.C.

K. O. SCHMUDE, Soil Scientist
Inventory and Monitoring Division, Soil Conservation Service, Washington, D.C.

JOHN F. TIMMONS, Charles F. Curtiss Distinguished Professor
Department of Economics, Iowa State University, Ames.

WILLIAM TONER, University Professor of Environmental Planning
College of Environmental and Applied Sciences, Governors State University, Park Forest South, Illinois

Contents

Preface

This book culminates what the Soil Conservation Society of America referred to as its agricultural land retention book project. The project began unofficially in December 1977 with the decision to assemble a book on the agricultural land retention question, foregoing in the process SCSA's usual practice of holding a conference as a means of generating material for publication. The project achieved more formal status several months later with the formation of a seven-member project advisory committee. That committee outlined the book in April 1978 during a day-long meeting in Washington, D.C.

In pulling together information on the agricultural land retention question, this book attempts to deal with three general questions: (1) What are the important facts and trends involved? (2) What are the issues and how important are they? (3) What are people doing about these issues?

Specifically, the book looks at why farmland is being converted to nonfarm uses, how the conversion process works, what the magnitude of the conversions are, and whether or not the loss of farmland constitutes a threat to the nation's ability to meet domestic and world needs for food and fiber. It hopefully summarizes what information is available and indicates what information is needed if people are to cope intelligently with the issues.

The book does not assume an advocacy role, either for or against the protection of farmland. Recognizing that the agricultural land retention question encompasses divergent points of view, it represents an information base from which readers can draw their own conclusions about the importance and imperativeness of farmland preservation.

Contributors to this book come from varied backgrounds. Some are research oriented, devoting their professional efforts to rigorous analyses of issues. Others are interest oriented, shakers and movers, who try to make things happen legislatively and otherwise. All are leaders in the national dialogue about the importance of farmland. Obviously, SCSA is indebted to them for their participation in the project.

Thanks are also due the members of the project advisory committee, without whose assistance this book probably would not have become a reality. They are Pierre Crosson, Resources for the Future, Inc.; R. I. Dideriksen, Soil Conservation Service; Robert G. Healy, The Conservation Foundation; Walter E. Jeske, Soil Conservation Service; Charles E. Little, American Land Forum; Dallas Miner, Office of Coastal Zone Management; and R. Neil Sampson, National Association of Conservation Districts.

Finally, I must thank SCSA's assistant editor, James Sanders, and our composition specialist, Betty Taylor, who assumed much of the responsibility and burden for guiding the book through the production process.

In spite of whatever shortcomings exist in the book, and there no doubt are many, I hope it will be viewed as a worthwhile contribution to the discussion about the importance of the nation's agricultural land resources and thereby represent a small step forward in SCSA's effort to advance the science and art of good land use.

Max Schnepf
Soil Conservation Society of America

October 1979

1

Agricultural Land Retention and Conversion Issues: An Introduction

John F. Timmons

For almost fifty years—from the 1920s through the 1960s—the United States experienced surpluses of agricultural products, with exception of the World War II period. During this nearly half century, public opinion and policy focused upon reducing these surpluses and the cropland that produced them. This focus spawned numerous programs to reduce planted crop acres in an effort to curb crop production. In this situation, the conversion of cropland to other uses, including irreversible uses, was not inconsistent with the national mood. Such conversions were readily tolerated and frequently accelerated by public actions.

During the early 1970s, however, an abrupt change occurred. A diverse and complex combination of domestic and international developments coalesced to increase substantially the demand for agricultural products. These developments, in turn, hampered agriculture's ability to respond to the new demands.

In the wake of this change, confusion and uncertainty has risen concerning the conversion of agricultural land to other uses, particularly irreversible uses. Citizens and public officials are finding it difficult to shift their thoughts and actions from crop surpluses in earlier eras to increased demands for agricultural products in the current era. Information and understanding are sorely needed by citizens and public officials in recognizing the need for change and in formulating future land policy concerning cropland.

This book is dedicated to providing a better understanding and appreciation of agricultural land retention and conversion through presentation of facts, ideas, and viewpoints by a variety of informed authors with varied backgrounds and orientations.

Transition from Surpluses to Possible Shortages

Current concern about agricultural land retention and conversion invites examination of factors responsible for the recent shift from chronic surpluses to increased demands for agricultural products. Two sets of factors are involved. One set is associated with increased demand. The other set is associated with limiting agriculture's capacity for responding to these increased demands. What direction and magnitude these factors take certainly will determine the future need and nature of actions for land retention.

Since the early 1970s, six important factors have been associated with increased demands for agricultural products. First, increased per capita income in developed and developing countries has altered and increased the effective demand for food and other agricultural products. Contrary to Malthusian reasoning, recent increases in per capita income have exerted greater influence on demand than has population growth.

Second, demand for food and feed grains within Communist countries has increased. These demands have penetrated the Iron and Bamboo Curtains and have extended into the United States and other nations with the abilities to produce and export these products.

Third, member countries of the Organization of Petroleum Exporting Countries (OPEC) have greatly expanded their effective demand for agricultural products, both for their own people and for people in other nations they are assisting with grants and loans.

Fourth, increasing population within the United States and throughout the world remains a positive factor in the demand for agricultural products.

Fifth, the United States is experiencing serious balance-of-payment problems resulting from imports of petroleum, vehicles, electronics, textiles, leather goods, and other products previously produced domestically. Agricultural exports increasingly are being relied upon to reduce the imbalance of payments, thereby strengthening the domestic economy and reducing inflation.

Sixth, recent imbalances in international trade have made U.S. agricultural products more attractive in price to those countries whose yen, mark, franc, and pound have increased in purchasing power relative to the dollar.

Another set of factors has adversely affected the ability of U.S. agriculture to respond freely to this increased demand for its products. First, weather conditions, particularly inadequate moisture during the middle

1970s, interferred with crop production throughout large sections of the nation.

Second, petroleum-based inputs, particularly fertilizers, pesticides, and energy, which are largely responsible for the crop yield increases in recent decades, have become increasingly scarce and expensive.

Third, environmental quality constraints, nonpoint water pollution control efforts in particular, threaten yield-increasing practices.

Fourth, interferences with agricultural production emanating from urban development have aggravated agriculture's ability to produce. The conflicts are between agricultural practices and reactions of urban people to noise, chemicals, and odors.

Fifth, there appears to be a levelling off of productivity increases per acre, due both to the above factors and possibly to inadequate research of a basic as well as an applied nature.

Sixth, this reduction in yield increases per acre necessitates bringing additional acres into cultivation to meet the increasing demand for agricultural products. These additional acres usually are less productive than existing cropland, hence, per acre output is less, particularly in terms of net value productivity. Also, additional acres converted to cropland frequently are more susceptible to water and wind erosion, which brings about adverse effects on environmental quality and on the soil's continuing productivity.

How all of these factors behave in the future is crucial in terms of the need for and extent of cropland retention (see Chapter 8).

Nature of Land Retention Problems

As mentioned, citizens and public officials find it difficult to comprehend and adjust to these demand and supply changes that characterize current and prospective agricultural production in the United States. Robert Coughlin (Chapter 3) discusses the historical inclination for urban settlements to occupy or be near good farmland. Coughlin points out that metropolitan areas occupy only 16.7 percent of the nation's land, but they have consumed 20.2 percent of the nation's best farmland.

Raymond Dideriksen and associates (Chapter 2) estimate that slightly more than 1 million acres of cropland were converted to nonfarm uses each year between 1958 and 1967. Between 1967 and 1977, however, the conversion amounted to 2.6 million acres annually.

J. Dixon Esseks (Chapter 4) identifies six types of nonurban uses of land that compete with farmland. Esseks estimates that these uses absorb about 500,000 acres of farmland a year.

The best agricultural land, according to David Brown (Chapter 6), is being converted to urban uses at twice the rate of poorer land. Brown also discusses impacts of population trends on agricultural land conversion.

The crux of the problem is how much cropland will be needed to meet future demand, domestic and foreign, for U.S. agricultural products. Prior consideration, however, concerns the nature and extent of this demand. Ancillary elements of the problem embrace what lands to retain in agriculture and what lands to convert to other uses. Means and mechanisms to retain whatever amount and kinds of land are necessary to meet future demand for agricultural products are crucial.

Words of caution must be sounded, however, lest the nation go overboard in responding to the demand and supply factors characterizing current and prospective conditions:

"Foreign demands for our agricultural products are very fickle and unreliable, depending upon such events as a drouth in Russia, the Anchoveta catch in Peru or a political change in China. Yet our agricultural production cannot readily be turned on and off in response to such changes. Such rapid changes leave in their wake waves of inflation for consumers and recession for farmers" (5).

It might be well to reconsider a statement made in 1962 at the U.S. Department of Agriculture's National Conference on Land and People, when the national attitude weighed heavily in favor of reducing crop production and cropland because of the actual and prospective crop surpluses plaguing the nation:

"Inasmuch as the science and art of predicting needs for lands well into the future are imperfect, the probabilities of uncertainty warrant the concept of a 'contingency reservoir' of cropland which does not get committed irrevocably to other uses. Of the land not presently needed for agricultural production, a to-be-determined amount, kind and location of land might be assigned to and kept within the contingency reservoir and used as uncertainties give way to certainty through changes as they unfold in population growth, technology, wealth, international affairs, and the like. Under this concept, the objective would not be just to idle land from the farm plant, but rather to take positive steps to provide for an uncertain future. Public investments in the contingency reservoir would constitute premiums paid for insuring the nation's future food and fiber needs" (4).

Considerable precision is required in monitoring and extrapolating directions and magnitudes of demand and supply factors. Because of the importance of agricultural productivity potential to our nation's welfare, prudence dictates that ample productive cropland be secured to meet all possible food and fiber needs in the future.

The contingency reservoir of protected cropland, recommended in 1962, which could increase or decrease in response to supply and demand changes affecting agricultural products, appears as viable a concept to-day as in the early 1960s.

Major Issues in Cropland Retention and Conversion

Several major cropland retention and conversion issues invite analytical attention. The concept of land use process provides a framework for considering these issues within an integrated framework.

The Land Use Process.
The process of land conversion from one use to another is not a random process. Elements within the process hypothesize existence of identifiable causal factors affecting uses of land, including land conversions from one use to another:

"Current land uses have evolved through processes involving decisions and actions in both the market place and the political arena. Land use does not just happen; rather, there is a rationale for present uses of land that requires understanding and analysis. Finally, normative elements of the land use process assume that land use goals can be articulated by society and implemented by institutions, taking into account identified causal factors" (2).

Viewed as an inherent part of the land use process, conversion from one use to another can be explained in terms of causal factors. Analysis of these causal factors is necessary in considering retention of land in a particular use because the causal factors must be modified to prevent conversion. Also, costs of retention may be estimated in terms of modifications brought about in other uses due to the effects on other uses inadvertently produced through manipulation of the causal factors.

Prime Land and Market Allocation Between Agricultural and Nonagricultural Uses.
The concept of prime land has come to be associated with agricultural use or, in a more limited sense, with crop use. Although the concept requires further explanation and more lucid definition, prime land has been defined in terms of capability classes, usually Class I or Classes I and II.

Physically speaking, particular lands may be equally adapted to several uses, agricultural or otherwise. The same land may be considered prime for two or more uses, as Marion Clawson points out (Chapter 9). But choices must be made among competing uses for particular pieces of land, and these are made in the land use process.

The usual mechanism for making this choice is the market system, which places priorities on land in the form of land prices. These prices reflect the present (discounted) value of future (estimated) income from land uses. Of course, there are imperfections within the market system, such as monopoly, imperfect knowledge, externalities, and so forth, which distort the land use allocation process. Because of these distortions, along with variations in the private and public accounting of utilities and disutilities, public agencies intervene through zoning, easement, acquisition, and other means to arbitrate choices. Robert Healy (Chapter 5) and, to a lesser extent, Coughlin (Chapter 3) deal with the land market issue in the land allocation process.

These economic and institutional dimensions thus join the physical dimension in the allocation of land among uses. Economist Philip Raup (3) wrote, "...the concept of prime agricultural land rests in the final analysis on economic criteria, not on physical characteristics of the land." Raup's observation embraces values and costs outside and inside the market, including social as well as private values of both ordinal and cardinal measurement. Therefore, the prime land concept, to be useful in cropland retention policy, must embrace analysis of other uses and the tradeoffs between retention and conversion among competing uses.

Production of Crops and Lots. The agricultural landowner increasingly experiences the option of producing crops or lots from his land. Usually the "crop" of lots is more remunerative in market terms. The landowner thus has the choice of participating in the conversion of agricultural land to urban development or keeping the land in agriculture. Frequently, relative values of the two uses favor lots over crops.

This issue extends deeply into the feelings and emotions of private ownership rights. But regardless of the private ownership issue, the incentive of owners to realize profits remains strong and is likely to bring about conversions of cropland to other uses. Or from a different perspective, the cost of cropland retention compared to conversion may well influence the landowner to sell or convert the land to other uses, albeit irreversible uses.

Cropland Conversion to Irreversible Uses. Cropland conversion can be reversible or irreversible. The concept of reversibility is determined primarily by economic and institutional factors. It would be physically possible to reconvert uses, albeit economically unwise or perhaps institutionally impossible to do so.

Major agricultural noncrop uses of land, including pasture, meadow, and forest, constitute reversible uses of land. Conversions between cropland and these other agricultural uses do not appear to be part of the cropland retention issue because land in these other uses constitutes potential cropland. It may be converted to cropland if and when justified by conversion costs relative to crop prices.

On the other hand, productive cropland converted to irreversible uses is not considered potential cropland because it is essentially eliminated from future crop use, excepting sufficiently high crop prices, which are unlikely.

Development Interferences with Agricultural Production. Retention of cropland by itself is not capable of insuring sufficient crop value productivity to meet demand increases because of developmental interferences with agricultural production. These interferences evolve from urban and industrial developments (adjacent to cropland) that are adversely affected by fertilizers, pesticides, motor noises, odors, silt movements in air and water, and other results of farm operations. William Toner (Chapter 15) discusses the nature of these interferences with agricultural production in more detail.

These adverse effects do not exist prior to urban development. But once development takes place, the new residents complain and bring actions against farmers, which discourages or seriously hampers agricultural production. As a result, efficient agricultural production becomes less efficient, a first step toward land conversion. Such interferences must be taken into account as part of the retention concept.

Intensive and Extensive Margins of Land Use. Using existing cropland more intensively through increased inputs, such as fertilizer, pesticides, water, improved seed strains, and increased plant populations, can increase crop production. Greater crop production can also be achieved by converting noncropland to cropland. A combination of both approaches is another possibility.

Between World War II and the early 1970s, increased crop production was achieved mostly through expansion on the intensive margins, that is, by using more and improved inputs. During this period, less cropland was required to produce a particular level of products. A chronic surplus of cropland resulted.

Since the early 1970s, increased crop production has come about mainly by increasing the acres of planted crops. Former cropland in acreage reserves and convertible uses has been reconverted to cropland. Land not recently in crops or perhaps never in crops has been converted to cropland also.

Pierre Crosson (Chapter 8) describes the technologies for expanding crop production on the intensive margin as land-saving technologies. These technologies require fewer acres to produce a particular amount of product.

Technologies for expanding production on the extensive margin are described by Crosson as land-using technologies. These technologies require more acres to produce a particular amount of product.

Potentials for expanding or reducing crop production on the intensive and extensive margins of use are important in considering the amounts and kinds of cropland to be retained, the amounts and kinds of cropland to be converted to other uses, and the amounts and kinds of noncropland to be converted to cropland or held as potential cropland.

Erosion Control Aspects of Cropland Retention. Available evidence points to the disproportionate conversion of level, more productive cropland, particularly in capability Classes I and II, to irreversible uses. This conversion means that additional land, as a replacement, must be added to the cropland base on the extensive margin, or remaining cropland must be used more intensively. In either event, the tendency will be to use more erosive land on the extensive margin and more erosive practices on the intensive margin.

Neil Sampson (Chapter 7) reports that erosion losses increase from less than 3 tons per acre per year on Class I land to 30 tons per acre per year on Class VIe land in row crops. It could be argued that retention of less erosive cropland would improve erosion control, prevent land deterioration, and reduce nonpoint water pollution. An alternative would involve expending funds for soil-conserving measures on the more rolling land remaining or brought into production to produce a given level of crops. Other alternatives would be to irrigate the more erosion-resistant land, or to invest in drainage on less erosive land to achieve a given level of production. These options invite further analysis to provide a factual basis for policy decisions on farmland retention as well as investment in cropland.

Export Trade Aspects of Cropland Retention. The crucial importance of agricultural exports to the nation's well-being enters the cropland retention scene. Dennis Cory and I (*1*) concluded, "Although agricultural exports help alleviate balance of payments deficits resulting from petroleum imports, expanded agricultural production appears to be accompanied by excessive soil erosion losses and water runoff, severe cropland deterioration, and environmental degradation." Our research revealed that increased crop production in the Corn Belt from a 1967-1969 base through 1985, because of estimated higher exports, would result in an estimated 29 percent increase in planted crop acres and an estimated 72 percent increase in soil erosion losses. These losses vary from 106 percent in Iowa to 40 percent in Illinois.

With recent increases in soil erosion accompanying increased exports from crop production, the United States has indirectly been exporting its soil, water, and land productivity. Of course, this situation cannot continue without impairing the cropland's ability to produce. Either large public and private investments must be made in erosion control improvements and practices or less erodable land must be retained within the cropland base if export potentials are to be satisfied.

Cropland Retention an Integral Part of Land Use Planning. Cropland retention is an integral component of land use planning and policy. Cropland retention cannot realistically be analyzed apart from other uses that compete for cropland or affect cropland management. Cropland retention policy must necessarily embrace tradeoffs with other uses. Otherwise, land uses tend to be treated as individual uses, which is unrealistic.

Norman Berg (Chapter 13) emphasizes the need to place land retention into the broader framework of land use planning. He traces federal efforts, particularly those by the U.S. Department of Agriculture (USDA), in land use planning from the 1930s to the present. He details the philosophy and efforts between 1973 and 1978 to reaffirm and extend USDA's responsibilities and interest in agricultural land retention as a part of land use planning.

Likewise, Richard Collins (Chapter 14) develops the necessity of integrating farmland retention into the broader settings of food and fiber policy and the processes of land use planning, environmental quality management, growth control, and overall development of land.

Private Ownership and Public Intervention. Practically all the nation's cropland is privately owned. This fact poses the most difficult problem in altering the land use process, including cropland retention and conversion. Landowners are motivated largely by prices offered them in the markets. This is true of factors as well as of products. The reasoning applies to land as well as to corn and other commodities. It would be unusual indeed if a landowner would sell his land at a crop use value if he were offered considerably more at a residential or industrial use value.

This attitude is understandable. Traditional rights in land evolved in a laissez faire manner during the pioneer period of natural resource exploitation in the United States. Fortified by revulsions against feudal tenures experienced in western Europe, our forefathers structured the foundations of a land tenure system that emphasizes individual freedom in the ownership, control, and use of land.

Although our land tenure system recognizes public rights in land as superior to private individual rights, individual landowners hold their rights tenaciously and guard them against public intervention. But individuals hold exclusive rights in land, not absolute rights. Society possesses the capacity to police, tax, or even take title to private land, providing constitutional guarantees of substantial public purpose, due process, and just compensation are satisfied. These rules provide the basis for public intervention as a last resort in the retention of cropland. To be acceptable and effective, however, this avenue must be accompanied by widespread understanding and support.

Another resolution of the problem consists of cooperative and voluntary participation in agricultural districts, as presently being tried in New York, through state-enabling legislation. Such an approach, to be successful, must also be accompanied by widespread understanding, support, and participation.

Cropland Retention Policy Considerations

Development of cropland retention policy begins with an analysis of policy needs. This includes formulating precise, unambiguous policy objectives and the means for achieving these objectives.

Issues outlined here and developed further in subsequent chapters must be resolved as an inherent part of developing policy objectives and means. Roles of education, research, and enforcement in pursuing objectives remain to be defined. Relative responsibilities of federal, state, and local governments require serious consideration.

Domestic and foreign experiences with land retention measures demand study as a foundation for further action.

Alternative policy means must be developed and appraised in view of retention policy objectives. Proposed policies require review and analysis in light of related existing policies and programs being carried out by local, state, and federal governments. Wendell Fletcher (Chapter 12) points out that state and local governments have taken initiatives to cope with cropland conversions. However, they have not received much federal assistance and cooperation in these initiatives. More recently, however, the federal government has taken steps regarding how federal programs and activities are inadvertently encouraging conversion of high quality cropland to other uses and assistance to state and local governments in developing and carrying out farmland protection programs. Berg (Chapter 13) reviews actions taken in 1973, 1974, and 1978 to reaffirm and extend USDA's responsibilities in agricultural land retention as an inherent part of land use planning.

Hector McPherson (Chapter 11) emphasizes inherent conflicts between landowners' interests and public interests in governmental intervention into the market allocation of land. The nature of these conflicts and their resolution are exemplified in 1973 Oregon legislation and subsequent actions.

According to Charles Little (Chapter 10), conservationists and agriculturalists have a common interest in maintaining an adequate land base for food and fiber production with efforts to retain acres in cropland and to conserve these acres through federal, state, and local actions.

Toner (Chapter 15) evaluates examples of local programs in California, Colorado, Illinois, Iowa, Maryland, Minnesota, New York, and Wisconsin that provide direction for federal and other state governments in dealing with cropland losses.

European experiences with agricultural land retention in relation to land use planning are provided for Finland, the Netherlands and Great Britain by Dallas Miner and Martin Chorich (Chapter 16). Emphasized is the fact that these countries regard agricultural land as a national resource, whereas land in the United States is considered a market commodity.

Most Americans do not relate the conversion of farmland to urban uses with the supply and price of food (Chapter 14). They still think in terms of unlimited land. Urban Americans see no connection between land use, state land use planning efforts, food prices, and availability of food for domestic or foreign consumers. While rural landowners realize the importance of land in relation to food, they may not relish infringements on their rights to sell land to the highest bidder. Collins (Chapter 14) emphasizes the need for facts and education on land retention and conversion as a foundation to policy-making.

Because of recent and prospective changes in the supply and demand for agricultural products, concern about maintenance of an ample, secure reservoir of productive cropland will likely become more widespread. This concern extends to farmers, consumers, urban as well as rural residents, national interests, and international interests. Reactions to this concern are needed in the form of information based on facts and analysis, as well as full consideration of the multifaceted nature of land retention and conversion problems and their solutions.

REFERENCES

1. Cory, Dennis C., and John F. Timmons. 1978. *Responsiveness of soil erosion losses in the Corn Belt to increased demand for agricultural products.* Journal of Soil and Water Conservation 33(5): 221.
2. Gibson, James A., and John F. Timmons. 1976. *Information needs and models for land use planning.* American Journal of Agricultural Economics 58(5): 903.
3. Raup, Philip M. 1976. *What is prime land?* Journal of Soil and Water Conservation 31(5): 180.
4. Timmons, John F. 1973. *Land and water resource policy.* Journal of Farm Economics 45(1): 100.
5. Timmons, John F. 1979. *Solving natural resource problems of food and energy.* Journal of Soil and Water Conservation 34(3): 122-123.

2

Trends in Agricultural Land Use

R. I. Dideriksen, A. R. Hidlebaugh, and K. O. Schmude

The face of America's nonfederal land is changing. Agricultural land that only a decade ago produced a variety of flourishing crops has been converted to space for living, working, and leisure. This happens because land suited to agriculture is also well suited to other uses. The result is intense competition for the best land in many places.

A comparison of the 1977 National Resource Inventories (*12*) with the 1967 Conservation Needs Inventory (*14*) shows that about 29 million acres, mostly agricultural land, shifted to urban and built-up uses or were committed to those uses between 1967 and 1977. Another 1 million acres of land changed to small water areas. Cropland declined 18 million acres, but the acreage irrigated increased 14 million during the same 10-year period. Pasture, native pasture, and rangeland increased 34 million acres, and nonfederal forest land decreased 74 million acres. Land in other uses increased 27 million acres. These figures do not include nonfederal lands in Alaska.

The number of farms declined 1.4 million between 1959 and 1974 (*1*). In this same period, average farm size increased 137 acres. Farm tenancy declined about 6 percent.

Nearly 135 million acres of land in pasture, range, forest, or other uses have potential for conversion to new cropland. However, more than 70 percent of this land has conservation problems requiring treatment before conversion could occur.

Projected trends (based on the Water Resources Council's OBERS projections) in use of nonfederal lands by the year 2000 suggest that, although agricultural land may decrease 7 million acres, cropland will increase 19 million. The new cropland will be of lower quality.

Situation: Land and Its Use

The total surface area of the United States consists of about 2.36 billion acres. Of this, 64 percent (1.5 billion acres) is nonfederal land, 32 percent (752 million acres) is federal land, and the remaining 4 percent (99 million acres) consists of water areas more than 40 acres in size and streams more than one-eighth of a mile wide (referred to as "census water"). Nearly all agricultural land is in nonfederal ownership.

The reservoir of rural, nonfederal land is abundant, but not endless. Most rural land is not suited to intensive agricultural uses. Agricultural uses include cropland, pasture and native pasture, and rangeland.

Although it varies in kind, there is more high quality land available for agriculture in the United States than in any other country. Of the total rural, non-federal land in the United States and the Caribbean area (excluding Alaska), about 414 million acres are level to nearly level, 422 million acres are gently sloping to sloping, and 599 million acres have moderately steep to very steep slopes. At least 269 million acres are

Table 1. Prime farmland in 1977, by land use and capability class.

Class and Subclass	Cropland		Native Pasture and Pasture Land	Range-land	Forest Land	Other Land	Total
	Irrigated	Nonirrigated					
			1,000 acres				
1	8,191	22,682	2,789	745	1,804	1,107	37,318
2E	6,085	71,349	16,871	5,774	17,771	4,126	121,976
2W	3,100	52,195	8,108	1,658	10,839	2,672	78,572
2S	7,086	7,422	1,563	825	1,103	471	18,470
2C	1,564	9,201	500	1,432	653	290	13,640
3E	2,381	16,032	6,032	9,614	3,975	748	38,782
3W	4,017	13,823	2,699	594	5,602	847	27,582
3S	1,340	806	387	619	202	351	3,705
3C	234	1,193	41	997	0	33	2,498
4E	59	1,300	440	962	111	41	2,913
4W	88	292	77	14	261	26	758
4S	24	79	25	14	49	0	191
4C	65	23	0	5	0	0	93
5	0	0	0	0	0	0	0
6E	0	0	0	0	0	0	0
6W	0	0	0	0	0	0	0
6S	0	0	0	0	0	0	0
6C	0	0	0	0	0	0	0
7 & 8	0	0	0	0	0	0	0
Total	34,234	196,397	39,532	23,253	42,370	10,712	346,498

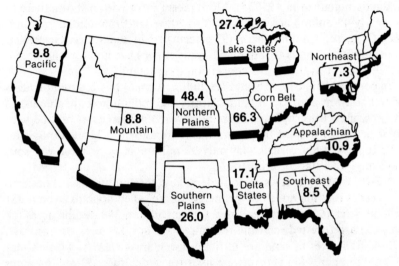

Figure 1. Prime farmland (million acres) in cropland use in 1977 (*12*).

naturally wet, and nearly 402 million acres are droughty or lack sufficient water to grow a variety of agricultural crops. Some land is not only sloping but wet. Other land is level but droughty. In many places, these conditions limit the use of land for agriculture.

A recent U.S. Department of Agriculture study (*12*) shows that there are about 346 million acres of prime farmland in the United States. Prime farmland is defined as land that has the best combination of physical and chemical characteristics for producing food, feed, forage, fiber, and oilseed crops. In general, prime farmland has an adequate and dependable water supply, a favorable temperature and growing season, acceptable acidity or alkalinity, acceptable salt and sodium content, and few or no rocks. It is permeable to water and air. Prime farmland is not excessively erodible or saturated with water for long periods of time and is protected from flooding. About 231 million of these acres are now cropped (Table 1).

The highest concentration of this best land for producing food and fiber occurs in the Corn Belt, followed closely by the Northern Plains (Figure 1). The amount of prime farmland in cropland use ranges from a high of 19 million acres in Illinois and Kansas to a low of 20,000 acres in Rhode Island.

Agriculture no longer can expand at the expense of other fragile resources. Wetlands are an example. Scientists estimate the nation's original acreage of natural wetlands on federal and nonfederal lands (excluding Alaska) at 127 million. Of these, 82 million acres of types 1 to 20 wetlands remained in 1956 (5). More recent information shows there to be nearly 42 million acres of types 3 to 20 wetlands on nonfederal lands (12). Of these, 40 million acres (97 percent) are in noncropland uses; half are forested wetlands. All these wetlands either have no cropland potential or are not available for conversion to cropland.

In contrast, the United States (excluding Alaska) has 269 million acres of wet soils on nonfederal lands. Nearly 105 million acres of these soils are now used for cropland. There remain 164 million acres of land with some degree of wetness that are available for agricultural and other uses. Yet, further study reveals that only 32 million acres of these wet soils have any potential for cropland.

Nearly 1.3 billion acres of nonfederal land (excluding Alaska) occur in landscapes that are not flood-prone. Most are called uplands. About 851 million acres (65 percent) are used for agriculture, 318 million acres (24 percent) are forested, and the remainder are in other uses. In contrast, 175 million acres of land are in flood-prone areas (12), of which about 103 million acres (59 percent) are used for agriculture, 52 million acres (30 percent) are forested, and the remainder are in other uses. Some floodplains that are frequently flooded are wetlands. As actions to restore and preserve the natural, beneficial functions of floodplains take place, agriculture's expansion onto floodplains will be limited.

Strippable coal deposits underlie 10 million acres of land in the United States. Most of the coal resources in the Midwest are beneath cropland and pasture. Eastern coal reserves are predominantly under forested land. In the West, most coal reserves underlie rangeland (3).

Data collected in 1977 by SCS indicate that surface mining of all kinds has disturbed 5.7 million acres of land. About 1.9 million of these acres have been reclaimed either by natural revegetation or through efforts by landowners. Of the 3.8 million unreclaimed acres, only 1.1 million acres are required by law to be reclaimed.

Use of Nonfederal Lands

In 1977, 36 percent of the 1.5 billion acres of nonfederal land was pasture and rangeland (541 million acres), 28 percent was cropland (413 million acres), 25 percent was forest land (370 million acres), 6 percent was urban and built-up areas (90 million acres), and 5 percent was in other uses (77 million acres). These 1.5 billion acres include small water areas less than 40 acres in size and streams less than one-eighth-mile wide (12).

Agricultural Uses of Land. Of the land available for grazing, about 133 million acres are in pasture, most of which occurs east of an irregular north-south line that cuts through the Dakotas, Nebraska, Kansas, Oklahoma, and Texas. Rangeland occurs predominantly west of that line.

Cropland occurs in every state. Amounts vary widely, ranging from 30,000 acres in Rhode Island to 30.4 million acres in Texas (Table 2).

Other Uses of Land. Nearly all other uses of land have some impact on land in agriculture. The impact of some uses is more pronounced than that of others. That is the reason for looking here at small water areas and land used for urban and built-up areas.

Small streams that dissect the land often determine the size of agricultural fields, and their acreage is generally constant over a period of time. Streams less than one-eighth-mile wide account for 4.6 million acres.

The acreage of small water bodies, such as ponds, lakes, and reservoirs, is not constant. Water bodies 2 to 40 acres in size comprised 3.5 million acres in 1977, compared to 2.5 million acres in 1967 (*14*). Water bodies smaller than 2 acres made up another 1.2 million acres. Some of this development took place before 1967. Thus, small water development used at least 1 million acres of land in 10 years (100,000 acres a year). About 10 percent of the land converted to new water areas each year comes from cropland (*9*). Many small water areas were built in support of agriculture. They occur within or adjacent to agricultural land.

There are 90 million acres of urban and built-up land (*12*), of which 65 million acres are in tracts larger than 10 acres. About 90 percent of the tracts are larger than 40 acres. These areas consist of towns and cities that, for the most part, provide the market place for agricultural products. They also use agricultural land as they expand. In the urban and built-up areas, 25 million acres are in rural transportation facilities (railroads and roads). Rural transportation provides access to the market place. Not included in the 90 million acres are another 4 million acres of very small built-up areas ranging in size from one-quarter acre to 10 acres.

Most small and very small built-up areas, as well as rural roads and railroads, are surrounded by agricultural land and are considered part of the rural setting. Some small and very small built-up areas represent scattered new-home developments, consolidated school or industrial facilities, and shops that are typical of major rural crossroads. Others, such as grain elevators, fertilizer distribution centers, and agricultural processing plants, are part of the agricultural use of land.

Changes and Trends in Land and Land Use

Cropland. There has been a continuing decline in the acreage of non-federal land used as cropland in the United States. From 1958 to 1967,

Table 2. Use of nonfederal land in 1977, by state.

State	Cropland	Pastureland	Rangeland
		1,000 acres	
Alabama	4,499	4,122	0
Arizona	1,312	11	35,091
Arkansas	7,990	5,628	248
California	10,073	1,127	17,554
Colorado	11,093	1,598	23,801
Connecticut	201	112	0
Delaware	542	23	0
Florida	3,189	5,483	3,017
Georgia	6,487	3,234	0
Hawaii	293	992	0
Idaho	6,287	1,112	6,589
Illinois	23,836	3,070	0
Indiana	13,320	2,147	0
Iowa	26,431	4,530	0
Kansas	28,806	2,701	16,276
Kentucky	5,428	5,735	0
Louisiana	5,899	2,945	326
Maine	907	249	0
Maryland	1,677	477	0
Massachusetts	282	91	0
Michigan	9,484	1,230	0
Minnesota	22,916	2,889	110
Mississippi	7,302	4,041	30
Missouri	14,573	12,823	35
Montana	15,355	2,647	38,834
Nebraska	20,699	2,899	22,001
Nevada	1,107	300	7,349
New Hampshire	273	95	0
New Jersey	777	144	0
New Mexico	2,282	382	42,096
New York	5,969	2,286	0
North Carolina	6,190	2,030	0
North Dakota	26,913	1,544	10,564
Ohio	11,762	2,615	0
Oklahoma	11,783	8,713	14,566
Oregon	5,148	1,767	10,110
Pennsylvania	5,661	1,797	0
Rhode Island	30	18	0
South Carolina	3,331	1,242	0
South Dakota	18,156	2,413	22,198
Tennessee	4,928	5,474	0
Texas	30,439	18,768	95,401
Utah	1,815	626	9,385
Vermont	597	534	0
Virginia	3,209	3,274	0
Washington	7,951	1,252	6,041
West Virginia	991	2,037	0
Wisconsin	11,741	2,738	4
Wyoming	2,970	736	26,169
Caribbean	363	863	64
Total	413,267	133,564	407,859

Forest Land	Urban and Built-up		Other	Total
	Greater than 10 Acres	Less than 10 Acres		
		1,000 acres		
19,792	2,204	129	812	31,558
1,803	1,027	26	1,429	40,699
14,072	1,467	98	711	30,214
9,855	4,880	86	10,132	53,707
3,343	1,356	55	1,554	42,800
1,416	976	51	349	3,105
360	159	12	126	1,222
12,140	4,830	43	3,283	31,985
21,566	2,354	111	1,372	35,124
1,443	156	1	890	3,775
4,230	590	19	625	19,452
3,028	3,382	110	1,775	35,201
3,534	2,183	169	1,269	22,622
1,487	1,858	61	1,308	35,675
788	1,793	43	1,309	51,716
10,648	1,602	70	821	24,304
12,595	1,314	149	4,440	27,638
16,520	588	76	1,369	19,709
2,157	1,257	78	525	6,171
2,756	1,283	66	498	4,976
15,323	3,764	321	3,168	33,290
13,806	2,381	88	5,289	47,479
14,412	1,831	79	979	28,674
10,832	2,346	85	1,338	42,032
6,341	1,123	20	1,696	66,016
444	1,288	35	958	48,324
230	335	6	1,309	10,636
3,976	350	76	299	5,069
1,965	1,192	51	537	4,666
3,426	982	69	2,067	51,304
15,445	3,311	286	3,063	30,360
16,820	2,636	166	1,440	29,282
366	1,237	18	1,938	42,580
5,865	3,964	194	1,494	25,894
4,931	1,798	79	951	42,821
10,066	1,035	78	945	29,149
14,349	3,635	344	2,317	28,103
301	249	11	61	670
10,770	1,898	84	865	18,190
330	977	12	1,698	45,784
11,638	2,166	115	872	25,193
9,240	7,063	196	3,777	164,884
1,071	702	19	2,986	16,604
3,928	363	53	180	5,655
13,233	2,289	106	1,060	23,171
12,382	1,704	95	950	30,375
9,805	931	78	482	14,324
13,248	2,152	174	3,080	33,137
1,164	535	7	1,071	32,652
428	314	30	102	2,164
369,668	89,810	4,398	81,569	1,500,135

cropland decreased 17 million acres, from 448 million acres to 431 million acres. This represents a rate of 1.7 million acres a year.

During the 10-year period from 1967 to 1977, cropland decreased 18 million acres, from 431 million acres to 413 million acres (Table 3). This represents a decrease of 1.8 million acres a year. The 100,000 acre per year difference between the reporting periods may not be significant.

Although the cropland acreage has declined, the amount of irrigated cropland has increased substantially. In 1958, 37 million acres of cropland were irrigated. By 1967, 44 million acres were irrigated. In 1977, just over 58 million acres of cropland were irrigated, an increase of 21 million acres in 19 years (12). The rate of change to irrigation accelerated to 1.4 million acres a year during the last 10-year period. Irrigation has been a key to agricultural development in the West, and supplemental irrigation is becoming more common in other areas.

Agriculture, primarily irrigation, accounts for 47 percent of all freshwater withdrawn and 81 percent of all water consumed in the nation (15). Water is also needed for energy, urban growth, recreation, and instream flows. Agriculture thus competes directly with other user demands for available water.

There are other changes in the cropland base than what is reflected in the total acreage decline and the irrigated acreage increase. Evidence indicates that the acres in cropland today are not necessarily the same acres that were cropped in previous years. The 1975 Potential Cropland Study

Table 3. National summary of trends in use of nonfederal land.

Land Use	1958*	1967†	1977‡
	1,000,000 acres		
Agricultural land:			
Cropland	448	431	413
Pastureland, native pasture, and rangeland	485	507	541
Forest land	453	444	370
Urban and built-up	51	61	90§
Small water	7	7	9‖
Other land uses	60	50	77
Total	1,504	1,500	1,500

*Source: (13).

†Unadjusted 1967 data. Adjusted data are published in (14). Bulletin 461 shows 430 million acres of cropland, 482 million acres of pasture and rangeland, and 462 million acres of forest land.

‡Source: (12).

§Four million acres of built-up areas less than 10 acres in size are not included. Total built-up area for the United States, excluding Alaska, is 94 million acres.

‖Water bodies less than 40 acres and streams less than one-eighth mile wide, which are considered part of land in census data. The 1977 data include water bodies less than 2 acres in size.

(9) showed that cropland losses to urban and water development amounted to 683,000 acres a year. Between 1957 and 1967, therefore, about 7 million acres (39 percent) of the 18-million-acre decrease in cropland were permanently lost insofar as crop production was concerned.

All the remaining acres should not be considered as a cropland reserve. A comparison of the quality of the land used as cropland during the period shows that about 4 percent of land converted to other uses was not suited for use as cropland. The 1975 study shows that 18 percent of the 1967 cropland had shifted to other uses by 1975. Some rangeland, forest land, pastureland, and land in other uses were brought into crop production, which partly offset cropland losses in the eight-year period. Thus, any interpretation of the changes and trends in cropland use must consider the fact that part of the cropland base is everchanging.

Grassland and Forest Land. More agricultural land is in grass now than 19 years ago. Of the nearly 1 billion acres of nonfederal agricultural land, more than half is in native pasture, pastureland, and rangeland. The acreage of grazing land (excluding grazed forest land) increased from 485 million acres in 1958 to 541 million acres in 1977 (Table 2). Most of this change (34 million acres) occurred in the last 10 years of the 20-year period. The change was due in part to a change in the definition of rangeland and forest land as well as adjustments in data from the 1958 and 1967 reporting periods.

Transitional ecosystems including such vegetation as brush, pinyon, juniper, and mesquite were generally categorized with rangeland in the 1977 data. Even with these differences, the overall trend is correct, and more land is now available for grazing purposes.

Although forest land is not a part of the agricultural land base, data in table 3 accounts for all nonfederal land. Nineteen years ago, nonfederal forest land comprised 453 million acres. In 1977, that acreage dropped to 370 million acres. Apparently the downward trend in the acreage of nonfederal forest land is correct, although its magnitude and rate are questionable. Part of the problem again relates to the definitions used at different reporting dates.

Urban and Built-up Land. Homes, factories, roads, and other urban and built-up uses absorb land at a rapid rate. Urban and built-up areas amounted to 51 million acres in 1958 and 61 million acres in 1967. This loss of 10 million acres of rural land during the nine-year period amounts to slightly more than a million acres a year.

Recent data show that in 1977 there were 90 million acres of urban and built-up areas larger than 10 acres (12). This suggests a gain of 29 million acres in 10 years and an average rate of 2.9 million acres per year, nearly three times the rate in the 1958-1967 period (Table 3).

The acreage of urban and built-up land in 1967 may have been underestimated. Some development outside incorporated cities and towns was excluded in the 1967 estimates. Thus, it is better to compare the rate from 1958 to 1977.

The rate of change for this 19-year period was about 2.1 million acres a year. It is reasonable to assume that the rate of change was higher in 1977 than in 1958. It was probably less than 2.9 million acres but more than 2.1 million acres a year.

Estimates are that each acre taken for development isolates at least one additional acre that is lost to farm production (2). The important farmland inventory map for Genesee County, Michigan, clearly shows this pattern of leapfrog development (8).

Another study (4) shows that 8 million acres of the 23 million acres converted from rural land to urban and water uses between 1967 and 1975 were prime farmland. This tendency for cities to expand at the expense of the best soils is not any new revelation (16).

Land Quality. The quality of land used for agriculture has changed significantly in the last 27 years. Quality of land for agricultural uses is commonly expressed in terms of land capability classes (7). Eight classes are recognized. Soils in Classes I through III are best suited to use as cropland. Soils in Class IV are marginal for cropland use, and soils in Classes V through VIII are not suited to use as cropland.

There has been a steady increase in the percentage of better land (Classes I-III) used as cropland (6). In 1950, 82 percent of the nation's cropland was Class I-III land. That percentage rose to 85 by 1977.

During the same period, the proportion of cropland not suited to that use (Classes V-VIII) declined steadily. In 1977, the proportion of cropland not suited to crop production was 4 percent, compared to 8 percent in 1950.

Neither did the acreage and proportion of marginal land (Class IV) used for cropland change significantly over the 27-year period, rising from 10 percent in 1950 to 11 percent in 1977. Alarmingly, though, the 15 percent (62 million acres) of cropland on marginal and unsuited land accounts for 24 percent (483 million tons per year) of the estimated sheet and rill erosion taking place on cropland in the United States (12).

Soils marginal or unsuited for cropland are typically less productive also and require greater amounts of energy per unit of production. For example, in Buena Vista County, Iowa, predicted corn yields for 1977 on Class I land averaged 106 bushels per acre; on Class II land, 92 bushels per acre; on Class III land, 75 bushels per acre, and on Class IV land, 35 bushels per acre (Figure 2) (10). If 100 acres of Class I land were lost from the cropland base in Buena Vista County, it would take 300 acres of Class IV land to maintain productivity, not to mention the ensuing damage to land and water quality resulting from increased soil erosion and the movement of fertilizers, herbicides, and pesticides.

Surface Mining. Surface mining on agricultural lands will continue. By 1965, surface mining had disturbed 3.2 million acres of land. The acreage increased to 4.0 million acres in 1972, then to 4.4 million in 1974, and to 5.7 million acres in 1977 (*11*).

These data suggest that the accelerating rate of land disturbance now averages about 400,000 acres per year. Clearly, more cropland, pasture, and rangeland will be temporarily removed from agricultural production. Because of the new surface mining legislation, however, all newly mined lands must be restored so that former cropland, for example, will again be available for agricultural use. Even the 1.1 million acres of old, abandoned mined lands are to be restored, but most of these will be used as pasture, rangeland, or forest land.

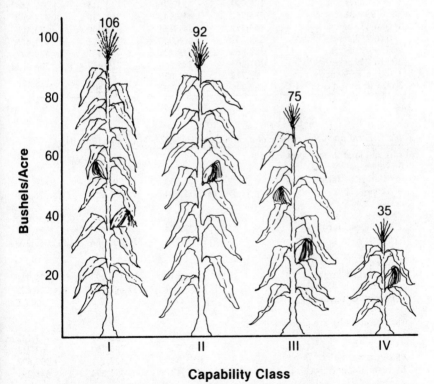

Figure 2. Predicted average annual corn yields in 1977 for Buena Vista County, Iowa, by capability class (*10*).

Number and Size of Farms. Number of farms declined sharply between 1959 and 1974, from 3.7 million to 2.3 million. Table 4 shows trends in the number of farms, land in farms, and size of farms (*1*).

Conversion of farmland to other uses is apparent in the land-in-farms acreage, which dropped more than 100 million between 1959 and 1974. Average farm size also changed significantly, from 303 acres in 1959 to 440 acres in 1974.

Table 4. Farms, land in farms, and size of farms, 1959 to 1974 (1).

	Year			
	1974	1969	1964	1959
Number of farms	2,314,013	2,730,250	3,157,857	3,710,503
Land in farms (acres)	1,017,030,357	1,062,892,501	1,110,187,000	1,123,507,574
Average farm size				
(acres)	440	389	352	303
Number of farms by size				
1 to 49 acres	507,797	635,576	820,015	1,057,544
50 to 99 acres	384,762	459,942	542,430	424,990
100 to 179 acres	443,122	541,764	632,940	772,508
180 to 259 acres	253,232	306,942	355,422	414,475
260 to 499 acres	362,866	419,421	451,301	471,547
500 to 999 acres	207,297	215,659	210,437	200,012
1,100 to 1,999 acres	92,712	91,039	84,999	} 136,427
2,000 acres and over	62,225	59,907	60,293	

Table 5. Farm operators, tenure and characteristics, 1974, 1969, and 1964 (1).

Farms and land in farms operated by:			
Full owners			
Number of farms	1,423,953	1,705,720	1,818,254
Acres	359,375,934	375,091,955	318,876,209
Part owners			
Number of farms	628,224	671,607	781,884
Acres	535,300,914	550,100,786	533,043,590
Tenants			
Number of farms	261,836	352,923	539,921
Acres	122,353,509	137,699,760	144,906,422
Percent of tenancy	11.3	12.9	17.1
Farm operators by age group			
Under 25	52,418	52,905	53,182
25 to 44	639,733	796,360	962,712
45 to 64	1,165,648	1,427,991	1,593,672
65 years and over	421,471	452,994	548,291
Average age	51.7	51.2	51.3

Significant trends also appear in the detailed breakdown by size of farm. Farms less than 500 acres in size dropped significantly in number during the 10 years between 1964 and 1974.

These Bureau of the Census data (*1*) on the reduction in acreage of land in farms parallel Soil Conservation Service data (*9*) on the conversion of rural land to other uses.

Number of Farm Owners and Workers. The number of farm owners declined at an increasing rate during the 1969 to 1974 period, compared to the 1964 to 1969 period (Table 5) (*1*). Farm tenancy declined about 6 percent, from 17.1 in 1964 to 11.3 in 1974.

The average age of farm operators gradually increased from 1964 to 1974, reaching 51.7 years in 1974. The age group of farm operators showing the greatest decline in number was the 25 to 44 year group, which dropped from 963,000 in 1964 to 640,000 in 1974.

Potential for New Cropland

There is a limit to the amount of land that can be used for agricultural purposes. Developing new, high-quality cropland is more difficult than developing land for other agricultural uses. What flexibility exists involves land of lower quality. If commodity prices, technology, water availability, energy constraints, and environmental concerns change, so will the potential for new agricultural land.

Of the 1.5 billion acres of rural, nonfederal land in the United States, 28 percent (413 million acres) is already used for cropland (Figure 3). Of the remaining rural land, 56 percent (548 million acres) has no potential for conversion to cropland at this time because of severe soil limitations or because it is committed to other relatively permanent uses. Thirty percent (299 million acres) is considered unlikely to be converted to cropland at this time because of social, economic, or resource-related problems. Examples of areas having conversion problems are densely wooded areas, highly erodible areas, small tracts, isolated tracts, or land committed to other uses.

This leaves 14 percent (135 million acres) of the nation's rural land that has a high to medium potential for conversion to cropland (*12*). The so-called abundant reservoir of rural land suitable and available for cropland is small.

Projected Agricultural Uses of Nonfederal Land

Projected uses of nonfederal land from 1977 to 2000 show a gradual decline in the acreage of agricultural land, despite an increase of 19 million acres used for cropland between 1977 and 1990 (Table 6). Acres in pasture remain about the same to the year 2000. Rangeland and forest land acreages are expected to drop.

The increase in cropland from 413 million acres in 1977 to 432 million acres in 1990 represents an average change of about 750,000 acres per year. As more land is used for nonagricultural purposes, the increase in cropland acreage will ultimately level off and the potential for new cropland will decline.

About 3 million acres per year of rural land, much of it suited to agriculture, is being converted to urban and built-up (2.9 million acres) and water (100,000 acres) uses. Assuming this rate of conversion con-

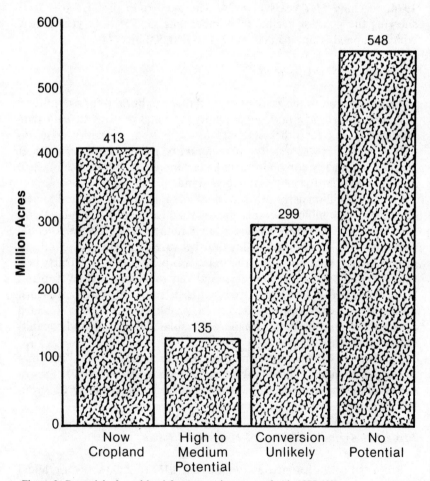

Figure 3. Potential of rural land for conversion to cropland, 1977 (*12*).

tinues from 1977 to 2000, agriculture and other rural uses of land will lose 69 million acres.

The picture is more vivid if the cropland converted to water and urban and built-up areas is examined. Currently, about 10 percent of the land converted to small water areas and 30 percent of land converted to urban and built-up areas each year is cropland (9). If these trends continue, 20 million additional acres of cropland, 60 percent of which is high quality land (Classes I-III), could be converted to water and built-up uses by the year 2000.

Table 6. Projected agricultural and silvicultural land. *

Land Use	Year		
	1977	1990	2000
	——— 1,000,000 acres ———		
Cropland	413	432	432
Pasture land	133	132	131
Rangeland	408	398	394
Forest land	370	363	360
Total	1,324	1,325	1,317

*Cropland projections are based on the Water Resources Council's OBERS projections, adjusted to final estimates of the 1977 SCS National Resource Inventories (12). Pasture land, rangeland, and forest land projections are based on estimates made by the U.S. Forest Service on federal land in collaboration with the Soil Conservation Service on nonfederal land and adjusted to nonfederal land using final estimates of the SCS 1977 National Resource Inventories (12).

Projected energy problems, a decline in population growth, and land use controls could modify these calculations. Therefore, they should not be considered predictions.

There are now 135 million acres of rural land with a high or medium potential for conversion to cropland. If current trends continue, urban and built-up uses will reduce this cropland reserve 15 percent by the year 2000. Equally important is the tendency for a greater proportion of high-quality land to be converted. The 1950-1977 trend toward cropping better lands could be reversed unless care is taken to select land for nonagricultural uses from the 848 million acres having cropland conversion problems.

Land well suited to agriculture or readily available for such purposes is limited. When evaluated over an extended period of time (1977-2000), it becomes evident that the 19-million-acre increase in cropland will consist of more marginal or near marginal land. Some low-yielding, erodible, wet, stony, shallow, and droughty soils may need to be farmed. Trying to achieve greater agricultural production in this setting could cause environmental problems, including water pollution, higher energy and water use, and soil degradation as a result of erosion. It could also mean the loss of fragile resources and other amenities important to our society.

REFERENCES

1. Bureau of the Census. 1978. *1974 census of agriculture.* Volume II: Statistics by subject, Parts 2 and 3. U.S. Department of Commerce, Washington, D.C.
2. Dideriksen, Raymond I., and R. Neil Sampson. 1976. *Important farmlands: A national view.* Journal of Soil and Water Conservation 31: 195-197.
3. Office of Surface Mining. 1978. *Permanent regulatory program implementng Section 501(b) of the Surface Mining Control and Reclamation Act of 1977.* Draft environmental impact statement. U.S. Department of the Interior, Washington, D.C.
4. Schmude, Keith O. 1977. *A perspective on prime farmland.* Journal of Soil and Water Conservation 32: 240-242.
5. Shaw, S. P., and C. G. Fredine. 1956. *Wetlands of the United States.* Circular 39. Fish and Wildlife Service, Washington, D.C.
6. Soil Conservation Service. U.S. Department of the Interior. 1953. *Land facts.* Technical Paper 123. U.S. Department of Agriculture, Washignton, D.C.
7. Soil Conservation Service. 1961. *Land capability classification.* Agricultural Handbook 210. U.S. Department of Agriculture, Washington, D.C.
8. Soil Conservation Service. 1977. *Important farmland inventory map, Genesee County, Michigan.* U.S. Department of Agriculture, Washington, D.C.
9. Soil Conservation Service. 1977. *Potential cropland study, 1975.* Statistical Bulletin 578. U.S. Department of Agriculture, Washington, D.C.
10. Soil Conservation Service. 1977. *Soil survey of Buena Vista County, Iowa.* U.S. Department of Agriculture, Washington, D.C.
11. Soil Conservation Service. 1979. *Basic statistics: Status of land disturbed by surface mining in the United States, as of July 1, 1977.* U.S. Department of Agriculture, Washington, D.C.
12. Soil Conservation Service. 1979. *SCS national resource inventories, 1977, final estimates.* U.S. Department of Agriculture, Washington, D.C.
13. U.S. Department of Agriculture. 1965. *Soil and water conservation needs—a national inventory, 1958.* Miscellaneous Publication 971. Washington, D.C.
14. U.S. Department of Agriculture. 1971. *Basic statistics: National inventory of soil and water conservation needs, 1967.* Statistical Bulletin 461. Washington, D.C.
15. U.S. Water Resources Council. 1978. *The nation's water resources, 1957-2000.* The second national water assessment, volume 1: Summary. Washington, D.C.
16. Vining, Daniel R., Jr., Thomas Plaut, and Kenneth Bieri. 1977. *Urban encroachment on prime agricultural land in the United States.* International Regional Science Review 2(2): 143-156.

3

Agricultural Land Conversion in the Urban Fringe

Robert E. Coughlin[1]

Metropolitan areas in the United States (as defined in 1975) contain 20.2 percent of the nation's prime agricultural land (Classes I and II) and 76 percent of its population. Together with the ring of counties adjacent to them, these areas account for 51.7 percent of prime land (*29*).

In recent decades, population growth has been concentrated within metropolitan counties, and during the 1970s, those counties just beyond the metropolitan boundaries have experienced rapid growth rates. This expansion of urban areas and the impact of spreading urban populations threaten a large proportion of the nation's stock of farmland.

In general, there is an historical bias for urban settlements to be near prime farmland. While metropolitan areas contain only 16.7 percent of the nation's land, they contain 20.2 percent of the nation's prime agricultural land (Table 1). A similar bias exists for metropolitan areas and adjacent counties taken together, which collectively contain 51.7 percent of the prime land but only 43.2 percent of all land. At the broad regional scale, therefore, the nation's prime agricultural land appears to be under somewhat greater pressure from urbanization than the nation's total stock of land.

The annual loss of prime agricultural land due to urbanization is beween 390,000 acres (*23*) and 760,000 acres (*27*). These losses, projected to the year 2000, suggest a further loss of between 2.8 percent and 5.5 percent of the nation's stock of prime land, as measured in 1975. To replace that loss, other prime land with "high or medium potential for conversion to cropland" (*27*) could be brought into production. However, this reserve of land is relatively limited in supply (about 46 million acres). Between 21.2 and 41.3 percent of all prime land in reserve would be need-

[1]This chapter is based largely on research conducted by the Regional Science Research Institute. My colleagues, especially David Berry and Thomas Plaut, provided many helpful suggestions.

ed to replace the anticipated loss of prime farmland due to urbanization between now and the turn of the century. If the losses due to urbanization are projected over a longer time period, one more appropriate to the evaluation of the loss of a resource that is vital to life and finite in supply, and if the remaining prime land is compared with increasing world population, whose demands for food are also rising because of increasing incomes, it becomes obvious that the loss of prime land due to urbanization presents a serious problem (23).

Forces Affecting the Loss of Farmland in the Urban Fringe

Forces affecting the loss of farmland in the urban fringe can be described under the traditional economic categories of supply and demand.

Demand for Land in Suburban and Rural Areas. Demand for agricultural land by urban uses is, in part, but only in part, a result of regional population growth and, particularly, new family formation. As new households are established, additional living space must be found. Since the industrial revolution, the overwhelming migration pattern has been from countryside to cities. But in the past few decades the reverse flow has grown, at first to nearby suburbs, later to "exurbs," and in recent years to small towns and rural areas beyond (2, 28).

Demand for residential land in rural areas has grown because of the enduring image of country life as having greater dignity and respectability, more permanence, and as being more healthful and less stressful than city life. The single house, with ample private living space and a lack of

Table 1. Concentration of prime farmland in metropolitan areas and adjacent counties (28).

Census Region	Percent of U.S. Prime Land in Region	In SMSAs		In SMSAs and Adjacent Counties	
		Percent of Region's Land	Percent of Region's Prime Land	Percent of Region's Land	Percent of Region's Prime Land
New England	1.4	22.6	24.3	41.5	40.7
Middle Atlantic	3.6	41.0	49.8	82.6	90.1
South Atlantic	10.0	24.8	20.9	51.7	61.7
East North Central	20.2	27.2	32.3	64.8	74.9
West North Central	33.5	7.2	6.2	23.8	24.5
East South Central	7.6	18.4	22.9	52.2	51.7
West South Central	16.2	17.5	23.8	55.9	65.8
Mountain	4.0	7.5	9.7	27.1	31.9
Pacific	3.5	30.5	46.8	51.3	72.3
Nation	100.0	16.7	20.2	43.2	51.7

community congestion, persists as the American ideal.

At the same time, disenchantment with city life has deepened. Rising crime rates and racial antagonisms in the 1960s, increasing tax rates and deteriorating public services, aging urban infrastructure, and more recently a heightened perception of environmental pollution have all led to the belief that a better way of life is possible in the suburbs and rural areas beyond. Inadequacies in urban school systems particularly have induced middle class families to look beyond the cities.

Despite preferences for the countryside over the city, migration to rural areas will occur only if people can make a living there. Some urban people truly move back to the land and become part of the rural economic system, but most commute to jobs in small cities and suburbs. Likewise, many established, bona fide farmers take up commuting to part- or full-time jobs in urban areas.

Living outside cities has been made possible by technological innovations that have changed the locational attributes of rural areas: by the automobile, which, beginning in the 1920s, has made almost all land accessible; by the construction of high-speed, limited-access highways in the 1950s and 1960s, which have brought vast areas within easy driving time of virtually every metropolitan center; by the development of package sewage plants and construction in the 1960s of community sewage systems (prompted by the objective of improving water quality); and by the availability of electricity, telephone, radio, and television, which have reduced the hardships and isolation of living in rural locations.

Increasing incomes have also fueled demand for residential sites in rural areas. Disposable personal income per capita, in constant (1972) dollars, rose from $2,696 in 1960 to $4,140 in 1976. The additional income has made it possible for both renters and homeowners in maturing urban areas to seek residences elsewhere. It has also led to a remarkable increase in the ownership of second homes and to the mushrooming of a second-home industry, which develops and merchandises large-scale communities in rural areas.

The impact of increased income on rural residential development has been multiplied by federal housing policies, which provide low-interest loans, and by tax policies, which allow mortgage interest payments to be treated as deductible expenses.

Supply of Land in Suburban and Rural Areas. Although the amount of land in the United States is fixed, the supply of land offered for sale in the urban fringe is not. First of all, the geographic definition of the urban fringe is continually changing, as new highways make more land accessible to existing urban concentrations and as residences, industries, and businesses locate in suburban and exurban areas, forming the nuclei of new urban concentrations. Second, the amount of land that rural landowners offer for sale at any time depends upon a set of economic, urban, and personal factors.

Economic factors generally receive the most attention. If farms are not economically viable, they will eventually be put up for sale. Land that is expensive to farm, because of low soil productivity or other reasons, tends to go out of agricultural production. It is replaced by more productive land hundreds or even thousands of miles away.

This process has been going on for over 100 years. For example, much of the loss of farmland in the Philadelphia region over the past generation has been attributed to poor quality soils rather than to the direct pressures of urbanization (4).

On the urban fringe, however, a number of additional factors typically force a farmer's costs up, reduce his profitability, and contribute to the probability that he will give up farming and sell.

Rising land prices affect farming in several ways. First, property tax assessments rise as land values increase. As urban development proceeds, local government must bear the higher costs of urban-level services. The resulting increases in property taxes hit farmers particularly hard because, per unit of output, the farmer typically requires a great deal of land. Second, existing farmers often cannot afford to add to their holdings, while prospective farmers cannot afford to purchase the necessary minimum amount of land. Third, rising land prices strengthen the speculative motive that is present in all landowners, farmers not excluded. As a farmer comes to believe that he can easily sell his land for a high price, he may cutback on maintenance and not make new investments in farm buildings, drainage structures, or other improvements to his land resource (9).

Farmers may experience difficulties in purchasing specialized equipment or replacement parts, supplies, and services as farming in the area declines and local suppliers reduce their stock or even cease operations. Such inconveniences and costs have been alluded to by a number of writers, but have not been quantified (10).

Interference with farming practices by neighbors who do not understand or are unsympathetic with the operating needs of the farmers can also increase the costs of farming and thereby reduce farming's profitability. Such "spillovers" from urban development may be either physical or legal and political. Physical effects result from the unwitting or willful acts of individuals: trampling or pilfering of crops, harrying of farm animals by suburban dogs, traffic interference with slow-moving farm equipment on roads, depletion of groundwater supplies by wells, and damage to crops by industrial pollution (19).

Legal or political effects tend to occur as the local political power shifts from people rooted in the rural economy and way of life to those oriented to the urban economy. As this shift occurs, local ordinances may be passed restricting normal farming practices that produce noise, odor, dust, or other pollution in the water or air. Legal restrictions, emanating primarily from urban-oriented state legislatures, may be imposed on rural areas statewide, regardless of whether a rural locality experiences urban growth.

Table 2 summarizes interviews with farmers, agricultural agents, planners, and others in five Northeastern counties under varying levels of urban pressure. The general increase of concerns with increase in popula-

Table 2. Perceptions of the importance of urban spillovers on agricultural production in five Northeastern urban fringe counties (19).

	Frederick, Md.	Cumberland, N.J.	Chester, Pa.	Howard, Md.	Hartford, Conn.
General characteristics					
Population density, 1974 (persons/square mile)	141	263	378	380	1114
Change in population density, 1960-1974 (persons/square mile)	33	49	101	236	181
Percentage of inventoried land in soil capability classes I and II	41	42	52	48	26
Percentage of land in farms, 1974	58	25	46	41	16
Percentage change in land in farms, 1959-1974	−20.7	−31.7	−23.9	−31.3	−42.5
Physical spillovers					
Vandalism	-*	-	P†	SC‡	SC
Traffic congestion	-	-	P	P	P
Water supply	-	-	-	P	-
Air pollution	-	-	-	-	P
Legal and political spillovers					
Drop in status in the community	-	-	P	P	P
Restrictive environmental regulations	P	P	SC	P	SC
Economic spillovers					
Real estate taxes	-	P	P	P	P
Land cost and availability	-	-	P	SC	SC
Availability of farm supplies	-	P	P	P	P
Summary of spillovers	1P	3P	6P, 1SC	6P, 2SC	5P, 3SC

*, not a problem.
†P, mentioned as a problem.
‡SC, strong concern.

tion density is evident. Few problems were perceived in the two most rural counties. Major complaints there were about the annoyance of statewide environmental regulations.

In the three more urbanized counties, the concerns expressed most strongly were those related to vandalism, restrictive environmental regulations, and land cost and availability. Concerning vandalism, the main culprits were seen to be children of newly arrived suburbanites who trample crops by foot and by motorcycle, who steal fruit and vegetables, whose pets disturb livestock, and who have little respect for the farmer. Statewide environmental controls (concerning the use of pesticides, disposal of manure, etc.) were mentioned most frequently, but a number of local ordinances (for example, regulating noise from nighttime operations) were also cited.

High land prices are perhaps the most serious and widespread effect of urban development. The resulting increase in property taxes was mentioned as a problem in four counties, but stronger concern was voiced about land cost and availability in the more urbanized counties. A Chester County, Pennsylvania, farmer observed that, as farming becomes more dependent on equipment whose cost is rising rapidly, the farmer must acquire more acres over which to spread these higher costs. Unless they inherit land, young farmers cannot afford to begin farming, particularly in areas where land prices have escalated. Rental of land is a short-term solution. Renting leads to insecurity for the established farmer and only provides a beginning farmer the opportunity to gain a few years experience before moving permanently to an area where land prices are compatible with agricultural productivity.

Personal factors also affect the decision to sell. Retirement or death is the direct cause of many farm sales. In situations of urban pressure, farmers near retirement age tend to be the most likely to sell, as are young farmers, who reinvest in other farms away from urban pressures and high land prices (8). Middle-aged farmers, who feel unable to start up a new farm and are not ready for retirement, tend to continue farming the longest as urban pressures mount.

Less closely related to age is a desire for a change in lifestyle, perhaps a desire for the shorter hours, and the lesser responsibilities of an urban wage earner. In the dairy farming area of southern Chester County, Pennsylvania, for example, farm wives tend to place higher values on the conveniences and increased leisure hours of urban living, while their husbands exhibit a deeper commitment to the farming way of life.[2]

Figure 1 diagrams the relationships (discussed above) among the fac-

[2]Personal communication with Daniel Rose, assistant professor of landscape architecture and regional planning, University of Pennsylvania.

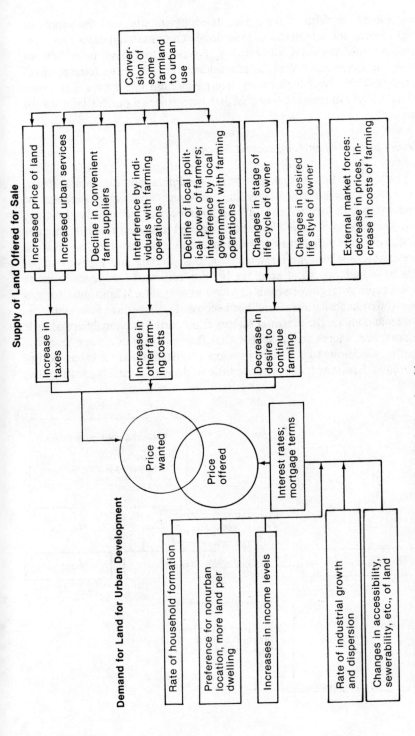

Figure 1. Urban factors that affect the market for land in the urban fringe.

tors that affect demand for urban development sites and the supply of land offered for sale in the urban fringe. The figure indicates how various economic, personal, and urban spillover factors may "push" a landowner to decide to sell his land at a price that coincides with the price offered. The relatively high prices offered by nonrural buyers may themselves be an inducement that "pulls" the owner to put his land on the market.

Actors in the Urban Fringe Land Market

The market, however, is not simply the interaction between abstract, anonymous demanders of building sites and farm-owner suppliers of land. Although farmers constitute a large portion of rural landowners, much rural land is owned by other rural residents, particularly absentee landlords, including large corporations, individual investors, and real estate syndicates. Among large corporations, mining and timber companies have had vast rural holdings for generations. More recently, large U.S. corporations have begun to invest in agricultural land, and foreign investment in agricultural land has become significant in a few locations. For such owners, the personal factors enumerated previously are of little importance, except to the extent that they increase costs and decrease profits. Decisions to sell or to develop are often based on broad corporate considerations that may have little to do with a farm's profitability.

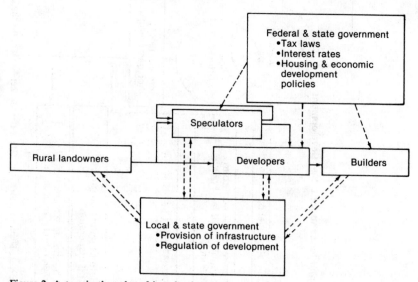

Figure 2. Actors in the urban fringe land market.

Often a relatively small number of owners, absentee or local, hold title to a large portion of undeveloped land in outlying areas. In this situation, a single decision to remain in farming or to develop can have a profound effect on the development pattern of an urban area and on the stability of the agriculture that remains (25).

The ultimate demanders of land for urban uses are builders, but speculators and developers function as intermediate landholders. Figure 2 illustrates the typical sequence of ownership from rural landowner to builders of urban structures.

Although distinct roles can be identified, one individual may play several roles. While the farmer may be the initial landowner, he may also play the speculator's role. Some developers act as builders, and both developers and builders may act as speculators.

The speculator seeks to invest his money where he can make the greatest return. He will hold or attempt to hold a particular parcel of land so long as the rate of appreciation in the land value minus the tax rate (plus any returns from farming the land) exceeds the rate of return from some alternative investment. The farmer-owner may begin disinvesting (that is, not making the necessary investment to maintain structures or to keep fields in good condition) and watching the value of his land appreciate when the possibility of urban development increases.

Professional investors may have a variety of choices open to them, but they choose a particular parcel of land because its rate of return exceeds the rate of return in other feasible investments. Of course, all speculators work in the realm of uncertainty, and their speculation entails risks. There is no guarantee that a buyer can be found for the land at the price they would like to sell it for. Nor is there a guarantee that the land will even be developed.

Although his decisions are based on maximizing investment return, with little regard for the long-run use of land resources, the speculator in some situations provides a useful social role by assembling land parcels into large, easily developed tracts and by filling the vacuum between the time a rural landowner is willing to sell and the time that the land is "ripe" for development. "Leap frog" development often results from speculation, however, as some speculators decide to sell to developers and others hold for higher returns.

Speculators behave differently because of their reaction to the uncertainty of development and because of their requirements for different minimum rates of return from their investment in land. Some speculators, having greater access to capital than others, can borrow money at lower interest rates. For high-income speculators, the real estate tax is not nearly the burden it is for low-income speculators because property taxes are fully deductible from a landowner's federal income tax liability.

The progression from rural owner to speculator to developer is not always direct (Figure 2). Sometimes the speculator is bypassed altogether. Often, there is a series of speculative owners.

Generally speaking, the active speculator strives to purchase as much rapidly appreciating land as he can in order to increase the volume of his returns. This implies that he would like to extend the purchasing power of his own money by spending someone else's money as well through various borrowing schemes. In other words, he seeks "leverage." This involves making as small a down payment on the land as possible and putting off as long as possible any payments on interest or principal borrowed so he can acquire more land with his initial funds. He anticipates that when he sells the land to another speculator or to a developer he will receive enough cash or notes to cover his own payments. Any unpaid notes on the original mortgage are passed on to the new speculator (20).

In his attempts to get leverage, he may obtain a mortgage from the previous landowner (a purchase money mortgage) rather than from a bank. In addition, to avoid large, immediate payments of interest or principal, he may pay a higher nominal price for the land in return for lower interest payments and a deferred payment schedule. Payments on the principal may not be made until years later. It is for this reason that recorded sale prices of land are often overstated in terms of the land's present market value.

Alternatively, the speculator may seek a sales contract or equity build-up sale. In this case, the seller retains use of the land until the buyer has paid a specified portion of the principal, for example, 25 percent. The deed is then transferred to the buyer, and the seller relinquishes use of the land. The buyer pays no interest during the equity build-up period, which may be five years, so he may pay a higher price at the beginning of the deal to obtain these terms (20).

These types of financial arrangements and sales to other speculators before mortgages are paid off can encumber the title to a particular parcel of land. In fact, the financial obligations of the various speculators and the web of liens, release clauses, subordination clauses, and exculpatory clauses can make land unusable from the developer's or builder's point of view (20). It is far too risky and imprudent to attempt to acquire land with so many complicated obligations if one is in the business of building houses, for example.

When land prices are no longer appreciating and buyers for properties are impossible to find, the speculative market may collapse. Then the financial obligations incurred by speculators can cascade into a tangle of legal conditions and possibly a series of defaulted payments that cloud the title to the land.

Land developers, the fourth group of actors, are "entrepreneur(s) en-

gaged in the activity of converting tracts of open land into improved...
subdivisions wherein the finished lots are ready for...building activities
to take place" (*18*). The developer buys undeveloped land from rural
landowners (or speculators); typically strives to change the zoning to
allow higher density development; assembles large tracts of land; installs
improvements, such as streets, sidewalks, sewers, and watermains; and
sells the land to a builder.

The developer's role in the land conversion process is a crucial one.
Once he has acquired a parcel of land, it is probable that it will eventually
be converted to urban uses (*17*).

Builders are those engaged in actually building the houses, apartments,
and commercial, industrial, and institutional facilities that constitute urban development. Builders and developers often work jointly, and a
single firm may assume both roles.

Actors in the land market operate in a financial and legal environment
set by federal, state, and local governments. The federal government,
through the Federal Reserve Bank and the Treasury Department, plays
an important role in setting the prime interest rates. State governments
control residential mortgage rates, but unless the rates are set in line with
the prime interest rate, sufficient capital may not be available for the
residential market. Through insurance of residential mortgages, the Federal Housing Administration and the Veterans Administration play direct roles in determining development patterns, as does the Federal Farm
Credit Service, which makes loans through its Production Credit Association to buyers of farmland (and at least during the early 1970s, when the
appraisal basis became market value rather than agricultural use value,
financing was provided to speculators as well as to bona fide farmers).

By funding highways, sewer and water systems, and other public facilities, both federal and state governments determine to a large extent
which areas become suitable for development. For the most part,
though, only local governments exercise direct control over subdivision
and land use.

Effects on the Land

These forces, as they are played out through the various actors and institutions, ultimately affect the land. Although conversion to urban uses
is the most irreversible and dramatic effect, other effects on agricultural
land often involve more extensive areas. A shift to different types of
farming and the premature idling of large areas may occur (Figure 3).
Depending on the demand for urban development sites and governmental policies, a long-run equilibrium may be reached in those areas that
have shifted to different types of farming, and idled areas may be left un-

disturbed while second growth matures into forest. On the other hand, succession from traditional farming to development may occur rapidly, without any period of change in type of farming and with only weeks or months between farm activity and urban construction.

A shift in type of farming involves at least two factors: a shortened planning horizon with consequent shift to farming requiring less investment, or at least shorter term investment, and a reduction in the amount of time available for farming as the farmer or members of his family take up part-time urban employment (5, 26). These two factors may explain the shift away from dairying and related activities in the Middle Atlantic region (4) and Lake States (12).

Idling of farmland after farming ceases to be economically viable, and for substantial periods before development takes place, is also generally acknowledged (15). The relationship between the amount of farmland idled and the amount built on has been analyzed in case studies of suburban counties in the Philadelphia metropolitan area and the Minneapolis-St. Paul area (Table 3). Causes of the variation from area to area have not been determined definitively, but may be due in part to differences in types of farming (10).

The ultimate stage in the cycle, and the stage that permanently destroys the farmland resource, is the conversion to urban uses. The amount of farmland lost to all urban uses per housing unit built was estimated in several farm production regions for the period 1959-1969. The results indicate a range of .25 to .63 acres for farmland and .11 to .38 acres for harvested cropland (Table 4). Two factors explain the varia-

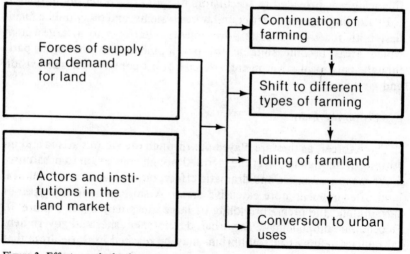

Figure 3. Effects on the land.

Table 3. The ratio between the number of acres of cropland idled due to urban pressures and the number of acres converted to urban uses.

Case Studies	Ratio
Six Suburban Counties in the Philadelphia Metropolitan Area, 1930-1970*	.50 or less
Exton Square Area, Chester Co., Philadelphia Metropolitan Area, 1965-1975†	0.97
Part of Dakota Co., Minneapolis Metropolitan Area, 1968-1975†	0.45

*Source: (*3, 4*).
†Source: (*10*).

tion: the greater the proportion of the area in farmland at the beginning of the period, the greater the loss per housing unit, and the greater the degree to which farmland is chosen over other rural land for development, the greater the loss of farmland (*24*).

Estimates of development's bias for farmland rather than for other rural land have also been made (Table 5). Although development appears strongly biased toward cropland, orchards, and nurseries in California, Massachusetts, and metropolitan counties containing no urbanized area, for most of the areas analyzed in table 5, other types of rural land are as likely or more likely to be developed. Most likely to be developed is the group "pasture and range, open idle, and farmsteads."

These results are consistent with knowledge that, for farm purposes, pasture and range are less valuable per acre than is cropland. They also conform with the observation that the shift from active farming to idle land is a stage in the development sequence that may have a long duration. There may be substance, therefore, to the popularly held understanding that developers prefer flat, open, well-drained farmland, even though development may replace crops only after an interval of unfarmed years.

Implications for Action

The concepts of supply of agricultural land placed on the market and demand for urban building sites are also helpful in discussing public programs used to retain farmland. Many types of programs have been suggested, experimented with, or instituted. They are classified as direct (controlling land use) or indirect (providing incentives) and related to the concepts of supply and demand (Table 6) (*10*).

Indirect approaches, concerned with strengthening agriculture and thus restricting the supply of farmland offered to the market, are the most widespread. The major incentive is property tax relief for farmers. Forty-four states have adopted some form of differential assessment to prevent property taxes on farms from rising in response to urban forces. Analysts agree, however, that these programs have had little effect in preventing development.

Partial relief from state income taxes is another method of reducing operating costs that may push a farm owner to put his land on the market. Programs involving reduced federal estate taxes (instituted in 1976) and reduced state inheritance taxes (presently instituted in only a few states) reduce the need of heirs to sell off part of their farms in order to meet initial, one-time taxes.

Other indirect measures provide incentives by protecting the farmer from disruptive urban forces—from front-foot assessment for utility line extensions; from local ordinances that restrict normal farming practices causing dust, noise, and other nuisances; and from the unconsidered placement in or near farming areas of state or local public facilities and institutions. New York State's Agricultural Districting Law combines several measures of this type.

Each indirect measure deals with a specific problem and thus, by itself, can deal with only one of the pressures forcing a farmer to give up farming. If combined, however, indirect measures may be able to maintain an environment hospitable to farming and capable of offsetting much of the disruption caused by urbanization nearby. This outcome is particularly likely if one of the indirect measures is an effective program of land use and facility planning that delineates extensive agricultural preserves encompassing areas of productive soil and that does not permit the construction of urban growth-inducing facilities in or near the preserves.

A location's agricultural viability has no effect on the demand for urban building sites, however. A site's potential return under urban devel-

Table 4. The loss to urbanization of farmland and cropland harvested per housing unit built and in relation to stock (24).

Farm Production Region	Per Housing Unit Built		Projected Losses, 1975-2000, as Percentage of Stock	
	Farmland	Cropland Harvested	Farmland	Cropland Harvested
Middle Atlantic	0.25*	0.11*	9.5	8.9
Appalachian	N.S.‡	0.10†	-	2.7
Southeast	0.26*	N.S.‡	3.8	-
Lake	0.63*	0.38*	4.2	4.3
Corn Belt	0.41*	0.27*	2.4	2.6
Pacific	N.S.‡	0.19*	-	10.1

Note: These figures may include some idling of farmland due to urban pressure.
*Significant at the one percent level.
†Significant at the five percent level.
‡N.S., not significant at the five percent level.

Table 5. Bias of development toward various types of rural land.

	Relative Liklihood of a Given Type of Rural Land to be Converted to Urban Uses			
	Cropland, Orchards, and Nurseries	Pasture and Range, Open Idle, and Farmsteads	Forest	All Con- verted Rural
Regional Groupings (1961-1970)*				
Seven counties in Northeast	.86	2.17	.84	1.00
Five counties in Maryland-Virginia	1.15	2.64	.50	1.00
Five counties in Piedmont	.90	2.39	.83	1.00
Four counties in Appalachian Fringe	.78	3.26	.39	1.00
Three counties in Florida Gulf	.49	1.51	.48	1.00
Eleven counties in Corn Belt	.83	2.75	.46	1.00
Six counties in Great Lakes	.96	1.63	.69	1.00
Three counties in South Central Prairie-Woodland Fringe	.49	1.31	1.12	1.00
Four counties in Texas Prairie	.92	1.14	1.06	1.00
Two counties in Colorado	1.12	.89	0	1.00
Two counties in California	3.79	1.12	.06	1.00
Groupings of SMSA Counties Based on Urban Orientation (1961-1970)*				
Containing no urbanized area	1.59	3.16	.25	1.00
Containing urbanized areas but none of Central SMSA city	.94	1.54	.72	1.00
Including parts of urbanized area and parts of Central SMSA	.61	1.22	1.24	1.00
Including the entire SMSA Central city	.86	1.83	.79	1.00
Case studies of suburban counties				
Anoka County (part), Minnesota†	1.03	.91	1.05	1.00
Dakota County (part), Minnesota†	.85	1.48	1.22	
26 towns in Massachusetts (1951-1971)‡	1.70	1.30	.80	1.00
Exton area of Chester County, Pennsylvania (1965-1971)†	1.09	1.09	.80	1.00

*Source: (30).
†Source: Regional Science Research Institute, Philadelphia, Pennsylvania.
‡Source: (14).

opment is what determines demand. It is this same factor that motivates speculators, developers, and builders. No matter how effective incentives for agriculture are, if an agricultural area has potential for development, it is likely that developers will be able to purchase some farms, and urban development will be injected into the farming community. The new development will intensify the pressures for additional conversion to urban uses. As other farm properties come on the market, the probability increases that they too will be purchased for development.

For these reasons, indirect measures are not likely to be enough, particularly in areas where development pressures are moderate or strong. Direct measures to control the use of land are likely to be necessary. These measures can be thought of as guiding the location of demand for urban development (Table 6). They consist of regulatory measures under the police power of government and the purchase of rights in land.

Most widespread of the regulatory measures is exclusive agricultural zoning. It differs from ordinary urban zoning in that permitted uses are much more limited (restricted usually to agricultural activity and farm-related dwellings), and very large minimum lot sizes (for example, 20 to

Table 6. Public programs for retaining farmland.

	Direct Programs (Control of Land Development)	Indirect Programs (Incentives)
Restrict supply of agricultural land placed on market		Differential assessment for property tax State income tax credits Differential valuation for federal estate tax Differential valuation for state inheritance tax Protection from urban effects • designation of farming districts of minimum size • restriction in rural areas of financing or construction by federal, state, or local government of urban institutions, facilities, and infrastructure • prohibition of nuisance ordinances • exemption from utility district front-foot assessment
Guide location of demand for sites for urban development	Regulation of land use • exclusive farm or rural use zoning • inverse condemnation • development permit systems Purchase of fee or lesser interests in land • direct purchase of development rights • purchase and sale with restrictions • purchase and lease with restrictions Regulation combined with exchange of development rights • transfer of development rights	Capital gains tax on land unless held for long period

80 acres) are often mandated. Exclusive agricultural zoning is common in the West, particularly California and Oregon. It is only now being introduced in the East and Midwest.

Purchase of development rights, on the other hand, is regarded with more confidence in the East. Several eastern states are experimenting with the technique. Purchase and sale or lease of land with restrictions have been less widely used in this country despite the fact that they are analytically equivalent to the direct purchase of development rights and have the practical advantage of depending more directly on the market for valuation (11).

An intriguing system for combining regulation with the exchange of development rights, the transfer of development rights, has been the subject of much academic debate. Thus far, however, few jurisdictions have adopted the system and even fewer have actually used it.

Just as indirect measures may make farming economically viable, but not prevent the conversion of farmland, direct measures may keep farmland undeveloped, but not prevent the cessation of farming. Both farmland and farming must be maintained if the whole range of relevant public values are to be saved—values related to environmental protection, retention of a landscape heritage, and energy conservation, as well as the production of food and fiber.[3]

Perhaps we are now entering a period when legislatures realize that single-measure programs are insufficient, that programs consisting of an integrated set of direct and indirect controls are necessary. The statewide program administered by Oregon's Land Conservation and Development Commission is an example. To preserve agricultural areas, it combines exclusive agricultural zoning with such indirect measures as differential assessment for property and estate tax purposes, exemption from utility extension assessments, prohibition of nuisance ordinances, and rigorous land use and public facility planning.

Another example is Wisconsin's program of state income tax credits, the magnitude of which depend upon the farmland owner's income and the extent to which a county commits itself to an agricultural preservation plan, exclusive agricultural zoning, and other measures (1).

Programs such as these, consisting of both direct and indirect measures, appear to be the nation's best hope of saving farmland and maintaining farming.

---

[3]Coughlin, Robert E. 1979. "The Public's Interest in the Preservation of Farmland." Paper presented at the Northeast Agricultural Leadership Assembly, March 21, Cherry Hill, New Jersey.

REFERENCES

1. Amato, Peter W. 1979. *Wisconsin hopes a new law will preserve its farms.* Planning 45(1): 10-12.
2. Beale, Calvin. 1976. *The revival of population growth in nonmetropolitan America.* Report ERS-605. Economic Research Service, U.S. Department of Agriculture, Washington, D.C.
3. Berry, David. 1976. *Idling of farmland in the Philadelphia region, 1930-1970.* Discussion Paper Series No. 88. Regional Science Research Institute, Philadelphia, Pennsylvania.
4. Berry, David E. 1978. *Effects of urbanization on agricultural activities.* Growth and Change 9(3): 2-8.
5. Berry, David E. 1979. *The sensitivity of dairying to urbanization.* Professional Geographer 31(2): 170-176.
6. Berry, David, E. Leonardo, and K. Bieri. 1976. *The farmer's response to urbanization: A study of the Middle Atlantic States.* Discussion Paper Series No. 92. Regional Science Research Institute, Philadelphia, Pennsylvania.
7. Blue Print Commission on the Future of New Jersey Agriculture. 1973. *Report of the Blue Print Commission on the future of New Jersey agriculture.* Trenton.
8. Brown, H. James, and Neal A. Roberts. 1978. *Land into cities: The land market on the urban fringe.* Department of City and Regional Planning, Harvard University, Cambridge, Massachusetts.
9. Conklin, Howard, and Richard Dymsza. 1972. *Maintaining viable agriculture in areas of urban expansion.* New York State Office of Planning Services, Albany.
10. Coughlin, Robert E., and David Berry. 1977. *Saving the garden: The preservation of farmland and other environmentally valuable land.* Preliminary report to National Science Foundation. Regional Science Research Institute, Philadelphia, Pennsylvania.
11. Coughlin, Robert E., and Thomas Plaut. 1978. *Less-than-fee acquisition for the preservation of open space: Does it work?* Journal of the American Institute of Planners 44(4): 452-462.
12. Cummins, D. 1970. *Effect of urban expansion on dairying in the Lake States: 1949-69.* Agricultural Economics Report No. 196. Economic Research Service, U.S. Department of Agriculture, Washington, D.C.
13. Dideriksen, Ray. 1976. *Potential cropland: A regional view.* Soil Conservation 42: 5-9
14. Foster, John. 1976. *Changes in agricultural land use in Massachusetts, 1951-1971.* Massachusetts Agricultural Experiment Station, Amherst.
15. Hart, John Fraser. 1968. *Loss and abandonment of cleared farmland in the eastern United States.* Annals of the Association of American Geographers 58: 417-440.
16. Hart, John Fraser. 1976. *Urban encroachment on rural areas.* Geographical Review 66: 1-17.
17. Kaiser, E. J., and S. F. Weiss. 1970. *Public policy and the residential development process.* Journal of the American Institute of Planners 36: 30-37.
18. Kenny, K. B. 1972. *The residential land developer and his land purchase decision.* Ph.D. Dissertation. University of North Carolina, Chapel Hill.
19. Leonardo, Ernest, and Robert E. Coughlin. 1977. *The farmer's perception of problems caused by nearby urbanization: A report on five field studies.*

Working Paper. Regional Science Research Institute, Philadelphia, Pennsylvania.

20. Lindeman, Bruce. 1976. *Anatomy of land speculation.* Journal of the American Institute of Planners 42: 142-152.

21. MacConnell, William P. 1975. *Remote sensing, 20 years of change in Massachusetts, 1951/52-1971/72.* Bulletin No. 630. Massachusetts Agricultural Research Station, Amherst.

22. Otte, Robert C. 1974. *Farming in the city's shadow.* Agricultural Economic Report No. 250. Economic Research Service, U.S. Department of Agriculture, Washington, D.C.

23. Plaut, Thomas. 1978. *Urban growth and agricultural decline: Problems and policies.* Bureau of Business Research, University of Texas, Austin.

24. Plaut, Thomas. 1978. Urban growth and agricultural decline: Problems and policies. Ph.D. Dissertation. University of Pennsylvania, Philadelphia.

25. Popper, Frank J. 1978. *What's the hidden factor in land use regulation?* Urban Land 37(11): 4-6.

26. Sinclair, R. 1967. *Van Thunen and urban sprawl.* Annals of the Association of American Geographers 57: 72-87.

27. Soil Conservation Service. 1975. *Potential croplands study.* U.S. Department of Agriculture, Washington, D.C.

28. Vining, Daniel R., Jr., and Ann Strauss. 1976. *A demonstration that current deconcentration population trends are a clean break with past trends.* Discussion Paper Series No. 90. Regional Science Research Institute, Philadelphia, Pennsylvania.

29. Vining, Daniel R., Jr., T. Plaut, and K. Bieri. 1977. *Urban encroachment in prime agricultural land in the United States.* International Regional Science Review 2(2): 143-156.

30. Zeimetz, Kathryn, Elizabeth Dillon, Ernest Hardy, and Robert C. Otte. 1976. *Dynamics of land use in fast growth areas.* Agricultural Economic Report 325. Economic Research Service, U.S. Department of Agriculture, Washington, D.C.

4

Nonurban Competition for Farmland

J. Dixon Esseks

Agriculture's rivals for the use of land extend beyond the residential development, industrial park, shopping center, and other forms of urbanization. Competition comes also from strip mining, reservoir-building, interurban highway construction, and other uses that, though tending to take considerable land out of agriculture, leave the environment essentially rural.

The focus here is on competitive situations that pit agricultural uses against six nonurban uses: transportation (roadways and rural airports), man-made reservoirs (for hydroelectric power, water supply, flood control, and/or recreation), wetlands (recreation, preservation of flora and fauna), forestry, strip mining, and other energy-industry uses of rural land (for power plants, transmission lines, pipelines) (22, 26). Not considered are the reforestation of abandoned New England farmland, strip mining of marginal southern Illinois cropland, and other conversions where agriculture is no longer a viable rival.

There are, of course, other rural, nonagricultural uses of land—parks, sand and gravel quarrying, solid waste disposal—but these do not appear to be major competitors of agriculture. Recreational homes may also consume much farmland. Because they tend to occur in subdivisions, however, this land use is more an urban phenomenon than rural (1).

For each competing use, I will look at the damage or hindrances to agriculture that the use can cause, the past and future significance of such effects, and the role government plays in shaping those effects. Among the negative impacts are the paving over or flooding (for a reservoir) of good cropland as well as yield reductions on adjacent land remaining in farming (for example, stormwater runoff from highways onto nearby cornfields and an excessive raising of water tables resulting from reservoir construction). Individually, these nonurban sources of farmland conversion do not appear significant on a national scale. But collectively, they are impressive; and for many local agricultural areas, nonurban conversions may undermine the viability of farming.

Government has a central role to play in these land use conflicts. In highway construction and reservoir-building, public agencies act as the developers. They choose whether and when to consume farmland with their powers of eminent domain and their access to tax revenues and public borrowing. In the location of private power plants and lines, government must approve siting plans and/or grant the right of eminent domain to private utilities. In strip mining the mine operators must obtain permits from government before they may extract.

Rural Transportation

Roadways. Roadways consume farmland directly for their paved areas and adjacent shoulders, medians, drainage facilities, and interchanges. The 40,000-plus miles of interstate highways completed by mid-1975 used an average of 40 acres per mile of right of way (*34*). Adjoining or nearby farms may suffer negative affects by disruption of established drainage systems, increased sedimentation both during and after road construction, barriers to movement of farm machinery and livestock posed by the road (especially if it is limited access), and even crop damage due to highway-derived air and water pollution (*15, 32*).

Secondary impacts of highway construction are often as great or greater in terms of farmland conversion or degradation. These result from stimulated urbanization, particularly around interchanges. Retailers of fuel, food, and lodging tend to appear first, followed by department stores, branch banks, offices, and/or commuter subdivisions (*4*).

Highway and other transportation construction has claimed substantial quantities of rural land in recent years. The amounts taken in the 1980s may be considerably less.

Between 1959 and 1969, land converted to rural roads and airports averaged about 130,000 acres a year nationwide (*15*). The bulk of that acreage went for roads rather than airports, and most of the roads were interstate highways. But in the early to mid-1970s, as the interstate system neared completion, the U.S. Department of Agriculture (USDA) estimated that the new acreage for rural transportation had declined to an estimated 50,000 to 100,000 acres annually. By 1975 the interstate system was 98 percent complete or under contract for construction (*34*).

Separate states may have their own land-extensive highway building plans, but rapidly rising construction costs are likely to limit the mileage that is fiscally feasible. Illinois, for example, in 1970 launched development of a 1,950-mile supplemental freeway system. By 1978, however, the state's Department of Transportation reported a serious lag in the program over the previous five years due to a "combination of declining state highway revenue growth, coupled with double-digit inflation within the road construction industry, long environmental and other preconstruction lead times, and even larger competing demand for limited resources" (24).

Government is the dominant actor in highway construction. In contrast to its role as a regulator of private housing or commercial development, government builds and maintains public roads. It chooses where to construct roads, and it designs the roads—two-lane, four-lane, wide or narrow medians, many or few access points, and so forth.

Most building is done by state and local governments. The federal government's construction activities are limited to roads on federal lands. However, Washington is the major source of funding for road building. In Illinois' fiscal 1979 highway budget, for example, the federal contribution was expected to be 68 percent of the total (24).

Federal review of state and local construction projects precedes federal check-writing. The reviewing agency, the Federal Highway Administration (FHWA), is mandated to evaluate projects at each major stage of their development, such as preliminary engineering, acquisition of right-of-way, then construction, with FHWA authorization needed to proceed from one stage to the next (20).

Has the FHWA exercised its review and authorization powers to protect farming? Its officials claim so, at least in following such design norms as siting rights-of-way to follow property lines rather than bisecting a farmer's holdings; preserving drainage tile systems; and building, at public expense, special underpasses for farm vehicles and livestock whose access to fields would otherwise be cut off by the new roadway (19). Farmers unsatisfied with such protective or corrective measures may sue for compensation.

Those farmers seeking more substantial changes, such as shifting rights-of-way sizeable distances or aborting an entire project or segment, are likely to face rough-going. The road-building lobby is strong, combining diverse economic interests, including trucking companies, automobile clubs, tourism industries, real estate developers, construction labor unions, and agricultural interests concerned about rapid transportation of produce to market.

A bureaucracy sympathetic to farmland protection could, of course, help to offset the political weight of the construction lobby. It is not clear, however, whether the FHWA performs this role. As of September 1979, there had been no FHWA policy statement, similar to those by the

Environmental Protection Agency (EPA) and USDA, committing the agency to protecting prime and unique agricultural land (*17, 40*). The FHWA's in-house directives for preparing environmental impact statements did not even list the loss of farmland as an impact worth consideration (*18*).

This situation may change. As of mid-1975, EPA had "no significant requirement...to consider the impact on crop production as an important criterion in facilities siting," for example, wastewater treatment facilities (*39*). Then in September 1978 the administrator issued a statement that recognized the need to assess such effects and committed EPA to protect "agricultural lands...wherever impacted by agency programs" (*17*).

A neutral or even hostile highway authority will probably consider agricultural impacts if formally requested to by farmers. Where federal money is to be involved, farm interests can invoke an August 1976 "Memorandum to Heads of Agencies" from the President's Council on Environmental Quality (CEQ). This memo calls for impact assessments when "prime and unique farmlands" are threatened by federal activities (*8*). For such assessments to influence right-of-way siting, they probably should come early in the planning process, before the highway agency expends considerable time, money, and professional ego on justifying a particular route.

How *not* to oppose highway construction is illustrated by the case of 162 farmers in four northern Illinois counties who contributed money and time in a vain attempt to block a 69-mile tollway extension. They had adequate funding, a good Chicago law firm to represent them, the support of all four county Farm Bureaus and the state Farm Bureau, as well as sympathetic media coverage. But they started too late.

Their organization, the Farmers Opposed to the Extension of the Illinois Tollway, was formed in May 1971. The extension's groundbreaking occurred shortly thereafter, in August 1971! The right-of-way already had been decided on and land acquisition was underway. After 10 months of legal and other efforts, the farmers' organization dissolved and paid back unused funds. For its pains, the group may have helped individual landowners to obtain more equitable settlements; but its chairman acknowledged that it had failed to prevent the bisecting of farms, to secure the realignment of overpasses, and to alter the tollway's design in other ways to reduce its disruptive impact on farming.

A successful case of opposition comes from central Illinois. Tazewell County farmers, led by a lawyer-farmer, began opposing a 15-mile freeway project at the first public hearing in 1969. A court suit followed, claiming that the environmental impact statement had been improperly prepared. The group delayed the project by suing for an injunction, losing their case at the federal District Court level in 1974, then winning two decisions at the appellate level in 1975 and 1976. In the meantime, road-building costs escalated, and a state study commission concluded in early 1976 that the transportation needs of the area in question could be adequately and more cheaply met by improving an existing state highway rather than building a freeway (41).

Another case of early and persistent opposition bearing fruit occurred in southwestern Wisconsin. In July 1973 farm and other local interests obtained a court injunction halting a 22-mile freeway project on the grounds that the project's draft environmental impact statement had failed to consider alternative construction designs, particularly an expressway that would take less land and give freer access to farm and other vehicles. An amended environmental impact statement was submitted, and in April 1975 the court lifted the injunction. Agitation for an expressway continued, and by early 1977 the state highway authority had shifted to that type of design and made adjustments to reduce the taking of farmland by reducing the median width and by making greater use of an existing state highway right-of-way (21). The authority acknowledged that these changes were responses, at least in part, to "public concern" over "land conservation" (21).

Also in 1977, and reportedly in response to this and other highway siting controversies, the Wisconsin legislature passed a bill requiring the Department of Agriculture to prepare "an agricultural impact statement whenever an agency having powers of eminent domain...proposes a project involving the taking of interests from any farm operation" (13). An agency is legally bound to notify the department "of any project involving the actual or potential exercise of the powers of eminent domain affecting a farm operation."

Rural Airports. Airports can have negative impacts on farming similar to those of highways, by direct conversion of land and by inhibiting farming on adjacent land (for example, disrupting drainage and blocking access to fields). Moreover, air traffic of significant volume tends to attract secondary development—restaurants, gas stations, and other service industries that may also consume good farmland and create adverse impacts on adjacent agriculture.

In the 1960s rural airports were estimated to have taken about 37,000 acres a year from other uses (22). USDA officials believe the conversion rate in the first half of the 1970s was about the same.

As with highways, developers of rural airports are public agencies. They can employ eminent domain for siting. However, airport projects, especially ones promising the noise levels of jets, if only executive jets, tend to be more vulnerable politically than highways. Farmers can win the cooperation of many, if not most, of their nonfarm neighbors in opposing airport construction.

In late 1978, 751 residents of rural Bureau County, Illinois, signed a petition that stated, "We the undersigned are opposed to the Illinois Port Authority using prime farmland for an airport when marginal land is available" (in an adjoining county). Targets of lobbying to defeat the site included both the Illinois agency and the Federal Aviation Administration, which would fund a portion of the construction cost.

Reservoirs

Man-made reservoirs may flood good cropland and prevent or hinder farming on land adjacent to the inundated acreage. The flooding may also turn adjoining land into peninsulas or near-islands that are too small or inaccessible for farming. Other nearby parcels, though of adequate size, can become water-logged because of the higher water table (6, 36). Where the reservoir project includes recreational facilities, considerable farmland can be taken for roads, parking lots, and other visitor facilities.

The acreage lost to reservoirs in the 1960s averaged about 300,000 per year (22). By the mid-1970s, according to USDA estimates, the pace slackened to about 200,000 acres flooded annually. Even less land may be taken in the 1980s because of fiscal and physical constraints. Construction costs have escalated rapidly, and most hydroelectric dam sites have been developed (6). Moreover, the Carter Administration, in search of budget items to cut, has favored reductions in water projects. A cheaper alternative to dam-building for flood control is a nonstructural approach, such as zoning to prevent development in floodplains.

Another cause for decline in reservoir construction has been opposition on environmental grounds. The Tennessee Valley Authority's proposed Tellico Dam, near Knoxville, was defeated largely on the basis of the endangered species issue. A supporting argument was that the project would flood some 16,000 acres of rich farmland (7).

The federal government's chief water resources development agency, the Army Corps of Engineers, has encountered fairly frequent opposition on farmland preservation grounds. In 1976, for example, the North Dakota Farm Bureau testified at Senate hearings against the Kindred Lake project, which would take an estimated 8,130 acres out of farming (36). At the same hearings, an Indiana county board president opposed the Big Walnut Lake project in part because it would convert 12,000 acres of "excellent farmland" (36). In 1977 a Virginia state legislator testified against the Verona Lake project partly because "10,000 acres of prime dairy and cattle farmland would be destroyed" (37). And in 1978 hearings, the president of a local "protection association" protested a lake-creating project (Falmouth Lake) also because of the loss of farmland—"4,500 acres of Kentucky's most fertile land" (38). In total, during these three years (1976-1978) of hearings on Corps activities, seventeen projects were opposed at least in part because of the threatened conversion of, or damage to, farmland (*36, 37, 38*).

The Corps does not appear overly concerned about protecting good farmland. As with the FHWA (but unlike USDA and EPA), its leadership has not issued a policy statement committing the agency to that objective. And like FHWA, the Corps' in-house directives for preparing environmental impact statements do not list, as important to assess, the impacts of agency activities on farming (*9, 29*). However, if questions about agricultural impacts are raised, as in public hearings, the Corps likely will respond to them in the draft or revised environmental impact statement. As with federally assisted highway construction, the earlier the farmland issue is raised, the more likely will the action affect decision-making.

Corps guidelines that became effective January 1, 1979, provide for three stages of planning prior to asking Congress for project authorization: reconnaissance, a preliminary assessment of the need for action; development of intermediate plans; and development of detailed plans. Public participation is supposed to occur at each stage (*11*). However, to assure participation early in the planning process, farmers and environmental groups may need to pre-register, as concerned parties, with the Corps' District Office. So listed, they should be automatically informed of public meetings held on a project in their area (*29*). Without taking this initiative, they risk being shut out of any review of early planning. The Corps acknowledges that some of its district officers are reluctant "to expose project plans, for which they are personally responsible, to the stringent and often hostile scrutiny of many potential opponents within a community."[1]

Wetlands

Wetlands are "lowlands covered with shallow and sometimes temporary or intermittent waters," including "swamps, marshes, bogs, sloughs, potholes, wet meadows, river overflows, and tidal overflows" (*30*). If properly drained, wetland acres can become highly productive for farming. If retained as wetlands, however, the land may be valued for its capabilities to support wildlife, to help recharge groundwater, and to protect the natural environment in other ways. The public policy question, therefore, is not (as with highways and reservoirs) whether land good for farming should be taken *out of* agriculture, but whether

[1]Ash, Grant C., chief of environmental policy, U.S. Army Corps of Engineers, in a paper, "Effects of National Environmental Policy Act on Water Resource Projects in the USA," presented in December 1978 at the Institute of Water Engineers and Scientists, London, England.

wetlands with the potential for agricultural productivity should be converted *to* farming.

Draining and clearing of wetlands has added significantly to the nation's supply of cropland. This has helped to offset losses of fertile land to urbanization, transportation, and other uses. From 1944 to 1964, an estimated 2.6 million wetland acres were converted to cropland in Florida and the lower Mississippi Valley (*15*). Much of the land conversion in Florida occurred around Lake Okeechobee, where a warm, humid climate promised good returns on agricultural investments, particularly from growing tomatoes, sweet corn, and other vegetables for winter markets (*15*). Along the lower Mississippi River and its tributaries, soybeans have become a profitable crop on reclaimed land (*5*).

Wetlands conversion to agriculture has also occurred in the prairie pothole region of North Dakota, South Dakota, and Minnesota. Between 1959 and 1966, an estimated 138,000 acres were reclaimed annually in this region for farming (*15*).

Soil Conservation Service (SCS) data for the 1967-1975 period indicate a slowdown in the conversion of wet soils to crops (*12*). One reason for this lower rate of conversion and the likelihood that it will carry over into the 1980s is that most feasible areas for reclamation in the lower Mississippi Valley have been developed.[2] Another factor may be the efforts by environmentalists to protect wetlands.

The Federal Water Pollution Control Act Amendments of 1977 empower the Army Corps of Engineers to restrict the drainage of wetlands throughout the country. The specific tool is the power to grant or withhold necessary permits for discharging fill material (for dams, levies, and other reclamation structures) into streams, lakes, rivers, and their adjacent wetlands (*27*). Under the implementing rules, the Corps is supposed to exercise this power so as to "avoid" discharges into wetlands (*10*).

Drainage activities undertaken or aided by the federal government should also be curtailed by President Carter's Executive Order 11990, issued May 24, 1977. This order requires all federal agencies "to avoid direct or indirect support of new construction in wetlands wherever there is a practicable alternative" (*30*). Among the federal programs resulting in wetlands drainage have been those of the Corps for flood control and SCS work in reclaiming organically rich wet soils for farming.

Agriculture versus Forestry

Competition between agriculture and forestry tends to be one-sided and dictated by the economics of farming. Agriculture takes forest land

[2]Interviews with USDA economists and forestry specialists.

when the income returns justify clearing. When the market is poor and/or the land becomes less fertile, farming may stop and the land revert to timber. For example, high soybean prices have attracted investments in the draining and clearing of hardwoods on large acreages of bottomland along the lower Mississippi River (35). However, this clearing tends to be offset by farmland reverting to forest.

USDA projections suggest that future conversions of forest land to agriculture will be too limited to add much to the cropland base or to threaten significantly the supply of timber (12, 26).

Coal Strip Mining

In contrast to forestry, coal strip mining can be a formidable rival to agriculture for the use of good farmland. By the early 1970s, surface mining of coal had disturbed (excavated, piled overburden on, etc.) 1.5 million acres; the amount of newly affected land each year was about 100,000 acres (15).

The major consumer of stipped coal is the electric power industry. Projections of demand for electricity in the year 2000 range from more than double to almost quadruple the 1975 level (3). Meeting power demands in that range will require an increase in coal output of two or three times, with strip mining's share of that increase probably disturbing an additional 1.8 million to 2.5 million acres (3).

Not all the land for strip mining will be taken from farming. From 1972 through 1977, an average of 52 percent of the land on which permits were granted for strip mining in Illinois was in cropland, 27 percent was in forest, and 21 percent was in pasture (23). However, in west central and northern Illinois, much of the strippable farmland is prime for agriculture.

Significant coal reserves also underlie large acreages of prime farmland in Indiana, western Kentucky, and North Dakota. In the Appalachian mining region, coal tends to lie on steep, unfarmable slopes, and in the western coal fields of Wyoming and Montana, "little land meets the definition of prime land."[3]

The potential damaging impacts on agriculture from strip mining include the excavation of farmland under which coal lies (as far down as 75 to 100 feet) and the bulldozing and/or filling of half again as many acres for haul roads, storage areas, and other mining purposes. Stripping may also disrupt drainage on adjoining land, and it can pollute surface or ground water used by livestock and farm families. In the mid-1970s, coal

---

[3]Letter dated March 18, 1977, from R. M. Davis, administrator, SCS to Bert Lance, director, Office of Management and Budget.

surface mines produced an estimated 6,000 tons of sulfuric acid daily, which found its way into about 13,000 miles of streams (3).

Moreover, surface mining has been called a "one-time harvest" (33). Unlike conversion of farmland to manufacturing or commercial uses, coal stripping tends to provide only short-term income benefits and, without government intervention, leaves the land unsuited for other uses.

State and federal governments have sought to prevent or mitigate surface mining's negative impacts through legislation requiring reclamation of disturbed land. For example, Illinois' Surface-Mined Land Conservation and Reclamation Act (as amended in 1975) provides that, on land capable of growing row crops (corn, soybeans), a permit is not granted unless the mining operator agrees to segregate out and store the topsoil during stripping, then replace it when grading the area back approximately to its pre-mining contours (23). The federal Surface Mining Control and Reclamation Act of 1977 focuses on prime farmland and makes even higher demands, including that "the topsoil and other soil horizons suitable for plant growth be segregated and replaced over spoil material" and that a permit be issued "only upon a finding that the operator has the technological capability to restore such mined area, within a reasonable time, to equivalent or higher levels of yield as non-mined prime farmland in the surrounding area under equivalent levels of management..." (28).

Where reclamation standards for prime land add substantially to mining costs, stripping may be diverted to land in forest or pasture or to lower grade cropland. Where high standards are adhered to, the land may be returned to farming, although there is considerable doubt that yield levels on prime land can be fully restored. A third possible outcome is that, because of such skepticism and pressure from coal companies about the economic hardships imposed on them by high reclamation standards, the regulatory authorities will relax the standards so that neither diversion nor restoration effects will be substantial.

Illinois' requirements for reclaiming land suitable for row crops became effective in 1976. In that year and 1977, 51 and 55 percent, respectively, of the total permitted acreage was to be reclaimed to row-crop standards, with capability assessments based on SCS soil maps (23). It is too early to judge if post-mining yields will match pre-mining levels. But one Illinois soil scientist cautioned in November 1978 that reclaimed land tends to suffer from inferior soil structure and excessive compaction (too dense to hold adequate moisture or to prevent normal root development, probably due to the weight of grading equipment).[4] Another specialist,

---

[4] Letter dated November 7, 1978, from I. J. Jansen, assistant professor of pedology, University of Illinois, to Jane Johnson, Land Use Committee, Knox County Board, Gilson, Illinois.

working on test plots of reclaimed land in western Illinois, also reported problems with "compactness and derangement of soil structure," which reduced yields in comparison to those on unmined plots (14).

Another problem that can frustrate restoration of yields is differential subsidence, which might preclude the use of some or most farm machinery (31). USDA's position in April 1977, prior to Congressional passage of the new surface mining act, was as follows:

"The reclamation of prime farmlands is, in our judgment, technically possible. It is not being done at this time, however, and it will take several years for the industry to gain equipment, technical skills, and operational capability." [5]

USDA sought a moratorium on permits for new mining on prime land, both to encourage diversion of stripping to other land and to enable further development of reclamation capabilities. However, as discussed previously, the legislation, as passed in August 1977, regulates mining on prime land by requiring operators to meet ostensibly high reclamation standards. If few can do so, the effect will be essentially the same as a moratorium. But only a few may choose to do so, given the likely high labor and equipment costs of meeting the federal standards as to "the systematic removal of soil horizons, stockpiling, site preparation prior to restoration, and systematic replacement of soil horizons" (28).

Opponents of strip mining on good farmland fear that the federal law will be watered down in implementation. Because the act allows states to substitute their own regulatory programs if they are as stringent as the federal government's, there is the concern that state bureaucracies will be less committed and/or technically unable to enforce regulations strictly. Another worry has been that federal as well as state regulators will relax standards in the face of mining company protests over the high costs and technological difficulties of cropland reclamation.

Good, if not indispensable, checks on tendencies toward weak implementation are likely to be undertaken by local or statewide political interest groups with the capacity to monitor the activities knowledgeably. For example, four county governments in southern Illinois have contracted with a nonprofit energy issues group, Illinois South Project, "to act as their advocates when dealing with the [Department of the Interior's] Office of Surface Mining and the State Regulatory Authority." [6] Illinois South Project people claim that by 1978 a "state-wide citizens network...was established to assure the implementation of the federal [surface mining] law in Illinois."

---

[5] Letter dated April 22, 1977, from Bob Bergland, secretary of agriculture, to Bert Lance, director, Office of Management and Budget.

[6] Mavrolas, Pamela J., staff member, Illinois South Project, in testimony prepared for the Office of Surface Mining Reclamation and Enforcement hearings, October 24, 1978, Indianapolis, Indiana.

Local, directly affected interests—farmers with fields adjacent to land acquired by coal companies, local government officials worried about the tax base and employment opportunities after land is mined out, and citizens concerned about the quality of ground and surface water—can probably make the most persuasive case for strict enforcement. They should be able to discredit, as too narrow, cost-benefit studies that compare only the high costs of reclamation to the likely modest direct income benefits of restoration, that is, the value of produce from the reclaimed cropland.[7]

Power Plants, Powerlines, and Pipelines

Power companies use rural land for transmission and generating purposes. Power plants require extensive acreages for varying needs—storage of coal, housing of generators, and cooling of water used to produce steam. Cooling ponds for larger plants (2,000-plus megawatts capacity) may exceed 2,000 acres (15). A nuclear plant southwest of Chicago required 4,480 acres, nearly all of which was once farmland (25).

Powerlines and pipelines consume rural land directly through their rights-of-way. Perhaps more burdensome for agriculture, however, are the disruptive effects on cropland adjacent to the lines. Also, pipelines may bisect farms, hindering field access and damaging tile drainage systems. Transmission line support poles and towers create nuisances to cultivate around. Where power companies have the right of eminent domain, these are nuisances or hindrances that farmers cannot reject, but for which they should be compensated at fair market value.

About 4 million acres are used for transmission line rights-of-way. One prediction is that another 1.5 million acres will be needed by the year 2000 (15). New coal and nuclear power plants may result in the permanent conversion of yet another 1.5 million to 2 million acres (3).

Government can play a decisive role in siting new plants and transmission lines and, thus, in determining the consequences of siting, including whether the facilities consume farmland or disrupt farming. Putting together a strip of parcels with the right alignment for a powerline or assembling enough contiguous parcels for a new power plant may require the use of eminent domain. The Environmental Policy Center calculated that in 1978 at least 19 states employed eminent domain for siting power plants and lines (16). This power is exercised by a public agency or by a private one, such as a utility company, to which government delegates

[7]McMartin, Wallace, "Western Coal: Energy vs. Agriculture," paper presented at the American Agricultural Economics Association annual meeting, August 1978, Blacksburg, Virginia.

the power, the use of which government can review, restrict, or cancel. A useful restriction might be to require that power companies publicize plans for siting before any property is purchased.[8] Without such a requirement, private utilities can quietly buy out enough landowners so those remaining, who might be inclined to oppose a power project, are discouraged by their small numbers and/or by the examples of their neighbors. Forewarned, they may be able to persuade those neighbors to join them in opposition. They might also have a better chance of swaying the power company's decision before it is too committed, financially and otherwise, to a particular site.

Conclusions

Conversions of cropland in the individual categories of nonurban uses discussed here have not been large. Collectively and cumulatively, however, they are reducing significantly the nation's supply of farmland. In the mid-1970s, 50,000 to 100,000 acres of rural land were converted each year to transportation uses; about 200,000 acres annually went into reservoirs; coal strip mining disturbed about 100,000 a year; and power plants, powerlines, and pipelines consumed another 120,000 acres or so.[9] Together, these four categories of rural land conversion were taking from 470,000 to more than 500,000 acres a year.

Is this rate likely to change in the 1980s? Probably not! While fiscal constraints are likely to reduce conversions for transportation and a combination of budgetary and physical constraints may cut the acreage consumed by reservoirs, there likely will be offsetting increases in the taking of farmland for coal surface mining and for electric power generation and transmission. Moreover, a once important source of land for agriculture, wetlands, may well diminish in significance.

It is not easy to assess what proportion of the roughly half million acres being lost is cropland. For surface mining in Illinois from 1972 to 1977, about 50 percent of the land so used was farmland. In the hilly Appalachian mining area, the proportion was much less. If a conservative 20 percent is used to represent farmland's share of the conversion of rural land to these four nonurban, nonagricultural uses, the loss is about 100,000 acres per year. With a 40 percent share, the loss reaches 200,000 acres annually. At these rates, over a period of 10 years, 1 million to 2 million acres of farmland will be lost or degraded (from strip mining);

---

[8]Suggested by David Ostendorf, Illinois South Project, to the First National Citizens Conference on Energy Facility Siting, September 17, 1978, Glenwood, Minnesota.

[9]Estimate for power plants, powerlines, and pipelines is based on the projected new acreage needed by the year 2000, about 3 million, divided by 25, the number of years between 1975 and 2000.

over a period of 20 years, 2 million to 4 million acres.

While such losses are significant on a national scale, they may be critical in local or regional agricultural areas. In La Salle County, Illinois, for example, construction of Interstate 80 bisected the county, east to west, for 40 miles, consuming about 40 acres per mile (a total of 1,600 acres). A nuclear power plant constructed in one of La Salle County's eastern townships took 6,680 acres. A state freeway, now being planned, would bisect the county north to south for about 19 miles, taking another 760 acres. Nearly all the affected acreage is cropland.

When the effects of both the actual conversions and the negative impacts on adjacent farming are felt, not enough profitable farms may remain to sustain needed agribusinesses. Feed, seed, fertilizer, and farm machinery dealers may move out of the area. Moreover, farmers may "lose neighbors [needed] for work and machinery exchange" (2). The critical mass required for a viable agricultural sector may be lost.

Protest groups of farmers opposed the nuclear power plant in La Salle County, a regional airport planned in neighboring Bureau County, a freeway project to the south in Tazewell County, and a tollway extension through four counties to the north. The protesters were concerned about good farmland being lost or disrupted and about their own fate of possibly having to relocate out of the area or be left with farms reduced in size and farmability. There would be monetary compensation at fair market value, of course; but for farmers unwilling to move out or to see an economic farm unit broken up, only prices that are considerably above the land's value in farming are likely to be considered adequate compensation. In reality, for cropland converted to highways, airports, reservoirs, and other public nonurban uses, the fair market price tends to be at or near the land's value in agriculture.

Where the rival use to farming is residential or commercial development, the compensation can be higher. For the uses discussed here, however, the capital gains to be made from converting agricultural land to other nonurban uses are likely to be modest. Hence, many, if not most, farmers see themselves as financially disadvantaged, and some may actively oppose the conversion.

The federal government can assist opposition groups at the local level by ensuring that federal projects or federally aided projects are publicized in the early planning phases and that the anticipated project impacts on agricure are thoroughly and fairly assessed in environmental impact statements. State governments can help in the same manner, perhaps following Wisconsin's example of requiring all state agencies that plan to acquire farmland to prepare agricultural impact statements. Also, where states delegate the power of eminent domain to private utilities, the latter could be compelled to announce early their intentions to purchase land and easements and to prepare impact evaluations.

Without adequate forewarning and information bases, farmers and other local interests are unlikely to make effective cases for preventing or mitigating negative impacts on farming. However, where local protests succeed, if not in aborting or modifying projects, at least in bringing into the open the full range and significance of the negative impacts, they may contribute to more public agencies, such as EPA, committing themselves formally to using their expenditure and regulatory powers to protect prime farmland.

REFERENCES

1. American Society of Planning Officials. 1976. *Subdividing rural America: Impacts of recreational lot and second home development: Executive Summary.* Council on Environmental Quality, Washington, D.C.
2. Anderson, Raymond L. 1978. *Urbanization of rural lands in the northern Colorado Front Range—1978.* Cooperative Extension Service, Colorado State University, Fort Collins.
3. Barse, Joseph R. 1977. *Agriculture and energy use in the year 2000: Discussion from a natural resource perspective.* American Journal of Agricultural Economics 59(December): 1,073.
4. Barton-Aschman Associates. 1968. *Highway and land-use relationships in interchange areas.* Chicago, Illinois.
5. Beltz, Roy C., and Joe F. Christopher. *Land clearing in the Delta region of Mississippi.* Forest Service, U.S. Department of Agriculture, New Orleans, Louisiana.
6. Blackwelder, Brent. 1976. *Benefit claims of the water development agencies: The need for continuing reform.* Environmental Policy Institute, Washington, D.C.
7. Christian Science Monitor. 1979. *When not to build a dam.* (January 26): 24.
8. Council on Environmental Quality. 1976. *Analysis of impacts on prime and unique farmland in environmental impact statements.* Washington, D.C.
9. Department of the Army, Corps of Engineers. 1976. *Civil works program: Environmental policies, objectives, and guidelines; revision.* Federal Register 41(October 29): 47,676-47,678.
10. Department of the Army, Corps of Engineers. 1977. *Regulatory program of the Corps of Engineers.* Federal Register 42(July 19) part II: 37,144-37,147.
11. Department of the Army, Corps of Engineers. 1978. *Water Resources Council (WRC) principles and standards, National Environmental Policy Act (NEPA) and related policies: Guidelines for conducting feasibility studies for water and related land resources; final rules.* Federal Register 43(July 13) part II: 30,228-30,231.
12. Dideriksen, Raymond I., Allen R. Hidlebaugh, and Keith O. Schmude. 1977. *Potential cropland study.* Statistical Bulletin No. 578. Soil Conservation Service, U.S. Department of Agriculture, Washington, D.C.
13. Division of Highways, Bureau of Environmental Analysis and Review. 1978. *Procedure: Agricultural impact statements.* Wisconsin Department of Transportation, Madison.
14. Doyle, John C., Jr. 1976. *Strip mining in the Corn Belt: The destruction of high capability agricultural land for strip-minable coal in Illinois.* Environmental Policy Institute, Washington, D.C.

15. Economic Research Service. 1974. *Our land and water resources: Current and prospective supplies and uses.* Miscellaneous Publication No. 1290. U.S. Department of Agriculture, Washington, D.C.
16. Environmental Policy Center. 1978. *Energy right-of-way/facility siting problems.* Washington, D.C.
17. Environmental Protection Agency. 1978. *EPA policy: To protect environmentally significant agricultural lands.* Washington, D.C.
18. Federal Highway Administration. 1976. *Federal-aid highway program manual.* U.S. Department of Transportation, Washington, D.C.
19. Federal Highway Administration. 1977. *Federal-aid highway program manual.* U.S. Department of Transportation, Washington, D.C.
20. Federal Highway Administration. *Your guide to programs of the Federal Highway Administration.* U.S. Department of Transportation, Washington, D.C.
21. Federal Highway Administration and Wisconsin Division of Highways. 1977. *Final supplemental environmental impact statement: Administrative action for Dodgeville—Mount Horeb Road, U.S.H. 18-151, Iowa and Dane Counties.* U.S. Department of Transportation, Washington, D.C.
22. Frey, H. Thomas. 1973. *Major uses of land in the United States: Summary for 1969.* Agricultural Economic Report No. 247. Economic Research Service, U.S. Department of Agriculture, Washington, D.C.
23. Illinois Department of Mines and Minerals. 1978. *1977 annual coal, oil and gas report.* Springfield.
24. Illinois Department of Transportation. 1978. *Proposed improvements for Illinois highways: Fiscal year 1979.* Springfield.
25. Jacobsen, Sally. 1973. *Land use dispute in Illinois: Nuclear power vs. crops.* Bulletin of the Atomic Scientists 29(January): 43-45.
26. Lee, Linda K. 1978. *A perspective on cropland availability.* Agricultural Economic Report No. 406. Economics, Statistics and Cooperatives Service, U.S. Department of Agriculture, Washington, D.C.
27. McCormick, Jack. 1978. *Ecology and the regulation of freshwater wetlands.* In Ralph E. Good et al. [eds.] *Freshwater Wetlands: Ecological Processes and Management Potential.* Academic Press, New York, New York.
28. Office of Surface Mining Reclamation and Enforcement. 1978. *Surface coal mining and reclamation operations: Proposed rules for permanent regulatory program.* Federal Register 43(September 18): 41,718.
29. Office of the Chief of Engineers. 1974. *Planning: Preparation and coordination of environmental statements.* Regulation No. 1105-2-507. Department of the Army, Washington, D.C.
30. Office of the Secretary. 1978. *Preservation of the nation's wetlands.* Department of Transportation, Washington, D.C.
31. Power, J. F., R. E. Ries, and F. M. Sandoval. 1978. *Reclamation of coal-mined land in the Northern Great Plains.* Journal of Soil and Water Conservation 33(2): 74.
32. Rollier, Maurice, and Marc-Auguste Erbetta. 1976. *Environmental impact of highways.* Ekistics 42: 248.
33. Smith, Janet M., David Ostendorf, and Mike Schechtman. 1978. *Who's mining the farm?* Illinois South Project, Herrin.
34. Spaulding, Brent H., and Earl O. Heady. 1977. *Future use of agricultural land for nonagricultural purposes.* Journal of Soil and Water Conservation 32(2): 89-91.

35. Sternitzke, Herbert S. 1974. *Eastern hardwood resources: Trends and prospects.* Forest Products Journal 24(March): 13.

36. U.S. Congress. 1976. *Senate hearings before the Committee on Appropriations: Public works for water and power development and energy research appropriations, fiscal year 1977.* 94th Congress, Second Session. Washington, D.C.

37. U.S. Congress. 1978. *Senate hearings before the Committee on Appropriations: Public works for water and power development and energy research appropriations, fiscal year 1978.* 95th Congress, First Session. Washington, D.C.

38. U.S. Congress. 1979. *Senate hearings before the Committee on Appropriations: Public works for water and power development and energy research appropriations, final year 1979.* 95th Congress, Second Session. Washington, D.C.

39. U.S. Department of Agriculture. 1975. *Recommendations on prime lands: From the Seminar on Retention of Prime Lands.* Washington, D.C.

40. U.S. Department of Agriculture. 1976. *Secretary's memorandum no. 1827, supplement 1, statement of prime farmland, range and forest land.* Washington, D.C.

41. U.S. News and World Report. 1979. *Blighted orphans of our road-building boom.* 87(February 19): 42.

5

Land Market Issues

Robert G. Healy

A basic concept in economics is the idea of the market. A market reconciles supply and demand, responding to new information about present conditions and new guesses about the future. A market allocates commodities to those people who want the commodities and are willing and able to pay for them.

Farmland is traded in such a market, yet the attention of people concerned with agricultural land retention traditionally has focused only on the outcomes produced by market forces, not on how the market itself works.

High Stakes in Land Markets

Perhaps the most striking thing about land markets is the immense amount of money involved. The estimated value of U.S. farmland as of February 1978 was $434 billion (*14*), just over $2,000 for each man, woman, and child in the nation. Attached to that land was another $90 billion in houses, barns, and other structures, a large portion of which would have little or no value unless associated with a working farm.

Despite modern agriculture's need for expensive machinery and equipment—tractors, combines, irrigation pipe—land remains by far the most significant asset for most farmers. In 1977 farm real estate accounted for 73 percent of all farm assets, up from 64 percent in 1960 and 57 percent in 1950.

Real estate also looms large on the liability side of the farmer's ledger. Total farm real estate debt increased rapidly in the past decade to last year's figure of $63 billion. This debt is rather unequally distributed.

Many farmers owe nothing, while others, principally those who bought high-priced land in the last few years, are deeply in debt (6).

For most farmers, land has been an enormously profitable asset. In fact, one hears stories in virtually any farming area about the farmer who was dirt-poor all his life but sold his land and retired a millionaire. Available statistics bear out the truth of this observation. Between 1971 and 1977, total net farm income ranged between $15 billion and $33 billion annually, a six-year total of $136 billion. This represented the fruit of the farmer's backbreaking labor, his risk-taking, and his management skill. During the same period, the value of *farmland*, with little or no effort on the farmer's part, rose some $223 billion. It is little wonder that land is jestingly referred to as "the farmer's last cash crop."

The land component of a farmer's assets significantly influences his attitude toward policies that might adversely affect its value. This concern emphatically extends to many proposed policies to retain productive land in agriculture. On one hand, the money a farmer has tied up in his land may be regarded as something of a windfall. Many farmers honestly find it difficult to believe their land is so valuable, or that, on paper, they are so wealthy. Farmers' patterns of consumption frequently reflect more closely their modest incomes than their considerable assets.

This sense that high land values are not quite real keeps many farmers from cashing in and leaving the business. A farmer readily responds to changing corn prices, selling when the price is high and withholding the crop from market when corn is cheap. The level of product prices may determine whether he plants corn or soybeans, or whether he keeps his calves or slaughters them. But when it comes to land, high prices often have little or no impact on a farmer's land use decisions. The decision to sell out and leave farming tends to be made because of retirement or death, not in response to fluctuating land prices.

On the other hand, the high stakes involved make farmers protective of their land asset, even when they have no intention of selling immediately. The price of the farmer's acreage is seen, quite accurately, as a function of supply and demand; and free market forces, which often seem to buffet him unfairly when it comes to selling his crops, have done well by him in producing a high price for his land. In the farm product market, as one West Virginia poultryman put it, "the farmer has to take the other man's price." In the land market, by contrast, the farmer often finds eager buyers hammering on his door. It is a satisfying feeling.

The Hierarchy of Demands for Land

If farmland is so valuable, from where does that value come? According to classical economic theory, the value of a particular parcel of land

Table 1. Land use hierarchy.

Use	Typical Land Value
Urban uses*	$5,000-50,000 +
Orchard, specialty crop	2,000-7,000
Rural residence	1,000-5,000
Corn, soybeans	1,000-4,000
Developed pasture	300-1,000
Wheat	200-500
Forestry (bareland value)	100-600
Rangeland grazing	50-200

*Urban uses include various intense land uses, including housing subdivisions, industry and commercial establishments.

is set by its usefulness when compared with all other parcels devoted to the same use and by the competition among uses (*10*).[1]

In considering how the present-day market allocates land, it is helpful to imagine a rough hierarchy of demands for land. These are ranked according to the maximum amount each is able to pay for the exclusive use of a given piece of land. At the bottom is rangeland grazing, the kind that uses several acres of land to support a single animal. Somewhat higher on the scale comes forestry; then growing wheat or oats; then more intensive grazing (that typically done on improved pasture); then corn, soybeans, orchards, and the more profitable specialty crops. At the very top are mostly nonagricultural uses: rural housing, industrial plants, suburban housing. Table 1 presents a rough approximation of the typical land values that these activities support.

All land, of course, is not suitable for all uses. But most land can support alternative uses. So the use of land is determined more by the competition among demands than by any unique suitability of land for a given use. For example, much of the agricultural land in the Southeast would make highly productive timberland, yet it is devoted to corn and soybeans. This is not because forestry is unprofitable, but because corn and soybeans are more profitable. Similarly, land in remote Utah valleys is used for extensive grazing, not because it is inherently good for nothing else, but because other lands are better for other uses.

Land remains sufficiently plentiful so that fierce competition among alternative uses for the same land is not readily apparent. Only at a few points in the land use hierarchy does the profitability of one land use overlap another enough to create open conflict.

[1] Land value is the capitalized value of land rent.

Historically the land market responds to the changing profitability of alternative uses. In the first half of the twentieth century, for example, increases in farm labor costs[2] and technological changes that favored larger farm units made millions of acres of cropland in New England, the Appalachians, and the South functionally obsolete. The market response, which took decades to work itself out, was falling land prices and wholesale farm abandonment. Indeed, in some cases land had so little agricultural value that it could not generate enough income to pay local property taxes, and the land was simply abandoned.

The same thing happened with forest land in the South and Upper Midwest. Denuded of its valuable timber in the early part of the century, the bare land had no value, and its owners simply walked away from it.

When the federal government began purchasing land for its eastern national forests, private owners and local governments alike were happy to unload several million acres of this "worthless" land on the government at prices averaging less than $5.00 an acre (*12*). Now, a new demand for this land—rural recreation and second homes—has prices high and rising.

More recently, increases in corn, wheat, and soybean prices in 1972 and 1973 helped trigger explosive jumps in demand for land suited to these crops. As a result, in five subsequent years land in the Lake States, Northern Plains, and especially the Corn Belt, consistently led the general advance in land prices (*13*).

Systematic studies of rural land price dynamics are virtually nonexistent.[3] However, it appears safe to assert, first, that market equilibrium is achieved slowly and, second, that prices adjust more rapidly than uses. The land market is not like the stock market, with multiple trades of identical securities each day. Instead it is riddled with imperfect information, misguided buyers, reluctant sellers, and high transaction costs. Prices of Midwestern corn land did not double overnight in 1972 and 1973 to reflect the quantum leap in the price of corn. Rather, land prices rose by large, yearly increments each year from 1974 to 1977, even as corn prices fell back from their 1973 high.

Similarly, land uses do not change instantaneously as the value of land changes. Many marginal farms in Appalachia hung on for decades after market forces rendered them economically obsolete as production units. On the other hand, virtually any large metropolitan area is ringed with land now growing crops or used for grazing that bears prices (based on

---

[2]Including the return the farmer requires for his own labor and that of his family.

[3]I am not aware of any study of long-term rural land price trends comparable to Homer Hoyt's classic urban land value study, *One Hundred Years of Land Values in Chicago*, published by the University of Chicago Press in 1933.

urbanization value) of $10,000 per acre or more. This is far beyond what current users can support or are likely to support in the future.

For example, the flower fields in northern San Diego County in California yield agricultural land rents of up to $200 per acre, exceptionally high for any agricultural use. Yet the land, which is in great demand for future housing construction, is so high-priced that even $200 per acre is inadequate to pay the yearly property tax levy.[4]

Similarly, thousands of acres of land are now growing corn in the eastern half of Loudoun County, Virginia, at the edge of suburban expansion in the Washington, D.C., metropolitan area. But despite their bucolic appearance, these lands are owned by homebuilding firms or speculators and bear values many times those of equally productive properties in more remote parts of the state.

Land Market Trends

The hierarchy of demands for land is not something fixed and immutable. In the Mississippi Delta, for example, the profitability of growing soybeans has led to the clearing of thousands of acres of what otherwise would be productive timberland. Yet it is not difficult to envision declines in soybean prices (or, less likely, huge increases in wood prices) that could erase that advantage and cause the land to be left uncleared. Likewise, millions of acres of farmland can be shifted fairly easily from pasture to crops and back to pasture in response to changes in the relative market prices of grains and livestock.

What is much harder to envision is agriculture outbidding urban uses in any situation in which the land market is allowed to operate unimpeded. Consider first that for several years agricultural uses have been stronger bidders for land than at any time since the early 1950s. Some strong years for crop prices, easy availability of credit for land buying, demand for farmland as an inflation hedge, and a rising demand among foreign investors have combined to cause land prices, *even in places remote from any possible urbanization,* to rise to record heights year after year (7). If ever there were a time that agriculture could be expected to compete head-to-head against urban demand for the same land, the early 1970s would have been that time.

Yet while farmland prices were rising, prices of land for urban expansion were rising even faster. There is no government series of raw suburban land price data comparable to the series for farmland, but bits and pieces of evidence suggest that prices of land suitable for homebuilding have risen significantly since 1970. One survey of prices of raw land

---

[4]I thank James L. Short, San Diego State University, for this example.

suitable for development found that between 1970 and 1974 alone land around Miami appreciated by 150 to 300 percent, around Denver by 100 percent, around Minneapolis by 44 percent, and around Washington, D.C., by 100 to 167 percent (3).

More discouraging yet are the absolute prices of land for housing compared with those for agriculture. A 1964 comparison of the price of raw suburban land in 259 U.S. cities with the average price of farmland in the state in which each city was located revealed that suburban land prices averaged more than 1,800 percent over farm value (11).

A simple calculation illustrates how difficult it is for agriculture to compete with housing for the same land. Consider corn land in Virginia, typical not only of that being urbanized around Washington and Richmond, but also of good farmland surrounding scores of American cities. Any suburban homebuilder would be delighted to buy such land at $15,000 per acre for use in building houses at, say, 4 units per gross acre.[5] Assume that the land yields, under average management, 90 bushels per acre of corn a year. Also assume that the farmer will be satisfied with a modest return on his land asset of 5 percent a year.[6] In order to support a land value of $15,000 per acre and, hence, compete with the homebuilder, the farmer, after deducting typical nonland production expenses, would have to receive nearly $11 per bushel for his corn.[7] Food would have to be scarce indeed to produce such an astounding price.

Even if such a price could be obtained, consider how easy it would be for the homebuilder to up the ante. At $15,000 an acre he must pay $3,750 for the raw land for each homesite. That amounts to 9.4 percent of a $40,000 suburban house. The builder need only raise the price of each house by $2,000 to be able to raise his bid for the land to $23,000 an acre.

In the unregulated market there are really only two ways in which agriculture can compete, head-to-head, against housing and other urban uses. In a few special places the combination of unusually productive land and heavy farm-related investment may raise the value of land to as much as $5,000 to $7,000 per acre. This would be true, for example, in the case of vineyards and citrus orchards, or truck farms that sell their produce on the premises. Such uses might just survive for a time if less productive, lower priced land nearby could be urbanized.

More commonly, the owners of agricultural land simply may not yet

---

[5]According to the Federal Housing Administration, the average single-family house receiving a FHA-insured loan in the second quarter of 1978 cost $41,638 and stood on a 7,798-square-foot lot. Allowing 25 percent of the site for roads and dedication of school sites, this would allow four house lots per gross acre.

[6]Between 1970 and 1975, the average ratio of farm rent to farm value was 5.6 percent.

[7]In contrast, corn currently is selling in the range of $2.00 to $3.00 a bushel.

be ready to cash in. This is particularly true if they have no mortgage on their land (or an old mortgage based on a very low purchase price and low interest rates) and if they can escape the full burden of ad valorem taxation. Such farmers, and they are by no means uncommon, are so committed to their occupation that they are willing to accept a lower income than they could earn by simply selling their land and banking the money. This situation is likely to be unstable in the long run because there is no guarantee that their heirs will share this commitment to agriculture.

Until recently, heirs often had little choice but to sell. Estate taxes were based on the land's full market value. In 1976 changes in federal tax law were made to give heirs who wished to continue farming the land the option of paying estate taxes on the land's use value rather than its development value.

If urban uses are so profitable compared with agriculture, how has farming survived at all? The simple answer, of course, is the lack of urban demand for the vast majority of the nation's land. Accessibility to city centers and to concentrations of jobs is the overwhelming determinant of residential land values. Beyond a certain distance from these centers, demand for housing traditionally tails off rapidly.

One nascent trend, however, might change this situation somewhat. Recent Census Bureau data indicate that for the first time since the Depression nonmetropolitan areas are growing more rapidly than metropolitan areas (2, 9).

A product of job dispersion, a search for low-cost housing, early retirement, a desire for a simpler lifestyle, and other factors, this so-called counterurbanization phenomenon has helped cause urban-like prices to be paid for rural land. So far most of the land affected has been marginal grazing land or woodland. Working farms are generally too expensive and too large to appeal to such buyers, and they often lack the rolling views that appeal to amenity seekers as well.

Scattered evidence on regional land markets suggests, moreover, that urban demand for rural land, whether for recreation, investment, or retirement, has been far greater than the actual urban-to-rural migration. Urban people apparently are bidding land away from traditional rural uses faster than the population growth figures themselves would indicate.

Of special concern is the parcelization phenomenon in which traditional-sized parcels of rural land are broken up into progressively smaller holdings, sizes more in demand by urban-to-rural migrants, recreationists, and investors (1, 8). Because land's economic potential for farming, grazing, or forestry frequently depends on the size of a land-holding, a closer monitoring of changing parcel size seems warranted nationwide.

Some Unanswered Questions

If policies intended to retain productive land in agriculture come to be vigorously implemented, they will of necessity change land market outcomes. (If a policy does not do so, it is simply irrelevant). Several pieces of information about the rural land market will be vital to their success. First, we should discover under what circumstances the market itself will protect farmland. I demonstrated earlier how difficult it is, at anything near present farm product prices, for farming to compete in the land market against urban demand for land.

Although it is hard to envision product prices high enough to change the outcome of that competition, perhaps a new factor may be injected into the urban-demand side of the equation. For example, will high energy prices or fuel rationing cause the demand for housing on the urban fringe to fall off? Or will new local policies on the extension and pricing of public utilities on the urban fringe reduce the price subdividers are willing to pay for raw, unserviced land? Will demand for prime farmland as an inflation hedge, by both Americans and foreigners, help agricultural uses compete in the land market? Will high wood prices, including the potential of wood as an energy source, create new competition between cropland and forest land?

Second, we need to know more about the market's reaction to declines in expectations based on development value. To what extent and at what price will farmers willingly sign away their development rights to a public authority (4)? Will the creation of exclusive agricultural districts, in which farm uses enjoy protection from laws limiting "accepted farming practices," give farmland within the district a market premium over other land not so protected?

Third, to what extent will the resettlement of rural areas, if it continues, bid land away from productive uses? Will farm uses be able to compete with this demand in the land market, or will the victory of sprawl over farming, nearly universal at the urban fringe, be repeated in more remote rural places?

REFERENCES

1. Armstrong, Frank, and R. D. Briggs. 1978. *Valuation of Vermont forests 1968-1977.* Department of Forestry, University of Vermont, Burlington.
2. Beale, Calvin. 1975. *The revival of population growth in non-metropolitan America.* U.S. Department of Agriculture, Washington, D.C.
3. Black, J. Thomas. 1974. *Land price inflation.* Urban Land 33(8): 29.
4. Boyce, Kohlhase, and Plaut. 1977. *Estimating the value of development easements on agricultural land: Methods and empirical analysis.* Regional Science Research Institute, Philadelphia, Pa.
5. Council of Economic Advisors. 1977. *Economic report of the President.* Washington, D.C.

6. Flanigan, James. 1978. *Question for Congress.* Forbes (May 1): 35.
7. Healy, Robert G., and James L. Short. 1978. *New forces in the market for rural land.* Appraisal Journal 56(2): 185-199.
8. Healy, Robert G., and James L. Short. 1979. *Rural land: Market trends and planning implications.* Journal of the American Planning Association 45(3): 305-317.
9. Houston, Jourdan. 1977. *How're they gonna keep 'em down in New York after they've seen Presque Isle?* Country Journal (April).
10. Ricardo, David. 1821, 1962. *The principles of political economy and taxation.* J. M. Dent, London, Eng. p. 39.
11. Schmid, A. Allen. 1968. *Converting land from rural to urban uses.* Johns Hopkins Press, Baltimore, Md.
12. Shands, William E., and Robert G. Healy. 1977. *The lands nobody wanted: Policy for national forests in the eastern United States.* The Conservation Foundation, Washington, D.C.
13. U.S. Department of Agriculture. 1977. *Farm real estate market developments.* Washington, D.C. p. 7.
14. U.S. Department of Agriculture. 1978. *Farm real estate market developments.* Washington, D.C.

6

Agricultural Land Use: A Population Distribution Perspective

David L. Brown[1]

Conversion of agricultural land to urban uses has become an issue of increasing public concern. The Citizen's Advisory Committee on Environmental Quality highlighted this issue in its 1974 report to the president, and numerous proposals for public action to control land use in agricultural areas have been offered.

Presumably, urbanization intensifies competition among alternative uses of land. Land use change in response to population pressure is expected to be particularly great in areas experiencing rapid growth. Population distribution trends in the 1970s indicate some of the potential impacts of this pressure on agricultural land.

Population Distribution Trends

Three population distribution trends during the seventies contributed to the current interest in agricultural land conversion: (1) metropolitan decentralization or suburbanization, (2) interregional shifts between the North and the South and West, and (3) renewed growth and vitality in rural areas. All three trends moved population and economic activity into less densely settled areas. Consequently, all three trends bear a potential relationship to the use of land.

Metropolitan Decentralization. Suburbanization is not a new phenomenon in the American demographic experience. Indeed, Adna Weber (*25*) wrote of an outward shift of residential population around certain

---

[1]Opinions expressed in this paper are the author's and do not represent the official position of the U.S. Department of Agriculture.

larger cities in the last quarter of the nineteenth century, and Leo Schnore (22) demonstrated that 10 American cities with 100,000 or more population in 1950 were already decentralizing before 1900—New York City by 1850. However, it was during the 1920s that a majority of U.S. cities began to experience lower rates of population growth than their surrounding suburbs (13).

The growth of suburban areas proceeds through outward movement of people from the central city and through in-migration to the urban periphery from nonmetropolitan and other metropolitan areas. Innovations in short-distance transportation and communication facilitated the outward movement of people from the central city. The reduction in costs associated with distance allowed central city workers to move away from their principal workplaces. Horsedrawn, steam and electric streetcars, the telephone, and later the private automobile were the principal innovations figuring in this outward movement.

Peripheral development first occurred along major transportation arteries and later in the rural interstices between these routes. The reasons for suburbanization are many and varied. Of crucial importance has been the availability of large tracts of relatively cheap land on which to locate residential developments. This is not to deny the importance of individual motivations among suburban dwellers. Congestion, crime, pollution, and noise (push factors), and "a yard for the kids" and access to open space (pull factors) have helped perpetuate the suburban trend throughout this century.

Table 1. Average annual rate of population change for central city and suburban counties by region, 1970 to 1977 (8).

Area	United States	Region			
		Northeast	North Central	South	West
			%		
Metro total*	+ .6	− .4	+ .1	+1.4	+1.6
Central cities	− .7	−1.6	−1.5	− .2	+1.0
Outside central cities	+1.6	+ .5	+1.4	+2.9	+2.1
Metro areas of 1 million or more	+ .5	− .5	+ .3	+1.7	+1.3
Central cities	−1.1	−1.7	−1.4	− .9	+ .3
Outside central cities	+1.6	+ .4	+1.4	+3.3	+1.9
Metro areas of less than 1 million	+ .8	†	− .1	+1.2	+2.3
Central cities	− .2	−1.0	−1.6	+ .1	+2.2
Outside central cities	+1.7	+ .6	+1.3	+2.5	+2.5

*Metropolitan status as of 1970.
†Less than .05 percent increase.

Suburban growth continued at a rapid pace during the seventies. Peripheral areas grew at an average annual rate of 1.6 percent between 1970 and 1977 (Table 1). This compares with an annual rate of growth of less than one percent (.9 percent) for the U.S. population overall. In contrast, central city portions of standard metropolitan statistical areas (SMSAs) declined by .7 percent a year during the period. This decline was mainly in central cities of SMSAs with a million or more population—the largest metropolitan areas. Central cities of smaller SMSAs declined much less rapidly.

There was little if any central city growth in any region of the country, except the West. There, appreciable growth occurred only in smaller SMSAs. In contrast, suburban areas grew in all regions, although their rate of growth in the Northeast was slight. Suburban growth was especially great in the South and West, regardless of metropolitan area size. Suburbs surrounding large SMSAs in the South grew at an average annual rate of 3.3 percent during the seventies, a rate comparable to that in many underdeveloped countries.

Indications are that rapid suburban growth and that slow growth or a decline in central cities will continue into the twenty-first century (*18*). Inhabitants in what is now defined as the suburban fringe are projected to increase between 62 and 75 percent by the year 2000. Central city residents are expected to increase only slightly (12 percent) or decline (about 4 percent). Consequently, the suburban land surrounding present metropolitan cities may have to accommodate as many as 135 million persons in the year 2000, 58 million more than in 1970.

Shifts in Regional Population Distribution. The South gained over 5 million persons between 1970 and 1975. This growth exceeded that of all other regions combined. The West grew by 2.9 million persons, slightly less than in the sixties, but nonetheless a continuation of past trends. In contrast, the North Central and Northeast grew only slightly, by 1 million and 400,000 persons, respectively. This is radically different than in previous decades (*7*).

Internal migration is the basic determinant of regional variations in population growth. This is increasingly so because natural increase, births minus deaths, is at a low point, thus contributing little to regional variations in population change.

In the South, recent population growth and in-migration contrasts sharply with history (*15*). Traditionally, the South has been an exporter of people. Poverty; economic underdevelopment; labor surplus in agriculture; and, among Blacks, prejudice, discrimination, and the abandonment of sharecropping have been strong motivations for leaving the region.

Migration from the South reached its peak during World War II and the following decade. During the forties, the region suffered a net loss of over 2 million persons. However, the South began to industrialize and modernize in the late fifties and early sixties, and the flow of jobs and people began to reverse their traditional course. Among the factors thought to be responsible for this reversal were low taxes, other investment incentives, cheap land and labor, and a relative lack of unionization.

Both increased in-migration and decreased loss of persons to other regions figured prominently in the South's shift to in-migration (16). However, in-migration to the South was selective during the sixties. Florida accounted for a large portion of the growth. In fact, had it not been for Florida, the region would have continued to show a net migration loss (7).

Table 2. Streams of migration between regions (5, 6).

	1965-1970	1970-1975
	——— 1,000 ———	
Net Migration Between:		
Northeast and		
North Central	− 53	− 67
South	− 438	− 964
West	− 224	− 311
North Central and		
Northeast	+ 53	+ 67
South	− 275	− 790
West	− 415	− 472
South and		
Northeast	+ 438	+ 964
North Central	+ 275	+ 790
West	− 57	+ 75
West and		
Northeast	+ 224	+ 311
North Central	+ 415	+ 472
South	+ 57	− 75

In-migration to the South accelerated during the seventies. More importantly, in-migration was characteristic of numerous areas throughout the region. Texas, the mid-South uplands (Tennessee, Kentucky, northern Alabama and Georgia) and the Ozark-Ouchita plateau (Arkansas and Oklahoma) recorded substantial growth (20).

California's dominance of in-migration to the West ended during the 1970s. Between 1965 and 1970, California was the destination of almost

70 percent of all migrants to the West. In contrast, during the first five years of the 1970s, the state's share dropped to less than a third (7).

The primary streams of interregional migration are from the North Central and Northeast regions to the South and West (Table 2). Migration between the North and South has increased markedly since 1965-1970, while the North to West stream has remained relatively stable. Also, the South to West movement has been reversed. Regardless of the region specified, the South is no longer a net exporter of population. On the contrary, it is a major locus of economic and population growth for the nation.

Nonmetropolitan Population Turnaround. Notions of metropolitan concentration and decline or abandonment of small towns and rural areas no longer characterize population distribution in the United States. In fact, from 1970 to 1976, 2.3 million more people moved into nonmetropolitan counties than moved out of them. In contrast, these same counties lost 3.0 million persons through out-migration during the 1960s (Table 3). Consequently, for the first time in the twentieth century, the rate of population growth in nonmetropolitan America (8.0 percent) exceeded that in metropolitan areas (4.7 percent) (1). This turnaround affects most regions of the country—remote and completely rural areas as well as those that are partly urbanized and dominated by large metropolitan cities.

The reasons for this turnaround are complex, but three interrelated factors appear to be at its root: (1) economic decentralization, (2) a preference for rural living, and (3) modernization of rural life.

1. *Economic decentralization:* There has been a decentralization of employment opportunities from metro to nonmetro areas (2). Between 1970 and 1977, nonfarm wage and salary employment increased 22 percent in nonmetro areas. In addition, the character of nonmetro employment has changed, with service jobs taking the lead in recent growth. Mining and energy extraction are new sources of employment growth in some areas, such as the Northern Great Plains. Also, people are no longer being displaced from rural areas by diminishing employment in extractive industries, as they were during the fifties and sixties. Commuting from nonmetro to metro areas brings additional jobs within the reach of rural residents.

2. *Preference for rural living:* National surveys repeatedly have found a decided preference for living in the country and in small towns, particularly within commuting range of a metropolitan city (28). This preference for rural living becomes increasingly important as employment constraints to living in rural areas are reduced. One evidence of the strength of nonpecuniary factors in recent metro to nonmetro migration

is the fact that almost one-quarter of recent migrants accepted an income cut in the process of moving to a smaller community.[2]

3. *Modernization of rural life*: All-weather roads, controlled-access highways, cable television, telephone service, and centralized sewer and water systems have helped modernize rural living. Such advances in transportation, communication, and public facilities increasingly render inappropriate the stereotype that rural areas are isolated and backward.

However, nonmetro America is extremely heterogeneous. Factors that bring about growth in one area may be of little consequence in another. Also, in the midst of this population turnaround, there are still about 500 nonmetropolitan counties that continue to experience out-migration and population decline. Most of these declining counties are in the Great Plains and Mississippi Delta.

Agricultural Land Conversion

The current population distribution trends suggest that significant pressure is being brought to bear on the nation's stock of agricultural land resources. However, it does not necessarily follow that large amounts of prime farmland are being irreversibly converted to urban (and transportation) uses simply because people are moving to areas that heretofore were less densely settled—the suburban fringe, the South and West, and small towns and rural areas. This may be true, but it could just as easily be true that in-migrants are occupying vacant houses, or settling on land not suited for agricultural use.

Analysts differ greatly in their estimates of the amount of agricultural

[2]Brown, David L. 1978. "Some Spatial Aspects of Workforce Migration in the United States, 1965-75." Paper presented at the Population Association of America meeting, Atlanta, Georgia.

Table 3. Population change by metropolitan status (1, 5, 6, 7).

| Area | Population | | | | |
| | Number (1,000) | | | Percentage Change | |
	1976	1970	1960	1970-1976	1960-1970
Total United States	214,658	203,301	179,323	+ 5.6	+ 13.4
Metropolitan counties†	155,901	148,877	127,191	+ 4.7	+ 17.0
Nonmetropolitan counties	58,757	54,424	52,132	+ 8.0	+ 4.4
Adjacent counties‡	30,433	28,033	26,116	+ 8.6	+ 7.3
Nonadjacent counties	28,324	26,391	26,016	+ 7.3	+ 1.4

*Net migration expressed as a percentage of the population at beginning of specified period.
†Metropolitan status as of 1974.
‡Nonmetropolitan counties adjacent to Standard Metropolitan Statistical Areas.

land taken each year for urban uses. In one of the first systematic studies of the issue, Donald Bogue (4) preducted that 372,000 acres of agricultural land per year would be lost to urban uses between 1955 and 1975 in metropolitan areas alone.

Bogue's figures were not unanimously verified over the 20 years of his prediction. Estimates of land loss by other analysts ranged from 1.1 million acres a year (26) to almost 3 million acres a year (17). However, an analysis by Robert C. Otte (19) in 1974 produced estimates that were similar to Bogue's prediction. Otte concluded that during the 1960s about 709,000 acres of land were converted to urban uses per year in SMSAs and that between 76 percent and 49 percent of this land previously had been in crops, depending on the region. Based on these estimates, and on information on changes in agricultural productivity and additions to the cropland base, Otte concluded that urbanization does not pose a serious immediate threat to the nation's supply of agricultural land.

Otte's conclusions have been reexamined several times since 1974. For example, John Fraser Hart (12), in analyzing data from the 1958 and 1967 Conservation Needs Inventories, found that relatively little land had been urbanized during the 10 years between the surveys. He concluded, "Little more than 4 percent of the nation's land area will be urbanized by the year 2000 and that urban encroachment will not remove significant acreages of land from agricultural production within the foreseeable future."

Daniel Vining and associates (24) at the University of Pennsylvania carried the analysis one step further by focusing exclusively on the conversion of prime agricultural land (Soil Conservation Service Classes I and II). The result: a radical increase in the rate of loss of rural land to urbanization between the periods 1958-1967 and 1967-1975. Moreover, prime land was converted to urban uses at twice the rate of nonprime land.

Net Migration			
1970-1976		1960-1970	
umber (1,000)	Rate (%)*	Number (1,000)	Rate (%)*
2,800	+ 1.4	+ 3,001	+ 1.7
545	+ .4	+ 5,959	+ 4.7
2,255	+ 4.1	− 2,958	− 5.7
1,328	+ 4.7	− 705	− 2.7
928	+ 3.5	− 2,253	− 8.7

To explain this shift, Vining and his colleagues investigated the hypothesis that in-migration to rural areas, which increased markedly after 1970, flowed predominantly to areas of high quality farmland. They could not support the hypothesis and concluded, "It is not the redistribution of population from high density to low density counties that is causing this large increase (in the rate of prime land conversion), but a higher rate of consumption of rural land for urban purposes at all densities." A bias toward prime land within counties was suggested as another factor. This explanation is plausible, but there is evidence that the increased rate of conversion of prime land may be due, in part, to procedural differences between the 1967 and 1975 studies, not to substantive reasons. Inventory procedures for the urban and water categories differed in the 1967 and 1975 studies. In 1967, inventory estimates of these categories were determined by county committees. In the 1975 study, estimates of urban and water land use were obtained by field personnel from point data.

Linda Lee (*14*), in an analysis of the issue, concluded that these procedural changes may have affected the comparability of estimates and, consequently, the measurement of land use change. For example, her analysis showed that some of the increase in urban and built-up land between 1967 and 1975 had already been built-up in 1967.

Even within the U.S. Department of Agriculture (USDA) differences exist on estimates of land converted to urban and transportation uses (Table 4). For example, the Economics, Statistics and Cooperatives Service (formerly the Economic Research Service) estimated from 1970 census data on urban areas that 950,000 acres of rural land were converted to urban and transportation uses annually between 1959 and 1974, less than half the annual acreage estimated as lost between 1967 and 1975 by

Table 4. Land converted to urban and transportation uses, 1959-1977 (10, 11, 23).

Estimates	Years	Acres Converted Annually to Urban and Transportation Uses From	
		All Sources	Cropland
		——————— 1,000,000 ———————	
ERS Major Land Use Series	1959-1969	.9	.3
	1959-1974	.95	.3
SCS Conservation Needs Inventory	1958-1967	1.2	Not estimated
SCS Potential Cropland Study	1967-1975	2.0	.6
SCS National Resource Inventories	1967-1977	2.9	1.0

the Soil Conservation Service (SCS) Potential Cropland Study and about one-third of the annual acreage estimated as urbanized between 1967 and 1977 in the recent SCS National Resource Inventory (*10, 11, 23*). Differences in data collection methods and in the definition of urban and transportation uses account for these varying estimates.

A possible solution to this confusion is to seek more direct case-study data on land conversion, but even here there is substantial variation among investigators as to the severity of the land loss problem. For example, Kathryn Zeimetz and her associates (*27*) at USDA analyzed aerial photographs of 53 rapidly growing counties and concluded that urbanization had not greatly encroached upon the supply of land used for crops between 1961 and 1970. In 1970 urban uses accounted for 16.4 percent of the land area in the counties, up from about 13 percent in 1961. Of the land developed for urban uses, 35 percent had been in cropland, 28 percent in forest, and 33 percent in open, idle land.

On the other hand, numerous local studies show a substantial loss of prime land to urbanization.[3] Thousands of acres of the best citrus growing lands have been converted in Orange County, California. In Illinois an estimated 505,000 acres of farmland will be converted to urban uses during the next 25 years (*21*).

In addition to land conversion itself, researchers are beginning to investigate other more indirect effects of urbanization on agriculture. For example, David Berry and his colleagues (*3*) suggest that regulations on farming activity spill over from urban areas into the countryside. These regulations, coupled with speculation in land, are thought to create a feeling of impermanence about agriculture's future.

Using qualitative data for areas in the Mid-Atlantic States, Berry and his associates demonstrated that the spillover effects of urbanization were strong and the impermanence syndrome was at its most intense level in rapidly developing areas where some land is still in agriculture. They concluded that in such areas the indirect effects of urbanization will drive out most types of agriculture and idle most farmland, some of which will be converted to urban uses.

Policy Implications

While population clearly is flowing to the suburban fringe, to the South and West, and to small towns and rural areas, it is not clear that migrants are consuming significant amounts of agricultural land. One cannot conclude, from the evidence, that changes in population distribu-

---

[3]David Berry reviewed these studies in a paper, "Population Redistribution and Conflicts in Land Use: A Midwestern Perspective," presented at the 1979 Conference on Understanding Population Change, held at the University of Illinois.

tion pose direct and immediate threats to the nation's supply of prime farmland.

Indications are that land resources are adequate to meet future foreign and domestic food and fiber needs (9, 14). The SCS Potential Cropland Study demonstrated that additions to the cropland base between 1967 and 1975 more than compensated for losses to urbanization and road and reservoir construction. About 4.5 million acres of cropped prime land were converted to these irreversible uses during the period, but the percentage of prime land used for crops actually increased. The new cropland was of high quality, not marginal land as might have been expected.

Moreover, urbanization of farmland does not appear to be a serious constraint to future growth in agricultural output. About 111 million acres of land has a high or medium potential for conversion to cropland, and indications are that crop yields per acre will increase, albeit at a dampened rate. The impact of urbanization on agricultural production thus is not a particularly critical issue at the national level.

However, one might reach a different conclusion by looking at the local situation. The amount of agricultural land converted to urban uses may not add up to a significant acreage in comparison with the national cropland base, but it may be substantial in specific communities. Whether this is viewed as an issue requiring public action or not is a question to be determined largely by local residents and interest groups.

Migration, particularly rapid, unanticipated migration, may create the potential for conflict among various community groups. It goes without saying that groups differ in the values they assign to certain issues. Some place economic development, quality housing, and the provision of an adequate level of essential services at the top of the list. Others accord the preservation of agricultural land first place. If the agricultural preservationists are strong enough, or well-enough organized, they may prevent a growing population from exercising its demand for new residences, industrial parks, and public and private infrastructure at the expense of agricultural land. As newcomers make their presence felt in the land market, increasing the competition between agricultural and nonagricultural uses of the land, preservationist groups are apt to mobilize against farmland conversion. In-migration pressures have induced some communities and states to regulate land use, to purchase scenic or conservation easements on rural land, or to provide incentives to rural landowners to keep their land in rural uses.[4]

Changing demographic conditions require adjustments in almost every aspect of community life and structure. Agricultural land conversion

[4]Ibid.

may be a crucial issue in some communities, even *the* crucial issue, but in general it should be understood that land use is only one of the complex set of conditions that covary with demographic changes. An ecological approach, one that emphasizes interrelationships among population, organization, environment, and technology, is necessary for a comprehensive understanding of land use change in rural America.

REFERENCES

1. Beale, Calvin L. 1978. *Internal migration in the United States since 1970.* Testimony before House Select Committee on Population, U.S. House of Representatives. Washington, D.C.
2. Beale, Calvin L. 1978. *Making a living in rural and small town America.* In *Rural Development Perspectives* (RDP 1). Economics, Statistics and Cooperatives Service, U.S. Department of Agriculture, Washington, D.C.
3. Berry, David, Ernest Leonardo, and Kenneth Bieri. 1976. *The farmer's response to urbanization: A study of the Middle Atlantic States.* Discussion Paper No. 92. Regional Science Research Institute, Philadelphia, Pennsylvania.
4. Bogue, Donald J. 1956. *Metropolitan growth and the conversion of land to nonagricultural use.* In *Studies in Population Distribution.* Scripps Foundation for Research on Population Problems, Miami University, Oxford, Ohio, and Population Research and Training Center, University of Chicago, Chicago, Illinois.
5. Bureau of the Census. 1973. *U.S. census of population, 1970.* Subject Reports, Mobility for States and the Nation PC(2)-2B. U.S. Department of Commerce, Washington, D.C.
6. Bureau of the Census. 1975. *Mobility of the population of the United States, March 1970 to March 1975.* Current Population Reports, Series P-20, No. 285. U.S. Department of Commerce, Washington, D.C.
7. Bureau of the Census. 1976. *Estimates of the population of states with components of change: 1970-1975.* Current Population Reports, Series P-25, No. 640. U.S. Department of Commerce, Washington, D.C.
8. Bureau of the Census. 1978. *Social and economic characteristics of the metropolitan and nonmetropolitan population, 1977 and 1970.* Current Population Report, Special Studies Series P-23, No. 75. U.S. Department of Commerce, Washington, D.C.
9. Cotner, M. L., M. D. Skold, and O. Krause. 1975. *Farmland: Will there be enough?* ERS-584. Economic Research Service, U.S. Department of Agriculture, Washington, D.C.
10. Dideriksen, Raymond I., Allen Hildebaugh, and Keith O. Schmude. 1977. *Potential cropland survey.* Statistical Bulletin 578. Soil Conservation Service, U.S. Department of Agriculture, Washington, D.C.
11. Frey, H. Thomas. 1977. *Major uses of land in the United States: Preliminary estimates for 1977.* Working Paper No. 34. Economic Research Service, U.S. Department of Agriculture, Washington, D.C.
12. Hart, John Fraser. 1976. *Urban encroachment on rural areas.* The Geographical Review 66(1): 3-17.
13. Hawley, Amos. 1956. *The changing shape of metropolitan America.* The Free Press, Glencoe, Illinois.

14. Lee, Linda K. 1978. *A perspective on cropland availability.* Agricultural Economic Report No. 406. Economics, Statistics and Cooperatives Service, U.S. Department of Agriculture, Washington, D.C.

15. Long, Larry H. 1978. *Interregional migration of the poor.* Current Population Reports, Special Studies Series P-23, No. 73. Bureau of the Census, U.S. Department of Commerce, Washington, D.C.

16. Long, Larry H., and Kristin A. Hansen. 1975. *Trends in return migration to the South.* Demography 12: 601-614.

17. Lutz, J. Fulton. 1973. *Agricultural land declining.* North Carolina Research in Farming 32(1-2): 11.

18. Morrison, Peter A. 1976. *The demographic context of educational policy planning.* Rand Paper P-5592. Rand Corporation, Santa Monica, California.

19. Otte, Robert C. 1974. *Farming in the city's shadow.* Agricultural Economics Report No. 250. Economic Research Service, U.S. Department of Agriculture, Washington, D.C.

20. Roseman, Curtis C. 1977. *Changing migration patterns within the United States.* Resource Papers for College Geography No. 77-2. Association of American Geographers, Washington, D.C.

21. Schneider, Roger. 1978. *Alternative for projections of non-agricultural land needs in Illinois to the year 2000.* Paper No. 78 E-57. Department of Agricultural Economics, University of Illinois, Urbana.

22. Schnore, Leo F. 1959. *The timing of metropolitan decentralization: A contribution to the debate.* Journal of the American Institute of Planners 25: 200-206.

23. Soil Conservation Service. 1979. *Preliminary data from phase one of the National Resource Inventories.* U.S. Department of Agriculture, Washington, D.C.

24. Vining, Daniel R., Thomas Plaut, and Kenneth Biere. 1977. *Urban encroachment on prime agricultural land in the United States.* International Regional Science Review 2(2): 143-156.

25. Weber, Adna F. 1899. *The growth of cities in the ninteenth century.* Macmillan, New York, New York.

26. Williams, D. A. 1956. *Urbanization of productive farmland.* Soil Conservation 22: 60-65.

27. Zeimetz, Kathryn A., Elizabeth Dillon, Ernest E. Hardy, and Robert C. Otte. 1976. *Dynamics of land use in fast growth areas.* Agricultural Economics Report No. 325. Economic Research Service, U.S. Department of Agriculture, Washington, D.C.

28. Zuiches, James J., and Edwin H. Carpenter. 1978. *Residential preferences and rural development policy.* In *Rural Development Perspectives* (RDP 1). Economics, Statistics and Cooperatives Service, U.S. Department of Agriculture, Washington, D.C.

7

The Ethical Dimension
of Farmland Protection

R. Neil Sampson

The United States food system dependence on increasingly fewer farmers, who in turn are dependent on a series of factors beyond their control, raises a basic question of farm sector resiliency to withstand supply-demand fluctuations without increasing Government assistance.

U.S. General Accounting Office (*10*)

In 1978 United States farmers reaped a bin-busting crop. Major grain commodities posted record levels of production despite government attempts to hold down crop acreage. Never before had American farmers produced so much, fed so many people per farmer, or talked so openly about an impending agricultural crisis.

Crisis? Impossible! Maybe. Maybe not. Let's examine some of the indicators and see if they lend credibility to efforts to protect the nation's farmlands.

Can we have a farmland problem in the middle of a farm production boom? The evidence is that we not only can, we do. But that problem is not well recognized. It is masked by analyses that measure resource adequacy on the basis of annual or average production figures.

Americans must begin to think about land, land quality, and land adequacy in a way that will allow us to evaluate the land's needs, irrespective of current agricultural commodity supplies and prices. That thinking should start with a basic statement of agriculture's relationship to land.

Agriculture is a man-made ecological system. Agriculture can no more escape certain ecological laws than Newton's apple could ignore the law of gravity. Any ecosystem, whether man-made or natural, must in the long run achieve a steady state with regard to both energy and materials.

89

Fertility, organic matter, energy, and water must flow into the system in relation to outflow, or the system is depleting. The soil is a living resource reservoir of constantly shifting dimensions. If the size and capability of that soil reservoir is shrinking, it is certain that, if the trend continues, problems will result.

Agriculture is to that soil reservoir what a pump is to a well. The food produced can be increased, as can the water from the well, by speeding up or improving the pump. But that will only be profitable so long as the level in the reservoir is maintained. If we begin depleting the reservoir, improvements in the pump and ever-increasing energy inputs become essential to maintain current levels of production.

American agriculture is in precisely that position today. Past productivity increases have come about through the adoption of new technology and a huge increase in the capital used, during a period when climatic conditions may have been unusually favorable. This has enabled a steadily dwindling number of farmers in America to stay in business by getting larger in size, adopting the latest techniques, and absorbing narrow (or nonexistent) profit margins. But how much more of this trend can we absorb? Is the pump running as fast as it will go? Evidence indicates the water level in the well is continuing to drop.

Unless we turn to the land that makes up the "reservoir" from which agriculture "pumps" food and find ways to reverse the damage and loss that is steadily depleting it, serious agricultural problems seem certain, and in the not-too-distant future. And those problems, because they will affect the nation's most basic economic industry, will reverberate throughout the entire economy, undermining every effort to slow inflation and imperilling our ability to produce enough export goods to pay for increasingly costly imported oil. The strength of the nation comes from the land, and the land is in trouble.

Stress on the Land Base

> The amount of cropland that will be paved over, built on, strip-mined, or flooded by a dam by the end of this century is unknown. However, if world population projections materialize, 2.3 billion people will be added between 1975 and the year 2000, a far larger increase than the 1.5 billion added during the preceding 25 years. Given those population projections and the projected gains in income, every nonfarm claimant on cropland—urbanization, energy production, transportation—is certain to be greater during the last quarter of this century than during the third.
>
> Lester R. Brown (*1*)

To get some idea of the magnitude of the current deterioration of America's farmland base, it is necessary to analyze and combine the major factors causing the land to lose productivity. It is not as simple as measuring the depth of the water in the well to see if it is dropping or holding steady.

The farmland resource is gigantic and complex. Over 20,000 kinds of soil are used for growing crops. While statistical indicators are often lacking, difficult to compare, or hard to interpret accurately, there are enough indicators to provide better insights than ever before, thanks to the accelerated work being done by the Soil Conservation Service (SCS) in their land inventory and monitoring efforts.

The two main causes of productivity loss are soil depletion and the conversion of farmlands to other uses. Both can be reversed, but the costs are such that it is prudent to consider both, for practical purposes, permanent.

Preliminary data from the 1977 SCS erosion and sediment survey (9) give some insights into the soil losses from cropland. The survey uses a broad definition of cropland, including row crops, close-grown crops, rotation hay and pasture, occasionally improved hayland, native hay, summer fallow, orchards, vineyards, bush fruit, and other.

On the 413 million acres included in this cropland category, SCS estimates the average annual soil loss via sheet and rill erosion at 2 billion tons. Predictably, erosion rates are lowest on Class I lands (just under 3 tons/acre/year average) and highest on Class IV and Class VI lands (averaging from 9 tons/acre/year on all Class IVe cropland to 30 tons/acre/year on Class VIe row-cropped land).

But what does this mean in terms of land loss? How important is a ton of soil anyway? There are few satisfactory estimates available. The many different situations that exist make it difficult to generalize. But we can draw some conclusions from this information by converting tons of soil loss into acre-equivalents of productivity loss.

A 4-inch layer of topsoil weighs about 650 tons per acre. Although this will vary for each kind of soil, let's assume that the loss of 4 inches of topsoil will badly compromise the productivity of most cropland, if not make it uneconomic to farm. Obviously, there are soils where this will not be the case, but there are many soils in America today that are already badly damaged by erosion, and another 2-inch to 3-inch loss will expose rock, clay, hardpan, or other subsurface layers that limit intensive cultivation.

It seems reasonable, therefore, to equate the loss of 650 tons of soil to the loss of one acre-equivalent of cropland productivity. The fact the soil loss is spread over many acres makes it no less a loss; it only changes the shape of the time-curve on which a specific parcel of land will become unproductive.

One fact becomes immediately apparent from table 1. That is that two-thirds of the productivity loss sustained by America's cropland today comes from Class II and Class III lands that make up the bulk of our cropland resource. At the same time, marginal croplands clearly are suffering erosion losses at a far more rapid rate. Class I land, about 9.5 percent of the cropland, suffers a productivity loss of about 4.5 percent. Equivalent ratios for the other classes of cropland are as follows: Class II, 45 percent of the cropland, 35 percent of the loss; Class III, 32 percent of the cropland, 35 percent of the loss; and Classes IV-VII, 15 percent of the cropland, 25 percent of the productivity loss.

These figures are not surprising. Recent trends in farmland use show that farmers have been slowly but steadily moving off marginal farmlands (Classes IV-VII) onto better lands. The erosion figures leave little doubt why: marginal lands are washing out from under the farmers.

When we look at the land lost to urban, built-up, and water storage areas, we get an estimate of the acres moved out of the cropland inventory on an immediate and fairly permanent basis. Instead of the insidious, unseen losses from erosion that rob productivity so slowly that few notice, the conversion of a tract of prime farmland from corn to houses is clearly apparent. Between 1967 and 1975, an estimated 5 million acres of cropland was lost in this manner (4). That's about 683,000 acres a year. In addition, another 1.6 million acres moved each year from cropland into "other" land, indicating that the magnitude of the impact of land use conversions on agricultural productivity is somewhere in the range of two to three times the actual acreage converted at any one time.

Of the land converted to urban and built-up uses between 1967 and 1975, 7 percent was Class I, 30 percent was Class II, 21 percent was Class III, and 42 percent was Classes IV-VIII. During the period, U.S. Department of Agriculture officials estimate, the impact of conversion affected about 5 million acres each year: 2 million acres were urbanized; 2 million were isolated, skipped over, or in some other way made unfarmable by the urban growth; and 1 million acres went into water impoundments (5).

In the 1977 survey, SCS officials estimate the average annual built-up

Table 1. Total annual soil loss, via sheet and rill erosion, converted to acre-equivalents of productivity lost from American cropland, by capability class.

Capability Class	1977 Cropland (acres)	Annual Soil Loss (tons)	Productivity Loss (acre-equivalents)
I	31,529,000	91,244,000	140,000
II	187,702,000	709,722,000	1,091,900
III	131,710,000	709,388,000	1,091,400
IV-VII	62,226,000	506,603,000	779,300
Total	413,167,000	2,016,957,000	3,102,600

Table 2. Annual losses of agricultural productivity due to urbanization, water projects, and other building activities in the United States, by capability class.

Capability Class	Percentage of Land Urbanized	Acres Affected	
		Cropland Base	Marginal Land
		acre-equivalents	
I	7	350,000	
II	30	1,500,000	
III	21	1,050,000	
IV-VIII	42		2,100,000
Totals	100	2,900,000	2,100,000

Table 3. Estimated annual loss of agricultural productivity due to soil erosion and conversion to nonagricultural uses, by capability class.

Capability Class	Loss to Erosion	Loss to Conversion	Total Loss	(%)
		acre-equivalents		
I	140,000	350,000	490,000	(8%)
II	1,091,900	1,500,000	2,591,900	(43%)
III	1,091,400	1,050,000	2,141,400	(36%)
IV-VIII	779,300	0	779,300	(13%)
Total	3,102,600	2,900,000	6,002,600	

acreage to be about 2.5 million. If the trends observed in prior years continue and one acre is put out of commercial agricultural production for every acre urbanized, we arrive again at the 5 million acre number. Assuming the percentages hold similar to what they were in the 1975 potential cropland study, table 2 indicates the land loss likely to be sustained in the different capability classes.

Not all the 5 million acres of urbanizing land comes from cropland or land that has a crop-producing capability. For purposes of this analysis, a conservative estimate of the loss would be to count only those lands in Classes I-III as having cropland potential. This would put the annual loss of agricultural productivity (Table 2) somewhere in the 2.9 million acre range. Of course, there would be a small loss of cropland from Classes VI-VIII. This would be minor, however, since these marginal lands account for so little of the future agricultural productive capacity.

Adding the two estimates of losses to productive capacity from erosion and conversion results in table 3. These figures represent a conservative estimate of the loss sustained by the nation's farmland base. They are not individual and discrete acres covered by asphalt or concrete in an absolute, permanent conversion, but they represent the productive capacity lost each year through the combined forces of erosion and conversion.

This loss of productive capability from soil erosion and land use conversion is large and will get larger at an increasing rate. Not only are both processes self-reinforcing, they are also interactive.

Soil depletion is not just a steady loss. It accelerates with each increment of topsoil that is washed away, resulting in less absorbtive capacity, organic matter, and plant growth to protect the soil when rain strikes again.

Farmland conversion, likewise, feeds on itself. Each plot of farmland lost not only breeds new houses that consume rural resources and services, it also creates another group of farmer speculators who decide that the time is coming soon when the land will make more money by being sold than by being maintained as a producing farm.

The interaction between the two processes is more subtle, but no less real. As erosion eats away the land's productivity, affecting the marginal acres first, it forces more reliance on the nation's prime farmlands. Yet these are the lands burdened with a disproportionate share of the urbanization and related development, so the competition for them is growing from two directions. As good land becomes urbanized and unavailable for food production, it forces agriculture onto more marginal land, which signals a new round of soil erosion and new pressures on the land and water base.

Losses from the nation's farmland base are not insignificant. Relative to the 413 million acres currently in the cropland inventory, they represent 1.5 percent annually. Of the estimated 135 million acres remaining as potential cropland, they represent over 4 percent annually, meaning the equivalent of the nation's cropland reserve could be lost in a 25-year period. These are alarming estimates and lead one to question why there is not more concern. A partial answer may lie in the way in which we value the land itself.

The Value of Land

> The real wealth of the planet is its natural resources. Our real wealth is our ability to use these resources without destroying their source. Money has no value unless it represents energy, food, materials, or products. No amount of monetary manipulation can create natural resources.
>
> Laurence J. Peter (7)

What is land's real value to man? Is it a store of basic wealth, a quarry to be mined for the products needed for survival, comfort, or pleasure? Certainly. But it is also more. It is the living, dynamic bridge where crops convert solar energy to human food. It spans the gap between death and life, between what was and what is to be.

There is a qualitative dimension to land also, as important as any quantitative measure. Not every soil is of equal value to man, or to nature itself. Varying from thin, stony, cold, or dry to deep, fertile, and loamy, the soils that mantle the landscape array themselves in an endless mosaic of value. Additionally affected by climate, slope, vegetation, and the changes wrought by man, the resulting landcapes can be readily categorized on a qualitative scale.

But what land shall be highest on that scale? What kinds of land will people decide are most valuable—most important for human needs? The choice is obvious: farmlands; those lands that produce food. On the qualitative scale, these lands have no peer in terms of their value to people. We treasure mountains, glaciers, deserts, swamps. They are of value in many ways. But is their value as basic as the value of the land that grows food? Hardly!

We treasure scarcity, and the fact that certain landscapes are unique justifies concern about their preservation. But are not food-producing lands more essential to man, and therefore of higher value?

We have, particularly in years of good weather, an abundance or even a surplus of food. Does this mean that food-producing lands are of less value? Does this mean we can waste farmlands without fear of future reprisal? Does the qualitative value of land rise and fall with annual rainfall, or technological breakthroughs, or man's tinkering with monetary or economic systems? Superficially, it can be argued that this is the case.

Measured in economic value, the price of land responds rapidly to economic events. When investors fear the stability of stocks, bonds, or other forms of investment, they turn to land. This demand drives prices up, making land look all the more lucrative, which attracts additional investors. But what does the resulting price spiral mean in terms of the land's real value?

When climate has been unfavorable, food stocks drop and prices rise. Land prices skyrocket as investors rush to take advantage of the food price bonanza. They inevitably over-produce when climate becomes more favorable. Stocks rise to glut proportions and prices plummet. But what of the land? Has it changed value?

We confuse price with value and money with wealth, and herein lies much of our inability to think straight about the value of farmland.

Clearly, farmland values are not measured simply by price. There is a fundamental difference between money and wealth. But economic analysis does not measure or even recognize these differences.

The Problem with Economics

Economics, as currently constituted and practiced, acts as a most effective barrier against the understanding of these (natural resource) problems, owing to its addiction to purely quantitative analysis and its timorous refusal to look into the real nature of things.

E. F. Schumacher (8)

The economic dimensions of farmland protection are important. They must be addressed carefully and properly. But farmland protection is not an economic issue. It is a conservation issue with an economic dimension. This difference, while perhaps appearing to be a play on words, is real and important.

The economic value of land resides in the profit, measured in dollars, that the land can return to its current tenant. If it is cheaper this year to import food from elsewhere and more profitable to build condominiums than plant corn, economic analysis tells us to convert or abandon farmland.

One problem with this elementary economic measure is that it treats natural resources the same as man-made resources. Land becomes an asset to be converted into dollars. The more dollars, the better; the faster, the better. Success, or "good," comes from profit.

In practical terms, this thinking too often has led economists to argue that land is best used by being destroyed, that foreclosing *for all time* the opportunities for people in the future to harvest food from the land is of no consequence so long as the current owner nets the maximum profit today.

But what are the real values involved? Should we convert prime farmland to housing tracts on the basis that mediocre land elsewhere can be exploited for food needs? Is it rational for people to treat prime farmland with the same attitude that they use in trading automobiles? Is $5,000 worth of prime farmland, which people did not make and cannot replace once it is lost, to be given the same value as a $5,000 car?

The obvious problem with such an approach means that some force other than simple economics must help guide the use of natural resources, particularly land. There are, after all, higher values than money and better measures of good and evil than costs and profits. But to find such measures, we must look at ethical, not economic, values.

The Ethical Dimension

An ethic, ecologically, is a limitation on freedom of action in the struggle for existence. An ethic, philosophically, is a differentiation of social from anti-social conduct.

Aldo Leopold (6)

The search for a land ethic in America is not new or novel. It has been the basis for the conservation movement from the beginning. But an ethic is a state of mind. It does not occur; it develops.

With the pressures of soil erosion and land use conversion threatening the land's productivity as never before, it is time for a new public debate to review the prevailing land ethic. The symptoms of land abuse indicate our current ethic is in drastic need of improvement.

We do not use a Van Gogh painting for a doormat. Not because doormats have no value; they are functional indeed. Not because Van Gogh paintings are prized for the dollar value of the canvas or the oil. No, we value the Van Gogh as a treasure, a delight to the eyes, succor to the spirit, a reflection of man's highest creativity. We give it a place of honor and protect it for people of all ages to treasure.

We must begin to look on farmlands in the same way. And farmlands, like paintings, have different values. Not all lands produce alike, given the same level of human management or economic input. Some farmlands obviously are of much greater real value than others. And these most valuable lands, as seen in the estimates made earlier, are being lost at the most rapid rate.

Americans must begin to assess the possibility that anti-social conduct in relation to the land is becoming a real and serious threat to society's continued existence. We have long assumed that our nation possesses the capability to produce ample supplies of food, far more than enough to feed our own people. But is it only Americans that we must consider?

The loss of 6 million acres of productive capacity a year equates to over 115,000 acres each week, over 16,000 acres every day! That means our weekly loss in productivity is greater than the annual production capability of many of the world's nations. These nations, where people starve when the weather turns bad, look to us as a reliable source of food when they need one. That may be an unfounded hope in the near future.

But how much suffering around the world and economic stress at home will be needed before we move toward a new ethical basis for treating our land? How long will we, as Robert Cahn has said, "take for granted that the waters, the soils, the trees, and the wildlife can be manipulated at will in the name of progress, even if that progress is short-lived and far outweighed by the loss of the land's long-term ability to benefit mankind" (2)?

What is needed, clearly, is a new land ethic, an ethic forged of our twin concerns for the land's proper use and care. We must begin to treasure the prime farmlands that have made us the world's richest nation, keep them available for agricultural use, help farmers survive economically and environmentally so that they can profitably produce from them, and insist that the lands be used in a way that minimizes soil depletion. That must be the nature of a new ethic.

But the emergence of a land ethic strong enough to offset our current proclivity to measure in narrow economic terms will not come easily. As Richard Collins pointed out, "An ethic powerful enough to alter patterns of land use must necessarily challenge other accepted habits and vested interests" (3). There are also important values that must be confronted, including individualism, liberty, property, the pursuit of happiness, and the right role of government.

It may be, as Collins proposed, that "The land, because it is so intrinsically important as a source of nurture for life and pastoral values, as well as being the basis for deeply rooted Jeffersonian ideals of individualism and human freedom, is the battleground for the nation's future."

If land and land use are to be a battleground, then facts, trends, and ideas must be the major weapons. The new land ethic must be a product of education and social evolution. It cannot be written, legislated, or imposed upon people. It must change, first, the way Americans think about land. Only then will it successfully alter the ways in which we use this vital resource.

REFERENCES

1. Brown, Lester R. 1978. *The worldwide loss of cropland.* Worldwatch Paper No. 24. Worldwatch Institute, Washington, D.C. 48 pp.
2. Cahn, Robert. 1978. *Footprints on the planet.* Universe Books, New York, New York. 277 pp.
3. Collins, Richard C. 1976. *Developing the needed new land use ethic.* In *Land Issues and Problems.* Virginia Polytechnic Institute and State University, Blacksburg.
4. Dideriksen, Raymond I., Allen R. Hidlebaugh, and Keith O. Schmude. 1977. *Potential cropland study.* Statistical Bulletin 578. Soil Conservation Service, U.S. Department of Agriculture, Washington, D.C.
5. Johnson, William M. 1976. *What has been happening in land use in America and what are the projections.* Journal of Animal Science 45(6): 1,469-1,475.
6. Leopold, Aldo. 1966. *A Sand County almanac.* Ballantine Books, New York, New York. 295 pp.
7. Peter, Laurence J. 1976. *The Peter plan: A proposal for survival.* Wm. Morrow & Co., New York, New York. 217 pp.
8. Schumacher, E. F. 1973. *Small is beautiful: Economics as though people mattered.* Harper and Row, New York, New York.
9. Soil Conservation Service. 1979. *National erosion and sediment survey.* U.S. Department of Agriculture, Washington, D.C. In press.
10. U.S. General Accounting Office. 1978. *Changing character and structure of American agriculture: An overview.* Washington, D.C. 152 pp.

8

Agricultural Land Use: A Technological and Energy Perspective

Pierre Crosson

The amount of land used to meet the demand for agricultural commodities depends on the technologies farmers employ. The more productive the technologies, the less the amount of land needed.

In U.S. agriculture the demand for commodities and the technologies used to produce them are related. The productivity of the technologies has an important bearing on production costs, hence on commodity prices. Prices, in turn, affect demand, particularly demand for exports, which account for 25 percent to 30 percent of harvested cropland. Future changes in technology, therefore, will influence changes in the amount of land used in agriculture in two ways: (1) through effects on yields and (2) through effects on demand for agricultural commodities, particularly export demand.

Agriculture uses land in three ways: (1) to grow crops, (2) as pasture, and (3) as range. According to the Soil Conservation Service (SCS) land inventory of 1977, there were 412.3 million acres of cropland in the United States that year, 133.1 million acres of pasture, and 408.5 million acres of rangeland.

These uses are interdependent. When crop prices are high and expected to remain so, some land in pasture, and perhaps some rangeland, is converted to cropland. When crop prices are low, conversions go the other way.

Technological change also affects the amount of land in each of the three uses. Increases in feed grain productivity for example, reduce the prices of feed grains and increase the profitability of feeding animals in lots. This reduces the demand for rangeland.

The agricultural land retention issue, particularly from a technological point of view, argues for considering the three agricultural uses of land jointly. At the same time the complexity of doing so weighs against this. The focus here is on technology's effects on the use of land for crop production. The core of the land retention issue is concern about the loss of cropland, not losses of pasture or rangeland. Moreover, the losses of concern are to nonagricultural uses. These are, by and large, irreversible. In contrast, conversions of cropland to pasture or range typically can be reversed at relatively small cost.

Technology and the Use of Cropland

Technological change affects both the demand for and the supply of cropland. Improvements in technology lower production costs and prices, which stimulates growth in demand for crops and for land to produce them. The improvements may be land-saving, land-using, or neutral. If they are land-saving, that is, the amount of land relative to other inputs declines, then the increase in demand for land will be less than if the improvements are land-using or neutral. If the improvements are sufficiently land-saving, this effect on the demand for land may more than offset the effect of higher crop demand, resulting in a net decline in the amount of land in crops even though crop production is higher.

Technological change may affect the supply of cropland by making possible the cropping of land previously unsuitable for crops. With irrigation, for example, land can be cropped in areas otherwise too arid for this purpose. As another example, minimum tillage permits the cropping of land unsuitable for tillage with a mold-board plow because of the erosion hazard.

Both the supply and demand effects of technological change on use of cropland are evident in the United States. Between the end of World War II and the early 1970s, these changes, on balance, were land-saving. Harvested cropland declined from 357 million acres in 1946-1950 to 297 million acres in 1970-1972, despite a 36 percent increase in crop production. The larger output on less land was possible, of course, because crop yields rose sharply over the period (at an average rate of about 2.5 percent annually) (9).

The Technological Revolution in American Agriculture

The increase in crop yields reflected a major change in the technologies employed by American farmers. The principal change was a massive substitution of agricultural chemicals (especially fertilizers and pesticides) and machinery for labor. In addition, the amount of irrigated land increased by 14.6 million acres, or 56 percent, even though the total amount of land in crops declined. The number of man-hours used annually in crop production dropped from 26.4 per acre in 1946-1950 to 9.6 per acre in 1970-1972, a reduction of 64 percent. In contrast, fertilizer applications rose from 21.4 pounds of nutrients per acre in 1946-1950 to 143.4 pounds per acre in 1970-1972, an increase of 570 percent. Inputs of machinery services per acre rose 68 percent over this same period (9, 12, 13, 14).[1]

These vast changes in crop production technology over two and one-half decades were unprecedented in the United States or any other country. The event can justifiably be described as a technological revolution. Should the revolution continue at the pace set between the end of World War II and the early 1970s, it is unlikely that there would be much pressure on the supply of U.S. cropland. In fact, the demand for land to produce crops likely would decline sharply from levels of the late 1970s.

However, from the early 1970s to 1978, the growth of crop yields slowed dramatically, suggesting that the pace of the technological revolution may also have slowed (Table 1). If this more recent experience should characterize the future, the demand for cropland likely would increase substantially from present levels.

Table 1. Average annual rates of increase (percent) in crop yields in the United States (11, 12).*

	Period	
Crop	1946 to 1972	1972 to 1978
Corn	3.2	1.1
Wheat	3.2	− .3
Soybeans	1.7	1.3
All crops	2.5	.2†

*Rates of increase were calculated from a regression of the logarithms of annual yields against time. Hence, they reflect the influence of the yields of each year on the trend, not just that of beginning and ending years.
†1972 to 1977.

Table 2 outlines the possible future demand for cropland. Should yields of grains and soybeans, the principal land-using crops, return to the rates of increase experienced between 1946 and 1972, the amount of cropland harvested in the United States in 2000 could be millions of acres less than in 1977. This would occur despite substantial increases in pro-

[1]The data for fertilizer consumption and machinery inputs refer to all uses, not just on crops; however, crop production is by far the most important use. Data for pesticide consumption are not available for 1946-1950. It is known, though, that pesticide consumption per acre increased substantially between those years and the early 1970s. The data on irrigated land are for 1949 and 1974.

Table 2. Harvested cropland in the United States, 1977, and alternative projections to 2000.

Commodity	Harvested Cropland 1977*	Alternate Projections	
		2000	2000
Wheat	66.2	56.3†	98.7‖
Coarse grains‡	107.0	68.0†	143.5#
Soybeans	57.9	64.8†	68.7#
All other crops	100.2	95.0§	90.0§
Total crops	331.3	284.1	400.9

*Source: (9).

†Based on production projections by USDA's Foreign Demand and Competition Division, and the assumption that yields increase from 1977 to 2000 at the same rate as between 1946-1950 and 1970-1972.

‡Corn and sorghum for grain, oats, and barley.

§In 1977 about 60 percent of the land in other crops was in hay; about 10 percent was in cotton. Land in these two crops has declined steadily for decades. The assumption here is that this will continue to 2000, with the decline more marked if the demand for land in grains and soybeans should rise in the way shown in the final column.

‖Assumes yields of 1971-1973, which were 7 percent higher than 1977.

#Assumes yields increase from 1977 to 2000 at the same rate as from 1971-1973 to 1977.

duction. U.S. Department of Agriculture (USDA) projections are that in 2000 coarse grain production will be almost one-third higher than in 1977, wheat production will be 62 percent higher, and soybean production will be 49 percent higher.[2] Even if actual production of grains and soybeans in 2000 were 20 percent greater than the projected amounts, the amount of harvested cropland that year would be slightly less than in 1977, assuming pre-1972 yield increases prevail.

However, should yields increase at the much lower rates established between 1971-1973 and 1977, meeting projected production in 2000 would require 70 million acres more than in 1977, or 117 million acres more than if yield increases return to the rates prior to 1971-1973.

Clearly, future pressure on the nation's cropland base will depend crucially upon the behavior of grain and soybean yields. Thus, it is important to consider the technologies underlying yield behavior and, in particular, to ask whether the yield experience since 1971-1973 reflects a basic change in these technologies relative to the period before 1971-1973.

Energy and the Technological Revolution

The yield increases achieved since the end of World War II resulted from the substitution of inanimate energy—fossil fuels and some

[2]The Foreign Demand and Competition Division of USDA released two projections of production in 2000. Table 2 is based on the higher of the two.

hydroelectric power—for human and animal energy. These new forms of energy were embodied in fertilizers and pesticides, gasoline and diesel fuel to power tractors and other farm machinery, natural gas and other energy sources for crop drying and driving irrigation pumps and electricity for various purposes. Because of the vast increase in these kinds of energy relative to the amounts of farm labor and land, it is common now to refer to American agriculture as "energy-intensive."

It is important to keep this assertion in perspective. Compared to most other countries, it is undoubtedly true that American farmers use more inanimate energy per worker and per acre. It is also true that they use much more energy in relation to land and labor than they did three decades ago. Despite the rapid increase in energy use, however, other inputs probably contribute three to four times as much to the value of agricultural production as energy does. A report prepared by USDA for the Senate Committee on Agriculture and Forestry (7) showed that in 1973 the cost of energy used in corn production, exclusive of the cost of human energy, was 35 percent of the value of corn production that year. This figure includes not only energy used directly in production, such as fuel to drive tractors, but also the energy required to produce fertilizers, seed, farm machinery, and all other inputs. Direct costs of energy were only 5 to 10 percent of the value of production.

A study by Norman Rask and D. Lynn Forster (6) of a representative cornbelt farm in 1976 showed that direct and indirect energy costs were about one-third of the total costs of corn production.

Corn is one of the most energy-intensive crops produced in the United States. Rask and Forster estimated that in soybean production, for example, energy costs were about 20 percent of the total costs.

Comprehensive data on the relation of direct and indirect energy costs to the value of agricultural production are not available. However, the Rask and Forster data suggest that these costs are in the range of 20 to 30 percent of the value of production, with direct costs being substantially less, perhaps in the range of 5 to 15 percent.

The energy used in agricultural production is a small proportion of total energy use in the United States, about 3 percent in 1974 (8). Agriculture uses about 1 percent of the natural gas consumed in the United States. Another 2 percent is used in production of nitrogen fertilizers (15). Estimates of agriculture's share in consumption of other fossil fuels and hydroelectric power are not available, but since the industry's share of all such energy sources is only 3 percent, these components cannot be large.

Two important inferences can be drawn from these data on patterns of energy use in agricultural production. First, because agriculture's share of total energy use is small, the demand for energy by agriculture will have little effect on the price of energy. With respect to energy, agriculture is a "price-taker."

Second, because the direct cost of energy is a small proportion of the value of agricultural production, the amount of energy farmers use likely will be insensitive to the price of energy in the short run. Over the longer run, however, after higher energy prices are reflected indirectly in the prices of farm inputs, the rise in energy prices likely will induce farmers to seek less energy-intensive technologies.

The second inference is more important here. It is supported by a number of studies done since the sharp increase in energy prices in 1974. One study (1) found the price elasticity of demand for energy by farmers to be − .05. In other words, a 100 percent increase in energy prices (all other prices constant) reduces demand for energy only 5 percent. This finding is consistent with a study (2) of the response of farmers growing irrigated crops in the High Plains of Texas.

These results suggest that, in the short run, substantially higher energy prices would have little effect in shifting farmers to less energy-intensive technologies. Over the longer run, however, after farmers have had time to adjust their operations to the higher energy prices, the effect likely would be significant. The principal effect of a doubling of energy prices (relative to other prices) would be a shift from irrigated to dryland farming (1). Irrigated acreage would decline about 22 percent and nonirrigated land would increase 1.7 acres for each acre taken out of irrigation. Nitrogen fertilizer applications per acre would not be affected much, declining only about 4.5 percent. Pesticide use per acre would be affected even less.

Higher energy prices restrict irrigation principally through their effect on pumping costs. But there are other forces likely to constrain the growth of irrigated agriculture also. Declining groundwater supplies and increasing competition for water from urban and energy developments not only threaten the expansion of irrigation but also the continuation of irrigation at current levels in parts of the West. In the Southern High Plains of Texas the acreage of irrigated land has declined since 1964 because of falling water tables. In other states urban growth already has resulted in the transfer of water rights from agricultural to urban uses. Because continued urban growth seems assured and the marginal value of water in urban uses is considerably higher than in agriculture, additional transfers can be expected.

Energy development in the West is also likely to increase pressure on the region's water resources. The transport of massive quantities of western coal as a slurry through pipelines to power stations is one possible source of pressure. Coal gasification and the production of oil from shale are other water-intensive activities being considered. Should these processes become competitive with conventional fuel production, the pressure to transfer water from agriculture to energy production likely would mount, although the quantities transferred probably would not be large relative to the water now used for irrigation.

Energy Alternatives to Fossil Fuels

If energy costs continue to rise and water becomes more scarce, the energy-intensive technologies that produced the rapid rise in crop yields since World War II may become increasingly less attractive to American farmers. Irrigation in particular would become more costly relative to dryland farming. Should this happen, farmers could respond in several ways. One would be to substitute other energy sources for the more expensive fossil fuels. So-called organic farming, for example, substitutes animal manure and leguminous (nitrogen-fixing) crops for nitrogen fertilizer and mechanical cultivation for herbicides. (There apparently are no fuel savings in organic farming because machinery use is about the same as on conventional farms.)

A study of organic and conventional farms in the Cornbelt (3) found that the value of production per acre was only slightly less on the organic farms, and net income per acre was the same. The organic farms used about one-third as much energy (in BTUs) per dollar of output as the conventional farms.

As far as it goes, this study suggested that organic farming might offer significant energy savings at little sacrifice in total output and no loss of income to the farmer. The study has several limitatons, however, as an indicator of what might be accomplished on a national scale. (The researchers involved recognize these limitations.) One is that all farms in the study, both organic and conventional, were mixed crop-livestock enterprises. All produced substantial amounts of manure. In fact, operators of conventional farms applied large amounts of manure to the land in addition to manufactured fertilizers. Much of the grain and soybean production in the country, however, is on farms with few or no animals. While manure is available that could be supplied to these farms, from feedlots, for example, the cost of transporting the material is high relative to the cost of manufactured fertilizers, even at the high prices for the latter prevailing in 1974 and 1975. This would limit the widespread substitution of manure for manufactured fertilizer.

Rotation of leguminous crops, such as clover or alfalfa, with a main crop, such as corn, significantly reduces the need for manufactured fertilizer on the main crop. Such rotations were more common on organic farms than on conventional farms in the Cornbelt study. Applied at the national level, however, this rotation would mean either that the amount of corn produced over a period of years would be less (because in some years land otherwise in continuous corn would be in the leguminous crop), or else, to maintain production, the amount of land in crops would be greater. In effect, to achieve a given level of corn production, the corn-legume rotation substitutes land for manufactured fertilizer. Whether this would prove economical from the farmer's standpoint would depend upon the relative costs of fertilizers and land, but adoption of the rotation clearly would increase pressure on the cropland base (for a given level of production).

There currently is some discussion and experimentation concerning use of crop residues or crops grown especially to generate energy organically in gaseous or liquid form. However, the cost of these technologies now is several times the cost of fossil fuels, and it is not clear that they will become competitive in the foreseeable future. If they do, the demand for land to grow crops for energy would increase the pressure on the cropland base already exerted by the demand for land to produce food and fiber.

Substitution of Land for Energy

On balance, it appears unlikely that energy alternatives to fossil fuels for use in agriculture will prove economical on a wide scale over the next couple of decades. In this situation rising fossil fuel prices likely will induce farmers to substitute other inputs for energy. Increasing the amount of land relative to energy is an obvious possibility. The rising scarcity of water also may increase the demand for land since, for a given amount of production, dryland farming requires more acres than irrigated farming.

From 1972 to 1975 the amount of harvested cropland in the United States rose about 45 million acres, almost 15 percent. This coincided with sharp increases in energy and fertilizer prices over those years, and the increase in land likely was, in part, a response to the higher prices. In other words, the higher prices for energy and fertilizer may have encouraged farmers to substitute land for these inputs. Fertilizer applied per acre of harvested cropland declined 12 percent in this period, the first decline in decades. Data on energy use per acre are not available, but it is unlikely that energy use increased as much as the acreage of harvested cropland. The experience since 1972, therefore, supports the argument that rising energy prices induce farmers to adopt less energy-intensive technologies, increasing the amount of land relative to energy inputs.

A consequence of this substitution is that crop yields rise less than they would with the more energy-intensive technologies, and they may fall. The shift to less energy-intensive, more land-using technologies after 1972, therefore, may explain the slower growth (and the decline in the case of wheat) of crop yields after that date (Table 1). There are other possible explanations as well, indicating that yield behavior since 1972 requires closer examination.

Crop Yields Since 1972[3]

As indicated, the rise in energy and fertilizer prices after 1972 may have encouraged farmers to substitute land for these inputs, resulting in sharply reduced growth of yields. Under these circumstances, that is, fewer energy and fertilizer inputs per acre, some slowdown in the growth of yields would be expected even if the additional land were of the same quality as land already in crops. In fact, much of the land brought into production after 1972 was of inferior quality. For corn and wheat this may account for 10 to 25 percent of the difference between actual yields in 1975-1977 and the yields that would have been obtained had pre-1972 trends continued. The additional land in soybeans does not appear to have affected the trend in soybean yields, however.

Weather also affected yields significantly after 1972, in two ways.[4] First, for corn and soybeans (not wheat), the weather in the 1960s generally was more favorable than in the late 1940s and early 1950s. This tilted upward the trend in yields established by new technology. Second, the weather in the mid-1970s generally was less favorable than in the 1960s and early 1970s, causing yields to drop below the trend established by technology. For corn, the adverse weather may have accounted for roughly 40 to 50 percent of the difference between actual yields in the mid-1970s and the pre-1972 trend in yields. Weather's effect on soybean yields was less severe. Estimates of weather's effect on wheat yields in the mid-1970s are not available.

Another possibility is that crop yield behavior after 1972 reflects a "playing out" of the yield potential of the energy-intensive technologies on which American farmers increasingly depended after World War II. This possibility was raised in a report by the National Academy of Sciences (4). The argument receives some support from the behavior of total agricultural productivity over the last several decades (Table 3). The steady decline in the rate of productivity increase over two decades prior to 1972 is evident. Experience after 1972 does not fit this pattern, although the rate of growth from 1972 to 1977 was well below that of the 1950-1972 period as a whole.

---

[3]The discussion in this section is based on research underway at Resources for the Future. The work is scheduled for completion in 1980.

[4]This analysis of weather effects on crop yields is based on work by Louis Thompson at Iowa State University.

The long-term relationship between fertilizers and crop yields also supports this contention. The National Academy's report, using USDA data, shows that over the 1910-1969 period the yield response to additional fertilizer declined as the amount of fertilizer per acre rose. In this connection, it is worth noting that the amount of fertilizer applied per acre increased 20 percent from 1975 to 1976, but yields remained unchanged (9).

Table 3. *Average annual rates of increase (percent) in agricultural productivity (9).* *

Period	Annual Rate of Increase
1950-1972	2.05
1955-1972	1.91
1960-1972	1.62
1972-1977	1.75

*Agricultural productivity is the ratio of an index of total output to an index of total in-put (i.e., land, labor, fixed and working capital).

Analysis of the corn yield response to fertilizer is inconclusive insofar as this hypothesis of diminishing returns is concerned. Per acre applications of nitrogen fertilizer to corn in the mid-1970s were well below what they would have been had the pre-1972 trend in applications continued. This explains most of the difference between actual and trend yields of corn in 1975-1977, after adjustment for weather. The question is, however, did fertilizer applications per acre fail to follow the trend because fertilizer prices were high or because the productivity of additional fertilizer was declining? Fertilizer prices in 1975 and 1976 were higher relative to other prices, including the price of farmland, than prior to 1972. The difference does not seem great enough to explain the marked slowdown in growth of fertilizer applications per acre, however. The data on corn yield response to fertilizer in the mid-1970s faintly suggest a decline in response, but no firm conclusion can be drawn.

Implications for the Future

There is much speculation and no consensus about trends in weather and their effects on crop yields. However, a group of experts surveyed by the National Defense University (5) concluded that the most likely trend to the year 2000 is a slight global warming, with climate generally resembling that of the last 30 years. The effect of this trend in weather on the trend in crop yields in the United States is expected to be negligible compared with the effects of trends in technology.

This suggests that over the longer term the demand for cropland in the

United States will depend primarily upon the prices of the inputs to alternative technologies and on the productivity of those technologies. Experience since 1972 indicates that if prices of energy and energy-intensive inputs rise relative to land prices, farmers will adopt less energy-intensive technologies than those prevailing before 1972 and, everything else the same, yields will grow more slowly than before 1972. For any given increase in demand for crops, the result will be more pressure on the cropland base than if energy prices did not rise.

The degree of pressure, of course, will be a function of the relative increase in the price of energy and energy-intensive inputs. No one can predict confidently how much these prices will rise, or even whether they will rise at all relative to other prices. The consensus is, however, that energy prices likely will increase more than other prices over the long term. There is less agreement about fertilizer prices. It is probably fair to say, though, that the weight of expert opinion is on the side of higher fertilizer prices over the long term also.

If these price expectations come about, American farmers likely will substitute land-using technologies for energy-intensive technologies. As a result, yields will grow more slowly than before 1972, other things being the same. If demand for crops grows according to the USDA projections underlying table 2, then demand for cropland could increase substantially from present levels. Should the demand reach the higher acreage projections in table 2 (which assume a continuation of 1972-1978 rates of increase in yields), then the agricultural land retention issue likely will become a major concern of national as well as local importance. Harvested cropland on the order of 400 million acres would exceed any previous acreage, and it would come at a time when demand for land for nonagricultural uses also would be substantially greater than at present. The issue is not the physical availability of land. It is the cost of bringing that much more land into crop production and the ramifications of that cost for the rest of the economy.

A rise in the price of energy and energy-intensive inputs may not necessarily induce farmers to adopt more land-using technologies if the productivity of those inputs were to rise fast enough. Judging from the shift to more land-using technologies, the rate of increase in productivity of energy and energy-intensive inputs after 1972 was not sufficient to compensate for the higher prices of these inputs. If these prices rise over the long term at the same annual rate as between 1972 and 1977, then, unless productivity of the inputs rises more rapidly than between those years, farmers will continue to favor more land-using technologies. Evidence is inconclusive as to whether the rate of increase in productivity of these inputs was declining after 1972, but no evidence suggests that it was accelerating. Of course, new technological breakthroughs may occur, for example, improvements in photosynthetic efficiency, which would permit fast-rising yields with no additional inputs of purchased energy. In fact, such breakthroughs are probable, but the date of their advent now seems far off.

The current outlook for both the prices and productivity of energy and energy-intensive inputs suggests that farmers will continue to favor land-using technologies more than they did prior to 1972. The likely increasing cost and scarcity of irrigation water in the Great Plains and arid West point in the same direction. The expected outcome of these developments will be a substantially slower growth in yields than prior to 1972.

This outlook, particularly if productivity fails to rise in step with energy prices and energy-intensive inputs, suggests rising costs of production for U.S. agriculture. Should this occur, the demand for U.S. exports likely will weaken enough to slow the growth of output and, hence, reduce the pressure on the cropland base. This situation is particularly likely if productivity grows faster in other producing countries than in the United States. Present levels of productivity in many developing countries are much lower than in the United States, and the potential for expansion is great.

On balance, it appears the 1970s and early 1980s may be a watershed period for U.S. agriculture. Demand for agricultural land may undergo a sustained rise after several decades of decline. When combined with the rising demand for nonagricultural uses of land, the result could be strong competition for, and heavy pressure on, the cropland base. Resolution of the consequent conflicts in a way consistent with all interests in the land likely will pose a major challenge to the performance of land markets and to the political institutions for resolving conflicts where markets fail.

REFERENCES

1. Dvoskin, Daniel, and Earl Heady. 1976. *U.S. agricultural production under limited energy supplies, high energy prices, and expanding agricultural exports.* Center for Agricultural and Rural Development, Iowa State University, Ames.

2. Lacewell, Ronald, G. D. Condra, and Brian Fish. 1976. *Impact of natural gas on irrigated agriculture.* In W. Lockeretz [ed.] *Agriculture and Energy.* Academic Press, New York, N.Y.

3. Lockeretz, W., R. Klepper, B. Commoner, M. Gertler, S. Fast, D. O'Leary, and R. Blobaum. 1978. *Economic and energy comparison of crop production on organic and conventional Cornbelt farms.* In W. Lockeretz [ed.] *Agriculture and Energy.* Academic Press, New York, New York.

4. National Academy of Sciences. 1975. *Agricultural production efficiency.* Washington, D.C.

5. National Defense University. 1978. *Climate change to the year 2000: A survey of expert opinion.* Washington, D.C.

6. Rask, Norman, and D. Lynn Forster. 1978. *Corn tillage systems—will energy*

costs determine the choice? In W. Lockeretz [ed.] *Agriculture and Energy.* Academic Press, New York, New York.

7. Senate Committee on Agriculture and Forestry, U.S. Congress. 1974. *The U.S. food and fiber sector: Energy use and outlook.* Washington, D.C.

8. U.S. Department of Agriculture. 1976. *Energy and U.S. agriculture: 1974 data base.* Washington, D.C.

9. U.S. Department of Agriculture. 1977. *Changes in farm production and efficiency.* Statistical Bulletin No. 581. Washington, D.C.

10. U.S. Department of Agriculture. 1978. *Crop production 1977 annual summary.* Washington, D.C.

11. U.S. Department of Agriculture. 1978. *Agricultural outlook.* Washington, D.C.

12. U.S. Department of Agriculture. Various years. *Agricultural statistics.* Washington, D.C.

13. U.S. Department of Commerce. 1949. *Census of agriculture.* Washington, D.C.

14. U.S. Department of Commerce. 1974. *Census of agriculture.* Washington, D.C.

15. White, W. C. 1974. *Fertilizer-food-energy relationships.* In Proceedings, Illinois Fertilizer Conference. University of Illinois, Urbana.

9

Land as a Factor
of Agricultural Production

Marion Clawson

All economic production, agricultural and otherwise, involves many inputs. The neoclassical economics of two generations ago classified these productive factors as land, labor, capital, and entrepreneurship (or management). In modern production economics the terminology has changed, but not the basic concept. Economists now speak of production functions and output as a function of many inputs.

Inputs can be grouped or subdivided according to the analyst's tastes. For example, one may speak of capital goods as a class of inputs, or one may divide this class of inputs into pesticides and other inputs. Still another possibility is to consider a particular pesticide as a separate input.

The resulting production function depends upon the grouping of the physically distinct inputs. For instance, if one uses irrigation water as an input but groups under this heading all factors associated with water, the result will be an apparent productivity of the water that is really a productivity of the package.

Production Functions

However one defines "input" and however the production function is expressed (algebraically, graphically, or otherwise), the overriding relationship is that all inputs affect output. Put another way, the output is the result of all inputs, not of any one input alone.

All productive factors but one can be held constant and that one varied with a consequent effect upon the output. To take a simple and absurd example: Assume a large area of cropland, plenty of labor and machinery, ample fertilizer and other chemicals, all in specified quantities, to which are applied varying amounts of seed, say wheat. If the seeding rate is a hundreth of a bushel per acre, the wheat crop will be small because the plants will be widely scattered and the land likely covered with weeds. As the seeding rate increases, all other factors remaining unchanged, the crop will also increase to some maximum. After that, more seed will reduce the crop, until perhaps at 100 bushels of seed per acre there would be little or no crop, the many plants competing so voraciously for the limited moisture and sunshine that none can mature.

In this sort of example, one factor varying while all else remain fixed, the relationship is typically not straight line. Small amounts of the variable may produce no end result. Results may increase more than proportionately for some range of inputs, then gradually level off and ultimately decline.

This type of all-but-one-fixed input factors, with that one varying, really does not make much practical sense. If one uses more of some productive inputs, then more of some others may be necessary for an appropriate or reasonable mix of inputs. If one uses improved seeds, then fertilizer may have a larger effect than for less productive varieties. But higher productive outputs may require better soil moisture control, by irrigation or by terracing, to retain natural precipitation; and surely one would want machinery capable of harvesting the crop that grew. Even this simple example omits productive factors that might be critical in some situation.

Faced with these relationships, many analysts refer to the synergistic effect of one variable in relation to others, the package approach. For instance, increasing each of four input factors separately by some specified amount may increase output 10 percent, but increasing all four at the same time in appropriate ratios to one another may increase output much more than 40 percent. The combined effect of the package is greater than the sum of the individual effects.

This synergistic or package effect is noticeable when dealing with badly run-down farms or with agriculture in an economically less developed country. Soil erosion must be halted, soil fertility built up, noxious weeds controlled, improved crop varieties introduced, crop disease controlled, better livestock breeding adopted, animal diseases controlled, crops and livestock products stored to reduce spoilage, better marketing introduced, more credit made available, and so on. The list is nearly endless. Each is important, and the effect on production of each depends on the others. Where does one start? Wherever one starts, the others are quickly involved, and one is likely in the end to come back to the input with which one started.

When one talks of package approaches, what happens to the old concepts of fixed and variable factors of production? In the long run, to the individual farmer, everything is variable. He can add more land, invest more capital, use more labor, etc. To the nation there may be closer limits; for example, there may be little or no land that can be brought into cultivation. Even when land area is fixed, most if not all other inputs are variable, at least over some time period. The composition of the package of inputs and the size of the total input package can vary, often within wide limits.

The production function is a physical-biological one—so much more fertilizer, of such and such a specification, produces so much more crop, with specified other inputs, etc. But there is an obvious economic relationship also—more inputs cost more money, while more output is more value, at least at the individual farm level. A maximum physical output per unit of a particular input can be calculated or estimated. This may or may not produce the maximum net economic return. If one input is relatively cheap, fertilizer for example, it may pay to use more of it than the maximum physical output ratio. Or, if it is relatively expensive, it may pay to quit using additional amounts at some level short of the maximum physical output ratio.

The farmer or the nation may thus vary different inputs in a known production function, with more or less predictable results as measured by the outputs. But sometimes the production function seems to shift. Old combinations of inputs seem to produce either more or less output than formerly. When has there been a shift of inputs along a known production function, and when has the function itself shifted? For instance, a new plant disease or crop pest reduced yields from a specified amount of all input factors, below what it has previously been; or a new chemical makes it possible to control an old plant disease or crop pest so that output increases, even while other inputs remain unchanged. Are these and similar situations shifts of inputs along the production function, or are they shifts in the function?

It might be argued that the apparent new factor of production existed all along, that it was in the old production function at a zero level of input. Or it might be argued that the new chemical, the new variety, the new disease or new pest, the new machine, etc., resulted in a new production function. The answer depends in part upon how detailed the input factors are specified in the production function. If highly detailed, then any new item that does not conform to the old definition represents a new production function. If defined in broad terms, such as labor or capital, then physically or biologically new factors can fit into the broad categories. It is to some degree a matter of taste or judgment how such things are defined. I prefer a reasonably specific definition of inputs with the consequence that the production function is shifting in American agriculture rather frequently.

Over the past two generations, or longer, science, industry, and farmers have developed or invented many new factors of production if one uses reasonably specific definitions. Every new farm machine is a new production function for it enables the farmer to do more work, or to do it better, or to do it cheaper, or all of these. But so is every new plant variety because it results in a somewhat different and often much better product from the same combination of inputs. But so are the many chemicals for pest and disease control or for soil enrichment.

One of the most dramatic new factors of production has been the discovery of the role of minor chemical elements in many soils naturally deficient in such elements and the application of such elements to these soils. With no other change in inputs, outputs have sometimes increased several-fold. But new sources of farm power, new farm machines, or both have sometimes enabled the cropping of soils previously too difficult to work, and often with dramatic results.

Sometimes the production functions are fully symmetrical in the sense that inputs can be increased or decreased with the same effect over the same range of inputs. A farmer could add more of some input one year, with a result conforming to the production function, and reduce it the next year, reverting to the position existent before the increase. But sometimes the expansion and contraction paths are different. This happens sometimes in the physical or biological sense—the increase or the decrease is irreversible because it changes the production function or the basic conditions in some manner. For instance, less fertilizer may have led to more soil erosion and permanently altered the soil situation. More commonly, the expansion and contraction phases are different for economic or social reasons. It is extremely unlikely that American farmers would ever go back to animal power, regardless of the economics of the situation, for instance. But in less dramatic examples farmers who have expanded output by some changes in inputs, in response to some favorable price situation, are unlikely to revert fully to the former situation even if prices revert to the old relationship.

Agricultural Experience Over the Past 40 Years

Agricultural output in the United States has risen dramatically and almost steadily for the past 40 years. The annual rates of increase range from 1 percent to 5 percent. At the same time the acreage of cropland first decreased, then rose about to its previous level, while labor input fell by two-thirds and capital input changed drastically in composition without corresponding changes in total amount. Weather conditions have affected year-to-year changes with modest declines in some years, yet the record generally is one of a dramatic, sustained increase in output.

Has the production function for American agriculture changed over this period, or has the higher output been the result of different inputs in the same old production function? This is a matter on which there can be, and has been, difference of opinion, at least to the relative degree of movement along the same production function versus shifts in the function itself. As noted earlier, no small part of a difference in conclusion arises out of how the production function is defined and, in particular, how finely the productive factors are specified. Surely, as the real price of fertilizer, especially nitrogen, fell for many years, more fertilizer per acre would have been used in the same production function. Was hybrid corn a new productive factor, or simply an old one at a new input level? It seems likely that both forces have operated. Some shifts in the production function cannot be ruled out.

More important than these definitional matters is that, for a considerable period of years, most of us came to expect annual increases in agricultural output. Several major commissions and groups of scholars in effect extended past upward trends in agricultural output, recognizing that such trends could not continue forever, but nevertheless extending past trends a generation or so into the future (1). I did more or less the same thing in some of my earlier research. Some analyses seemed more complex, but almost all relied on historical relationships between input factors and output. While output could indeed not continue to rise forever at any constant rate, the fact is that over these past 40 or more years trend extenders have as often underestimated as overestimated future agricultural output. For the short run—a decade or two—trend extension may be fully as accurate and more simple than complex methods of forecasting future agricultural output.

But this complacency about continued increases in agricultural output, even in the middle term future, was seriously challenged by the National Academy of Sciences report (1). For some crops, such as corn, the yield per acre had been steadily upward. There was no sign of a levelling off by 1972. For other crops, the yield increases were smaller or nonexistent. For some outputs, such as eggs per hen, a definite ceiling seemed to have been reached; and crop yields in general seemed to have levelled off in response to fertilizer use. Could the United States really count on continued increases in total agricultural output over the long run, or without further increases in inputs? It is significant that the Academy report did not answer this question unequivocally. Instead, the report tried to analyze the factors likely to result in a continued rise in agricultural output and the factors likely to result in an eventual levelling off.

Nonagricultural Land Use

The concept of production function applies equally well to land used for forestry, outdoor recreation, residences, and factories. In every case other factors or inputs are combined with land to produce an output or a range of outputs.

Forestry is often thought of as a form of production that depends almost wholly on natural forces operating over a considerable land area. But labor and capital can often be invested profitably to insure prompt regeneration of a timber stand following harvest. The same general input factors can often be used effectively in thinning the stand to insure the optimum number of stems per acre. Fertilizer is increasingly applied, and other productive inputs can increase timber growth. Forestry is a capital-intensive form of production. Standing trees represent a substantial amount of capital that can be used to grow more timber or to be released through timber harvest for investment elsewhere.

Outdoor recreation on any area requires service facilities for visitors, such as toilets, roads, trails, picnic tables, etc.; and recreational use is possible only with a continuing expenditure of money and a continual application of labor to service the visitors—to clean up their garbage, if nothing more. Residential use of land is a relatively intensive form of land use, with substantial amounts of capital invested on small areas of land. Many a suburban yard has more labor, more fertilizer, more insecticides, and more of other inputs added per unit of area than almost any type of farm would use. Industrial use of land is also an intensive use, generally.

At least for forestry and outdoor recreation, there is evidence that the production function has shifted over the past generation. Wood growth in American forests in 1977 was 370 percent of the wood growth in 1920, from almost exactly the same area of forests. While there has been a significant increase in productive inputs over that period, the forestry production function has shifted also. Forestry now stands on the threshold of a production revolution similar to the production revolution agriculture experienced over the past 40 years.

Recreational use of parks, forests, reservoirs, and other outdoor recreation areas has also increased dramatically over the same 40-year period. Again, more inputs in the form of more capital and more labor have been expended in management of many parks; but again, the production function has shifted considerably over these years. A campground for trailers can accommodate several times as many people as an old-fashioned campground where tent camping was the mode.

Preservation of Prime Agricultural Land

Where does the preservation of prime agricultural land fit into all of this?

Land is clearly one factor in agricultural production—an indispensable factor for almost all agriculture. Prime land, by definition, is better suited for agricultural production than is any other kind of land. It is important, therefore, that prime land be preserved for agriculture to the extent feasible.

But this contention glosses over some important and serious issues. First, how shall prime land be defined? Soil texture, depth, slope, and fertility have been important in the past, and are likely to be so in the future, but so is climate and location relative to population or transportation centers and other factors not inherent in the soil.

Changing technology may change the importance of one or more of these variables. For instance, sprinkler irrigation using groundwater has drastically changed the productive capacity of many areas during the past generation or so. Land that once would not have been rated prime now seems to be so, at least as long as the groundwater lasts. The role of trace chemical elements in some soils has been noted, as has the effect of increased mechanical power in making some soils productive that were too difficult to handle with animal power.

Land classification is not a once and forever matter, but a changing element. A prime land classification at one date is not necessarily a prime land classification at some other date.

One important factor, often not considered explicitly in agricultural land classification, is the ability of particular land to respond to inputs. For instance, many sandy soils in the Southeast are not very fertile, yet precipitation is adequate, they respond well to fertilizer, they are easily worked, and they are well located with respect to major urban markets. Their capacity to respond to inputs would lead to their higher classification than would their inherent qualities under a relatively extensive system of cropping.

Agricultural people tend to think of prime land only in agricultural terms, but every land use has its land requirements and its land grades. What is prime for one use may not be prime for another. Other factors being the same, level or gently sloping land in the Corn Belt is more valuable for cropping than is steeper land, in part because the soil erosion hazard is less and the power requirements are lower. Roughly broken areas in the same region may be far more attractive for outdoor recreation than are the flatter areas. This is an example of land requirements for different land uses being so different that the competition for land between the uses is greatly reduced.

A similar relationship exists for at least some forested areas. Rougher mountainous areas may make good to excellent wilderness areas, whereas flatter areas with better soils are better suited to growing timber. The land's classification and its productivity rating thus depend in large part on the use to be made of the land.

While it is important to think of the preservation of productive lands in terms of agriculture only, it is also important, perhaps equally so, to think in terms of other land uses. Many conservation groups are concerned about preserving outstanding forests; watersheds; marshes; and recreational, historic, and other special sites. A number of organizations exist whose major function is the preservation of such areas. Substantial sums of money are expended annually for this objective. Many laws and appropriations at federal, state, and local levels have been enacted for the preservation of such areas. The people concerned about the preservation of ecologically or historically valuable areas get just as upset over the prospect of a suburban residential subdivision gobbling up the land as do the agricultural interests when a "prime" farming area is threatened in a similar way.

Two conclusions emerge from this interest of other groups. First, agricultural use of land cannot be looked at and decided upon without consideration of other land uses. After all, people must live somewhere, and residential subdivisions, to use but one example, must be put somewhere. Second, agricultural groups concerned with preservation of the land they value most highly might well communicate and perhaps ally themselves with the other interest groups involved. Preservation of the best farmland must be part of a general land use planning and management process.

Other Productive Factors

Stressed thus far is the fact that agricultural output is the result of many production inputs, of which land is but one. A logical extension of this point is to stress that concern, perhaps equal concern, should be directed at the inputs other than land. For instance, protection of modern agriculture's high technology may be as important as protection of the best farmland. Among other matters, protection of technology involves a continuation of agricultural research on an adequate scale. The problems of agriculture are never solved once and for all. New problems continually arise. Even when no obvious problem exists, research may be able to develop new techniques or new production functions that are more productive than the old ones. There may be no obvious problem, but an inherent or incipient one.

American agriculture's greatest single asset is its backup research community. The research organizations have developed over many years as their body of knowledge grew, their staffing increased, staff members were better trained, and as the organizational structure itself grew. One need not consider this research community perfect. It has been criticized by many persons from many viewpoints, and there is no point here to enter into an appraisal of its strengths and shortcomings. But one need only think for a moment about what modern agriculture would be like if there were no agricultural research establishment at all to arrive at a conclusion that the contribution of research has been very great indeed.

The more advanced agriculture is, and the more intensive the methods of agricultural production are, the more important agricultural research becomes. A more primitive agriculture was like the Model T Ford, which many of us could and did repair and adjust with little more than a screwdriver and one simple wrench. Agriculture today is like the modern auto, the innards of which I gaze at in bafflement when I lift the hood. The highly productive farm machine must be finely tuned and adjusted by agricultural experts, as the modern auto must be serviced by experts.

A single illustration may help clarify this point. In 1970 a leaf blight reduced corn yields substantially in some parts of the country. This was the result of a too narrowly based genetic inheritance in corn, with the dominant genetic strain vulnerable to leaf blight. What might have been an agricultural crisis was averted in just one year by the application of research, and yields immediately rose above their previous trend line. We must assume that similar problems will arise in the future and that agricultural research will continue to be a major national asset.

But input factors other than agricultural research may merit some attention for preservation. For instance, the availability of other inputs, such as fertilizers, insecticides, and other chemicals, is extremely important. Many American farmers do not realize how fortunate they are, compared with farmers in many other parts of the world, on this matter of input availability. With reasonable foresight, the average American farmer can buy the kinds and amounts of all productive inputs he thinks will be profitable, and he can get them when he wants them. In many countries this is not the case. Materials are unavailable at all or available only after long delays that reduce their productivity in seasonal processes. Or, substitutes have to be accepted.

Conclusion

Preservation of prime agricultural land is important, but so is the preservation of land prime for other uses. Agricultural land use must be viewed in a wider context than agriculture alone. Prime land is important, but so are all the other inputs in the agricultural production equation. Agricultural research in particular must be fostered and protected.

REFERENCE

1. Committee on Agricultural Production Efficiency, National Academy of Sciences. 1975. *Agricultural production efficiency.* Washington, D.C.

10

Farmland and the Future

Charles E. Little

Never has the conservation community and the agricultural establishment been caught so thoroughly out of position as it has on the agricultural land issue. Although not well publicized, recent revelations by the Soil Conservation Service (SCS), along with demographic analyses by the Economics, Statistics, and Cooperatives Service (ESCS), constitute as important a warning to policy-makers about farmland and farming as the U.S. Department of Agriculture (USDA) has issued since the dust and depression-ridden 1930s.

After decades of agricultural surpluses, which exist to this day, it is perhaps understandable that policy-makers would, for a time, either misconstrue or ignore both the statistics and the on-the-ground evidence that pertain to the loss of agricultural land to urban development. But sooner or later, conservationists and agriculturalists must face up to the fact that they have an issue in common and that they must come to grips with it forthrightly and effectively.

The Issue

What is the issue? Simply this: the United States is losing a great deal more cropland to urbanization and, correspondingly, has a great deal less cropland in reserve than anyone previously thought. SCS research showed that between 1967 and 1977 some 29 million rural acres, mostly agricultural land, were converted to urban uses. At the same time, a 1967 estimate of 266 million acres of reserve farmland had to be adjusted downward in 1977 to 135 million acres of land with a high or medium potential for use as cropland. Not all this land is immediately or easily

123

put to use as cropland, however. Seventy percent of it has soil or water conservation problems to be overcome before tillage could begin.

In any case, and aside from conservation requirements, having only 135 million acres in reserve means that, in the best circumstances, only 14 percent of America's rural land can be pressed into service to make up for the 3 million acres per year of cropland lost to other uses. Importantly, this attenuated cropland is comprised of land most vulnerable to urbanization because it is fairly level, easy to build on, and in areas of benign climate. Moreover, the 3-million-acre rate of conversion is likely to increase in the future.

An analysis of Census Bureau statistics by ESCS demographers has revealed that for the first time since the beginning of the Industrial Revolution population growth trends have all but reversed themselves. Instead of a declining rural population in favor of growing urban centers, census figures now show that rural areas are increasing in population, and increasing far faster than cities or their suburbs. This is not merely a failure in the definition of what a city really is, for even counties that themselves are not adjacent to metropolitan areas are growing faster than counties within metropolitan areas.

The statistical evidence of a shrinking cropland reserve, together with an exponentially urbanizing rural environment, is underscored by the visual evidence. Sprawl is not a phenomenon confined to the edges of cities. It is a pervasive pattern of development in many parts of rural America, and it weakens the highly specialized and fragile agricultural economy and family farm ownership structure.

Because the ecology of agriculture is not endlessly elastic, it may now be asserted that, for the first time in this nation's history, each new subdivision, highway, dam, factory, power plant, or shopping center threatens to reduce permanently the productive capacity of American agriculture.

It is possible to substitute fertilizer for land, unless, of course, the next increment of fertilizer costs more than the increased yield will bring in prices. It is possible to substitute pesticides for land, unless it costs more to kill the pests than to lose the crop they destroy. It is possible to substitute water for land, diesel fuel for land, new genetic stocks for land, but only to a point. And many believe industrial agriculture, as practiced in western nations, has reached that point. If indeed this is the case, then the loss of cropland relates directly to yield.

The Export Connection

The importance of joining these issues—land and food—is crucial because the United States is, once again, an agricultural nation. Those who are either bemused or disbelieving of such an apparently retrograde status are invited to take a look at the foreign trade figures of recent years. After increasing slowly during the fifties and sixties, food export income suddenly doubled in the early 1970s, then doubled again. And the fiscal year just passed, 1978-1979, holds the record: $27.2 billion worth of food sold abroad, 20 percent of all exports, which provide the major offsetting income for increased expenditures for oil. Were it not for food exports, the nation's largest export category, it is nearly certain that the dollar abroad would be even spongier than it is today and inflation at home would be even more onerous. And upon what does this international balance sheet rest? Many things, of course, but agricultural land is not among the least important factors.

Family Farming and the Land Price Problem

United States agriculture is celebrated as the most efficient in the world, based in large part on the fact that it is an economically decentralized, proprietary enterprise. In the main, it is still possible to describe this enterprise as family farming. There is a good case to be made also that the agricultural land problem derives from the same set of factors as the family farm problem, that is, the disappearance of such farms as the mainstay of United States agriculture. It is truly said that there is no value in preserving the resource base without preserving the economic activity that sustains it. Therefore, if the resource base of the United States is in trouble, it is because the resource users, family farms, are in even worse trouble.

What may be at the heart of both the family farm problem and the urbanization problem is the land *price* problem. In fact, the price of farmland has been increasing at a rate two and one-half times that of inflation. An important reason for this is that farmland is an attractive, sheltered investment for urban-industrial wealth. The flow of investment dollars into farmland has been encouraged by favorable tax laws and exacerbated by fear of inflation. The result? Farmland is in the process of being priced out of the market for farm use.

Discontinuous urban development, far from metropolitan areas, is both a cause and effect in this equation. That land can be sold for development *somewhere* suggests to each and all that land can be sold for development *anywhere*. Therefore, the prices go up *everywhere*, making the marketing of land for nonagricultural use almost mandatory. The effect of all this is to make paper millionaires out of some farmers and to provide others with mortgagable value to borrow against in order to afford high-cost machinery. But there is another effect, and that is to preclude the nonestablished farmer from full participation in agriculture because the price of farmland is just too high.

Logic would require that if farmers cannot enter or fully participate in the business of farming it is only a matter of time until there are no farmers farming at all. For most this is a nightmare vision of vertical integration, super-agribusiness, and absentee ownership carried to the final degree. The nightmare will not be analyzed here, but it is safe to say that the land resource base is wholly implicated and perhaps has a controlling role in the kind of agricultural and rural future the United States will have.

The National Interest in Farmland Preservation

This is why the efforts of states and counties to protect their farmland resources are not, as some would have it, quixotic, faintly amusing, financially unsustainable, and of only local importance. It is also why the rapid expansion of such efforts is urgent and in the national interest.

How should this national interest be expressed? Some would say that the greatest need is to create a federal policy that can keep federal programs from causing the loss of farmland. One way to put the federal house in order, so called, is not to create urban investment opportunities by putting roads, sewers, and other urban amenities into rural areas. Another would be to take away the income tax advantages of speculating in farmland. A third would be to create a proper urban policy in the first place so that people and businesses would not be so anxious to flee to the wide open spaces.

But tidying up the federal house may not by itself be dynamic enough to protect farms and farmland, given contemporary pressures on the land base. What states and localities seem to need is a foundation for mediating the use of land that not only protects farmland but farming as well. This can be done via tax abatement and regulatory schemes in agricultural areas that strike a bargain with the farmer. If the farmer protects the land for the community, then the community is willing to help protect the farmer in terms of current profitability and future farm value.

Another way is for the community to become a part owner in the land, a silent partner, providing recapitalization to the farmer in return for a deeded right forever precluding improper conversion of the land to nonfarm use.

A third way, not much used in the United States, but well-tested in Europe, is for the community to intervene in the actual market mechanism of buying and selling land. In Sweden and France, effective programs providing local public or quasi-public bodies with the right of preemptive purchase have been in place since the late 1940s. After a preemptive purchase is made, the land is resold with appropriate restrictions on the new buyer in order to protect the stability of farm districts.

All of these approaches have their good and bad points. Some approaches may be better in some situations than in others. Understandably perhaps, there is a tendency for analysts to evaluate specific farmland protection techniques on an all-or-nothing basis. This is true, for example, of the purchase of development rights—negative easements over the land to preclude subdivisions. Because the purchase of development rights is not affordable nationally—and it isn't—the tendency is to devalue the technique. In some places, though, it may be the only way left to secure permanent protection of farmland resources.

Similarly, because the regulation of farmland via the police power, as the planning and zoning process is called, might unconstitutionally deprive an owner of significant land value in some places, this does not mean that such regulation would be unconstitutionally restrictive everywhere.

Perhaps the problem lies not in faulty analysis of techniques, but in the failure to see the techniques in the larger policy context. Significantly, there is as yet no persuasive assessment of the intrinsic value of agricultural land resources to the nation as a whole, nor is there a reliable examination of the various approaches at the state and local levels that can protect this resource fairly, affordably, and permanently. These are not difficult tasks, but they are necessary so that policy-makers can come to grips with the loss of agricultural land before it becomes a thoroughgoing crisis.

In this regard, the farmland issue is a curiosity. The decision the nation makes about its resource base is actually being made now, at a time when the crucial importance of the resource is practically invisible to the average citizen. The trouble is when the problem does become critical it may well be beyond remedy, at least of the kind under consideration today.

There are many political historians who believe the United States is on the verge of losing its pre-eminent position of world leadership, from lack of arms superiority, from lack of domestic energy resource alternatives, from lack of technological innovation. Maybe one more lack should be added to the list: the lack of ability to protect the greatest body of farmland in any nation on the face of the earth.

But then again maybe this incredible resource *can* be protected, especially if, as stated at the outset, conservationists and agriculturalists see that they have an issue in common and that this issue is only as intractable or soluable as they wish to make it.

11

A Farmer/Rancher View
of Agricultural Land Retention Issues

Hector Macpherson

Few issues divide farmers and ranchers more sharply than do attitudes on governmental intervention in the land market. Many equate planning and zoning with Communism and antichrist. A minority at the other extreme argues that the world will eventually starve unless the United States locks up every last acre of potential farmland.

A little history of Oregon's struggle toward a public land policy not only illuminates the emotions involved but foretells the difficulties of implementing strong measures elsewhere.

Acceptance of Planning and Zoning

Prior to the 1960s, planning and zoning were thought to be city inventions, neither necessary nor practical in allocating rural land. During the 1960s, rural leaders in Oregon and elsewhere, alarmed about urban sprawl, sought to install planning and zoning at the county level. Rural people's acceptance of planning was guarded but friendly until the impact of zoning with its limitations on the property sales became apparent.

County commissioners, lauded when they appointed planning commissions, suddenly found themselves on the defensive. Some who pushed too fast were voted out of office. Others faced recall elections. The landowning public, farmers and others alike, was not ready to accept strict zoning if it meant a possible loss of value in the marketplace.

Oregon's legislature entered the fray in 1969. In an effort to bolster job security for embattled county commissioners, the legislature decreed that the entire state should be planned and zoned by 1971. This allowed much of the heat to be passed to the state level but left the argument about the kind and quality of the zoning strictly local.

The 1969 law brought the first of three statewide referendums on planning and zoning, and each time the voters reaffirmed the need for state intervention in the process. In 1973 the legislature adopted Senate Bill 100, which created the Land Conservation and Development Commission with power to impose standards on local planning, called goals. The second referendum, in 1976, would have repealed Senate Bill 100 in its entirety, but the bill survived by a greater margin than the previous law.

The third challenge came in the 1978 election. Opponents of land use planning by this time recognized the futility of a frontal attack and devised Ballot Measure 10, which appeared to enhance local planning and zoning but in fact stripped the Land Conservation and Development Commission of most of its powers. Voters responded with a crushing defeat of the measure, 61 percent to 39 percent.

The debate over what rural zoning should accomplish rages on to this day. Preservation of farmland in Oregon by what is called exclusive farm use zoning has always been a central issue. After 10 years the argument has shifted, however, from the need to preserve to how much.

Support for Farmland Preservation

Are farmers and farm organizations solidly behind efforts to preserve farmland? Unfortunately, no. Both the Grange and the Oregon Farm Bureau endorsed Ballot Measure 10. While the Grange is no longer an organization of active farmers, the Farm Bureau is. It has a policy position that endorses planning at the local level but, true to its long-standing opposition to big government, opposes any state supervision. None the less, a growing minority of its members supports a stronger position on the farmland retention issue.

Among nonfarmers farmland preservation gets top priority. A recent poll found 80 percent of the people in support of zoning that would protect farmland. Stopping urban sprawl, a related issue, came in second. Given this kind of support, the agricultural goal seems relatively secure.

Some Prejudices

An examination of attitudes among active farmers on the land use issue uncovers a number of prejudices. Most pervasive is the feeling that government should stay out of people's business lives. Farmers feel they have enough to do to cope with the vagaries of the weather and the market place. Government should help them, not create stumbling blocks, be they unemployment compensation, the Occupational Safety and Health Act, or zoning. Most farmers believe government is run by an urban-oriented majority that is unresponsive to their specific needs. They point to the Environmental Protection Agency as the prime example of government taking away needed pesticides and passing regulations on air and water quality that are both unnecessary and burdensome.

I once remarked that if you scratch a farmer you will find a subdivider. While this statement is less true now as Oregon's laws settle into place, it still accounts for some of the most vehement opposition to exclusive farm use zoning in rural communities. Farmers who dream of cashing in on the swing to rural living feel cheated when told they can't sell to subdividers. The rapid rise in zoned farmland prices has only partially alleviated this feeling.

Any analysis of attitudes must recognize that a strong minority of rural leaders now believes in the need for laws to protect farmland. Most are willing to fight for such laws with the zeal of a knight on his first crusade. This group argues persuasively that bringing nonfarmers into farming communities creates problems for the remaining farmers with complaints about dust, odor, and noise. Farmland prices are driven up, making it difficult for existing operations to expand. The world needs food and the United States depends on the sale of agricultural products for foreign exchange. Therefore, no land should be taken out of commercial production. These arguments are gradually winning converts to the point that it is now safe to predict that the farm community will grudgingly accept, in time, what is surely in its best interest.

Oregon's Law in Action

Oregon is still in the trial and error position of attempting to identify which lands must be locked up in exclusive farm use zones. The agricultural goal says that all land classified by the Soil Conservation Service as Class I through IV in well-watered western Oregon must be considered for such zoning. This does not apply to land within the urban growth boundary of a city or to land already so parceled or developed that it is impractical for commercial farming. There is little argument about the desirability of preserving Class I and II land. But unresolved is the disposition of Class III and IV land, some of which is unproductive and unattractive for commercial operation because of steep slopes, limited field sizes, thin soils, and broken topography. Purists say it too should be protected from rural subdivision because of future needs.

The owners of such land take the opposite view. They point to the demand for rural living and see far greater opportunities in subdividing and selling the land than in the limited kinds of farming possible under these conditions. They point to the greater productivity of more problem-free soil types and the recurring surpluses of agricultural products in the

United States as proof that this kind of land is not really needed.

In the end it will not be farmers and rural landowners in Oregon who will decide the issue. Land use restrictions are clearly a public issue that will be decided in the political arena. The public in Oregon has spoken, and tough restrictions are here to stay. Only the details remain unresolved.

How has this come about in Oregon but failed so miserably in most other states? First, the environmental awareness of the early seventies bloomed more vigorously in Oregon than in many places. Land use legislation was preceded by laws protecting ocean beaches, air and water quality laws, and the bottle bill. Oregon has so much scenic beauty to protect that politicians could exploit local pride to overcome the resistance of affected economic interests.

Another often overlooked factor has played a large part in keeping tough laws on the books despite the increasing number of people whose ox has been gored. That is the basic resistance to change by individuals whose economic well-being is not threatened by a lack of growth. This manifests itself in neighborhood associations that block every major new development. Collectively they opt for a no-growth or slow-growth policy for cities and routinely vote down annexations. With a population of 2.5 million, Oregon is the victim of tremendous in-migration, yet the newest immigrant is the first to want to slam the gate.

Oregon's Senate Bill 100, with its mandated citizen involvement, is considered the bulwark against unwanted change. However, Oregon's land use legislation can also be used to force needed development. The law is blind on the growth issue. It requires housing to be provided if the need is demonstrated. Other economic interests must be accommodated also. As a result, home builders are attacking building moratoriums in the courts, and their chance of winning is good.

Growing support at the polls points to the increasing statewide acceptance of a rational yet politically acceptable approach to land use allocation. Farmers, traditionally more independent and conservative, have been slow to grasp the full implications of the pressures on their land base. They are reluctant to accept governmental control. In Oregon, however, such control is here to stay. It promises to bring a major departure from national trends.

A recent study by Oregon State University revises earlier predictions that a megalopolis would develop on the West Coast from Seattle to the California border. The new study indicates this won't happen in Oregon so long as Senate Bill 100 remains on the books. Farmers should rejoice that most productive valley bottomland will be spared from housing developments and the concrete wastelands of freeways and parking lots.

12

The Changing Role of the Federal Government in Farmland Retention

W. Wendell Fletcher

Conversion of high quality agricultural land into highways, housing subdivisions, water reservoirs, and other uses is increasingly viewed as a nationally significant problem. This is a departure from the view that has prevailed in recent decades, a view holding that the loss of farmland is a local or, at most, a regional problem, about which the federal government need not, or should not, concern itself.

In fact, few federal agencies have concerned themselves with the loss of farmland to any great extent, even when their projects and activities have inadvertently forced the conversion of high quality farmland. Nor have those state and local governments with farmland protection programs received much federal assistance or encouragement over the years. Until recently at least, it would not have been a great exaggeration to use the terms "benign neglect" and "laissez faire" to characterize the federal government's posture toward the loss of farmland.[1]

In recent years, mounting concern about the loss of farmland has increasingly challenged this traditional federal posture. To an extent that few people would have anticipated a decade ago, both the Congress and the Executive Branch have actively begun to consider new federal policies that could facilitate retention of high quality agricultural land in the future. This consideration already has resulted in new policy directives of potential importance. While these policy changes do not yet constitute a major redirection of federal policy, their adoption, along with the seri-

---

[1]This does not mean the federal government has been unconcerned about other farmland resource problems, however. The U.S. Department of Agriculture (USDA) administers many programs designed to encourage use of conservation management practices on farmland to reduce soil erosion and related land degradation problems.

ous consideration being given to farmland retention policies that have yet to progress beyond the proposal stage, suggests that the loss of farmland is now widely viewed as a national concern that merits federal attention.

Agricultural Land: A Significant National Resource

Unplanned development of land on the urban fringe has long concerned regional planners anxious to curb urban sprawl and preserve open space. Conversion of farmland to urban uses often affects local farm economies adversely as well.

Only recently, however, has widespread concern been expressed about the potential impact of cropland conversion on the overall, long-term productive capacity of American agriculture. This concern has grown out of a conviction that the nation's prime agricultural lands constitute an irreplacable but finite national resource. USDA's Soil Conservation Service (SCS) estimates that 384 million acres of land across the country have the proper soil quality, growing season, and moisture supply to produce sustained crop yields using modern methods.[2]

During the 1950s and 1960s, an era of unprecedented advances in agriculture, there seemed little reason for such concern. At the time, it was widely held that any declines in production resulting from cropland conversion could be offset through advances in agricultural technology or by bringing irrigated land into production.

During the 1970s, however, a combination of factors—escalating world demand for food, unfavorable weather, evidence of farmland's increasing vulnerability to development pressures, soil erosion and other "limiting" factors, as well as more conservative estimates of land that could be easily and inexpensively brought into production—has elicited closer scrutiny of the cropland base and its relationship to national agricultural production goals.

Perceptions of this relationship are changing significantly as a result of escalating world demand for food produced in the United States. Figures 1, 2, and 3, published by USDA for the 1970-1977 period, show the significant increase in both the quantity and prices paid for agricultural exports during the period, and the growing importance of agricultural exports in partially off-setting the enormous trade deficits the nation is experiencing. While agricultural exports are difficult to anticipate, there is every reason to believe that they will remain high. For example, Secretary of Agriculture Bob Bergland has noted on several occasions the potential for expansion of trade with the People's Republic of China.

Not surprisingly, therefore, recent projections suggest that more crop-

---

[2]Only 65 percent of this land—250 million acres—is currently cropped, however. The rest is used for pasture, range, forest, or other purposes (2).

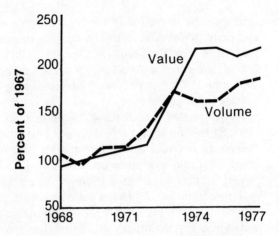

Figure 1. Value and volume of U.S. agricultural exports.

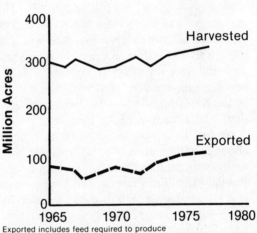

Figure 2. U.S. exports from harvested acres.

Exported includes feed required to produce livestock products exported.

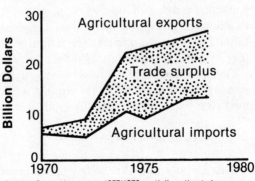

Figure 3. U.S. agricultural trade balance.

October-September years. 1977/1978 partially estimated.

land must be harvested in the future than was anticipated in the 1960s and early 1970s. A 1978 USDA report, for example, compared two projections of cropland needs (4). One, based on conditions in the 1950-1972 period, projected a need for 346 million acres of harvested cropland in 1985 and 354 million acres of harvested cropland in the year 2000, assuming moderate export demand. The other, assuming high export demand, estimated a need for 407 million acres of harvested cropland by 1985, 81 million acres more than was harvested in 1974. Some of this 81 million acres could come from pasture and unused cropland, but new cropland would have to be developed to reach the 407-million-acre level.

Yet, we may have less land in ready reserve for this purpose than we had once thought. USDA has substantially reduced its estimate of the nation's reserves of high and medium potential cropland. Based on physical capability, USDA initially estimated that 266 million acres of noncropland was suitable for cultivation (7). This estimate, based on soil capability, was more than halved when other considerations, such as location and ownership, were assessed. The revised estimate (4) identified only 135 million acres of land nationwide with a high or medium potential for conversion to cropland. About one-third (40 million acres) could be converted without application of conservation practices. Much of the potential cropland is likely to be less suited for crop production than land already used for this purpose.

As for the actual loss of land to other uses, USDA estimated that about 24 million acres of rural land, not just farmland, were converted to urban uses or innudated with water during the 1967-1975 period (6). Roughly 13 million acres of this land were in soil capability Classes I, II, and III, land with high or medium value for crop production. USDA's latest estimate is that slightly under 1 million acres of cropland were converted annually to other uses during the period (7).

But not all agricultural experts are convinced that the availability of land for crop production will become a significant problem. The present situation, and that of most of the post-World War II period, is one of agricultural surpluses. Furthermore, technological breakthroughs, a system of international grain reserves, and improvements in agricultural production by other countries could reduce future pressures on the land.

Given limited cropland reserves and high export demand, however, it appears that concern about the cumulative, long-range impact of continuing conversion of high quality lands is increasingly justified.

The Objectives of Change

Those who would like the federal government to assume a greater role in the effort to protect high quality farmland have focused their energies to date on achieving two separate but related objectives: adoption of policies by federal agencies to govern their own programs and activities that might inadvertently encourage the conversion of high quality farmland and provision of assistance to state and local governments who wish to carry out their own farmland protection programs.

Federal Activities and Farmland Conversion. Federal projects and federally assisted projects for highways, water resource development, sewage treatment facilities, and assorted other public works often are implicated as contributing to indiscriminate conversion of farmland, not only because of the farmland used for such projects, but because of the additional development that may be stimulated by major public works programs. While the loss of some high quality farmland because of such projects is inevitable, few agencies have factored farmland protection considerations into their planning processes.

Other federal objectives can at times interfere with farmland protection needs also. Federal tax policies, for example, are thought to affect the pattern of rural land development (9). A federal commitment to increasing domestic energy production could also result in adverse consequences for high quality agricultural lands unless special care is taken to accommodate agricultural needs.[3]

It is not surprising, then, that many people feel a major priority in any national effort to conserve farmland should be to put the federal house in order first, or, if not first, at least concurrently with other efforts.

While some federal agencies have begun to scrutinize the impact of their actions on farmland more closely, most have not yet changed their procedures sufficiently to ameliorate such impacts. Some foresee the need for a presidential directive, ordering the agencies to develop policies related to farmland protection, or Congressional direction to prompt further executive agency action on the issue.

Federal Assistance to State and Local Governments. The second objective of those who seek a greater federal role in the effort to protect farmland is to encourage state and local governments to adopt their own

---

[3]Federal energy development scenarios suggest that major commitments of land may be needed to meet domestic energy production goals. For example, the Federal Energy Administration (FEA), now part of the Department of Energy, estimated in 1974 that between 37.1 and 38.5 million acres of land could be used for energy production purposes by 1985 if the assumptions in the proposed Project Independence were borne out. This was more than double the 15.8 million acres of land that FEA estimated was dedicated to energy-related purposes in 1972. The following year, FEA, as part of its environmental assessment of President Gerald Ford's proposed Energy Independence Act, upped its estimate of energy-related land needs to 45 million acres. Neither assessment specifically addressed impacts on farmland. While these estimates are not necessarily reliable indicators of what is likely to happen, they do suggest the potential for conflict with agricultural land needs.

farmland protection programs, or to incorporate farmland protection objectives into more comprehensive land use planning and regulatory programs. State and local governments are also looking to the federal government for better information about high quality agricultural land.

A more direct federal role, while feasible, is considered politically unrealistic by many or unnecessary, mainly because, under our system of government, state and local governments are generally thought to be responsible for the regulation of private land use.

With the exception of differential property tax programs,[4] however, only a few state and local governments have put into effect farmland protection programs that specifically attempt to reduce the conversion of high quality agricultural lands. With few exceptions, most of the programs in effect are intended as pilot programs or are otherwise limited in effect. Nonetheless, these programs, which differ from earlier efforts to preserve open space or curb urban sprawl because they focus upon the land's value for agricultural production as well as environmental or aesthetic concerns, indicate an increasing recognition of the need for state and local governments to provide greater protection for farmland.[5]

The Federal Role in Transition

Recent actions by Congress and certain Executive Branch agencies suggest increasing awareness of the importance of farmland to the nation.

Restrictions on Surface Mining. Concern that the nation's effort to develop its coal resources could jeopardize high quality farmland has prompted the Congress to place special restrictions on the surface mining of high quality agricultural lands. This limitation, part of the 1977 Surface Mining Control and Reclamation Act, is the most significant Congressional commitment to the protection of prime farmlands to date.

The decision to restrict surface mining of prime farmland was, in part,

---

[4]Over 40 states have adopted differential property tax programs. While the efficacy of these programs in providing property tax relief to farmers and other landowners is uncontested, the programs have not been particularly successful in curbing farmland conversion. For an analysis of these programs, see *Untaxing Open Space*, a 1976 report prepared for the Council on Environmental Quality by the Regional Science Research Institute (5).

[5]Wisconsin, New Jersey, Massachusetts, Maryland, Connecticut, and New York are among the states that have adopted farmland protection programs. Other states, most notably California, are considering legislation. A number of local governments, including Suffolk County, Long Island, and Black Hawk County, Iowa, also have adopted programs. Both the scope of these programs and the degree of implementation varies greatly from case to case. Other states, including Oregon, Vermont, Florida, and Hawaii, have adopted more comprehensive land use programs, some of which factor agricultural land concerns into the overall planning process. In addition, all but one coastal and Great Lakes States are in the process of developing planning programs for their coastal areas. While only a fraction of farmland is on the coast, some coastal programs address farmland issues.

a reaction to plans to expand coal mining activities in the West and Midwest and to the increase in surface mining that has occurred in recent years. By July 1, 1977, according to SCS, 1.7 million acres of land, not just farmland, had been surface mined for coal. About 570,000 of these acres were under legal reclamation requirements.

While the SCS figures did not provide a breakdown of surface mining activities on high quality agricultural lands, a significant amount of coal surface mining has occurred in the Corn Belt: 158,000 acres in Illinois, 79,000 acres in Missouri, 42,000 acres in Kansas, 14,000 acres in Iowa.

While the federal surface mining law does not ban surface mining on high quality agricultural lands, the act does have several significant provisions that will likely limit surface mining on prime agricultural lands in the future. Among other things, the act specifies that surface mining can only proceed where there is a technological capacity to restore the mined area so it is able to produce yields equivalent to or higher than those on nonmined prime farmland in the vicinity.

Agricultural Land Retention Proposals in the 95th Congress. Legislation was proposed, but not enacted, in the 95th Congress that would have established a commission to study the farmland conversion issue and set up a demonstration program to fund innovative state and local approaches for protecting farmland from indiscriminate development.[6] The House Agriculture committee in July 1978 reported a version of this legislation that would have established an Agricultural Land Review Commission but not the grant program. Congress ultimately adjourned without considering the issue further.

Although it could be argued that such legislation, by encouraging state and local action, could reduce the likelihood of a more direct federal role in the future, the proposal proved controversial because of concern about federal influence over private land use decision-making. Opponents believed that even modest federal support of this kind would constitute an erosion of deeply held traditions of local autonomy over land use decision-making.[7] While a number of federal programs involve far more direct influence over land use decision-making processes than this

[6]Among the bills introduced in the 95th Congress were: H.R. 11122, S. 2757, and S. 1616. For a discussion of H.R. 11122 and the issues involved, see House of Representatives Report 95-1400. Hearings on the legislation, held by the House Agriculture Committee's Family Farms, Rural Development, and Special Studies Subcommittee in 1977, are reproduced in House Serial No. 95-L.

[7]The Carter Administration also opposed the $220 million demonstration grant program in the original legislative proposal on budgetary grounds. It argued that it would be premature to provide federal funds for such a program until the farmland study commission proposed in the bill had completed its study. The administration supported the concept of the study commission.

proposal,[8] there is little doubt that an effective federal support role would have to be fully sensitive to state and local authorities and traditional American attitudes about landownership.

Proposed Legislation in the 96th Congress. Support for the concept of farmland retention legislation carried over into the 96th Congress. Two major bills have been introduced, H.R. 2551, sponsored by Congressman James M. Jeffords and over 40 colleagues in the House, and S.795, introduced by Senator Warren G. Magnuson and 17 colleagues in the Senate. On May 31, 1979, the House Agriculture Subcommittee approved a revised version of H.R. 2551 (with a new bill number) for full Committee consideration. The Senate Agriculture, Nutrition and Forestry Committee had not yet begun its consideration of S.795 in early June.

Like their counterparts in the 95th Congress, both bills would fund state and local pilot projects to test innovative methods of protecting farmland. But there are several salient differences between the bills in the 96th Congress and those proposed in the 95th Congress. For one thing, both S. 795 and H.R. 2551 address the impact of federal agency activities on farmland to a much greater extent. The bills would require federal agencies to develop methods to factor farmland retention objectives into their decision-making. Both would require these agencies to report to the president instances where existing authorities and policies appear inconsistent with farmland retention objectives. The bills also would require federal agency activities to be consistent with state and local farmland retention objectives to the extent possible.

Both bills would authorize a program of technical assistance for state and local governments interested in developing farmland protection programs. This assistance would not be limited to pilot projects. S. 795 would authorize financial assistance to these states and localities as well.

Finally, the bills would provide guidance to USDA for the preparation of a report on farmland protection. Because the administration has initiated such a study, the National Agricultural Lands Study described below, the independent study commission approach proposed in the 95th Congress was deleted from S. 795 and the version of H.R. 2551 approved by the Family Farm Subcommittee.

Federal Executive Actions. Even without a specific congressional directive, Executive Branch agencies have considerable opportunity to re-

[8]Examples are the National Flood Insurance Program, which prescribes floodplain management guidelines for local governments participating in the program; dredge and fill permit requirements under the Federal Water Pollution Control Act; and approval processes associated with the siting of major air polluting facilities in "clean air" areas under the Clean Air Act.

direct their existing authorities and programs to protect farmland. Some federal agencies have, in fact, begun just such efforts.

1. *National Agricultural Lands Study (NALS).* In June 1979, USDA and the President's Council on Environmental Quality (CEQ) agreed to co-sponsor a "study of the availability of the nation's agricultural lands, the extent and causes of their conversion to other uses, and the ways in which these lands might be retained for agricultural purposes."[9] Eight other federal agencies are also participating in NALS. The 18-month $2.1 million study will result in a report to the President on January 1, 1981.

NALS will assess, among other things, the impact of federal programs and policies on farmland availability. It will also produce a handbook comparing ways of protecting farmland at the state and local levels.

2. *Council on Environmental Quality.* CEQ provides guidance to federal agencies in their preparation of environmental impact statements required by the National Environmental Policy Act. The impact of federal agency activities on prime farmland has been identified by CEQ as a consideraton that should be included in environmental impact statements. At this time, however, CEQ's suggestion, set forth in an August 30, 1976, memorandum to heads of federal agencies (*1*), is non-binding in nature, and federal agencies have considerable discretion as to whether they wish to include prime farmland in their statements.

CEQ is planning a study to assess the consideration given to prime agricultural lands in the impact statement process.

3. *U.S. Department of Agriculture.* As the department in charge of the federal farm programs, USDA has an interest in the protection of high quality agricultural lands. USDA also has major responsibilities for rural development, housing, and rural electrification that may have, at times, conflicted with farmland protection objectives.

During the 1970s, USDA has begun to assert a leadership role among federal agencies concerned about the loss of prime agricultural lands. In 1976, then Secretary of Agriculture Earl L. Butz announced a departmental land use policy. That policy urged all federal agencies to use prime agricultural lands only when no suitable alternative site existed and when the use met an overriding public need.

On October 30, 1978, Secretary of Agriculture Bob Bergland issued a revised version of this land use policy (*8*), under which USDA agencies are to avoid proposing or assisting activities that are likely to force the conversion of high quality agricultural lands. Bergland also indicated that he expected USDA agencies to increase their efforts to assist private citizens and state or local governments in efforts to retain important

[9]From a memorandum of agreement between USDA and CEQ, signed on June 14, 1979.

farmlands, as well as forestlands, rangelands, and wetlands.

Among other things, the secretary's memorandum directs agencies within USDA that administer grants, loans, regulations, or technical assistance programs to review their activities and to make necessary changes to minimize the impacts of their programs on farmland. These changes are to be made within one year.

The policy statement also indicates that USDA will "intercede" in "decision-making by other federal agencies where conversions of important farmlands and forestlands, prime rangelands and wetlands are caused or enabled by an agency of the federal government, or where conversions require federal licensing or approval." This intercession apparently will involve "participation in the planning of projects where invited" and review and comment on environmental impact statements, or other authorized review processes associated with federal and federally assisted projects.

4. *Environmental Protection Agency (EPA)*. Like USDA, some programs managed by EPA exert growth-stimulating effects. This stems from the fact that EPA is not just the nation's chief pollution control authority, but also administers the federal government's largest public works program, the sewage treatment facility construction grant program set up by the Federal Water Pollution Control Act in 1972. Under this program, and subsequent amendments, Congress has authorized $42 billion for local sewage treatment facilities through 1982. Since sewage treatment facilities are major inducers of growth and often a precondition for new development, the way in which these facilities are planned has significant implications for farmland.

On September 8, 1978, EPA Administrator Douglas M. Costle approved a new EPA policy "to protect, through the administration and implementation of its programs and regulations, the nation's environmentally significant agricultural land from irreversible conversion to uses which could result in its loss as an environmental or essential food production resource" (*3*).[10]

The memorandum indicates that EPA will "apply the policy to the full extent of its authorities in implementing Agency actions." Each agency office and regional office is to modify its operations accordingly, and staff are to be designated by EPA to assure that the requirements are carried out. The implementation effort will be monitored by EPA's Office of Federal Activities.

---

[10]As defined in the memorandum, "environmentally significant" farmland includes prime farmland, unique farmland, farmland identified by state or local agencies as being of state or local importance, farmland contiguous to environmentally sensitive areas, farmlands of waste utilization importance, and farmlands with significant capital investments to achieve soil erosion, nonpoint pollution best management practices.

Assistant administrators and regional administrators for EPA are to ensure that their actions and the actions of staff "clearly advocate protection of agricultural lands." Specific agency actions stated in the memorandum include, among other things, consideration of agricultural land concerns in developing agency regulations, standards and guidelines, and in planning specific projects.

The policy memorandum states that, in the future, EPA-funded sewage interceptors and collection systems "should be" located on agricultural land only if necessary to eliminate existing discharges and serve existing habitation.

Other provisions of the policy specify that EPA permit actions requiring an environmental impact statement "shall ensure that the proposed activity will not cause conversion of environmentally significant agricultural land" and that primary and secondary impacts on prime agricultural land shall be considered in EPA impact statements, or in EPA's review of the impact statements of other agencies.

Finally, the policy calls for a public awareness program that recognizes the environmental value of prime agricultural land, future research and study of the environmental roles of agricultural lands, and encouragement of state and local farmland protection programs.

Related Federal Measures. In addition to federal laws and programs that specifically provide for the protection of farmland, there are a number of other programs that could foster farmland protection in certain circumstances.

1. *Federal Coastal Zone Management Act.* Most coastal state governments are developing land use planning and regulatory programs for their coastal areas. A major impetus for this state coastal planning effort has been the Coastal Zone Management Act, first passed in 1972 (P.L. 92-583) and significantly amended in 1976 (P.L. 94-370). The program is administered by the National Oceanic and Atmospheric Administration in the U.S. Department of Commerce.

Participation in this federal planning assistance program is voluntary. However, all but one coastal and Great Lake states are participating in the program.

Protection of high quality coastal agricultural lands may be a component of some state programs, but it is not a specific requirement of the act. Furthermore, since the coastal zone only covers a small proportion of a state's total land area, the impact of even a strong farmland protection component would have only modest impact on the overall loss of farmland.

Nonetheless, the experience gained from these state coastal planning efforts could have application elsewhere.

2. *National Flood Insurance Program.* The National Flood Insurance Program, administered by the Federal Insurance Administration in the U.S. Department of Housing and Urban Development (HUD), may, in some circumstances, have the effect of protecting farmland through its goal of limiting new development in flood-prone areas. Under the program, most of the nation's flood-prone communities are adopting floodplain management guidelines developed by HUD. With restrictions on new development in high hazard areas, some farmland in floodplains that might otherwise be developed could be retained in farm use.

3. *Programs Affecting the Quality of Farmland Resources.* In addition to planning assistance programs, the federal government conducts a number of programs that provide farmers with assistance in managing their farmland or in maintaining or improving its quality. Examples are programs to reduce soil erosion and prevent water pollution. Because these programs can affect the productive quality of the land, they may indirectly affect land needs.

4. *Soil and Water Resource Conservation Act of 1978.* This law, a version similar to a proposal that was pocket-vetoed by President Ford at the end of the 94th Congress, is not a farmland protection measure. Nonetheless, the information this act requires could result in a better information base for defining farmland resource issues and problems.

The law calls on USDA to conduct a ''continuing appraisal'' of the ''soil, water, and related resources of the nation.'' This appraisal is to include, among other things, data on the quality and quantity of these resources; data on the resource capabilities and limitations, given current and projected needs; and data on federal and state laws, programs, and policies that affect the ''use, development and conservation'' of these resources. The act also calls for the implementation of a national soil and water conservation program.

Future Policy Options

Current debate over the federal government's role in agricultural land retention suggests several issues that may be of concern in the future.

Information and Technical Assistance. Of all the roles the federal government could play in assisting state and local efforts to protect farmland, this may be the least controversial. By providing, upon request, useful information and technical assistance to communities that are developing their own farmland protection programs, the federal government could be of considerable assistance without infringing upon traditional state and local prerogatives concerning the use of land. In fact, USDA and EPA have significantly upgraded their efforts in this regard in recent years. Nonetheless, some believe that an explicit congressional directive for an assistance program of this sort might be beneficial.

Federal and Federally Assisted or Approved Activities. The impact of federal public works programs, tax policies, and other direct federal activities on farmland is, by most accounts, substantial. Yet, to date, only USDA and EPA have developed explicit policies to review such impacts. Given national concerns about farmland resources, more widespread adoption of such policies and review processes by other federal agencies may be desirable. Furthermore, many who would oppose an attempt by the federal government to influence private land use decisions may feel it appropriate for the federal government to get its own house in order.

Of a more controversial nature, the federal government could also adopt policies that would require the consideration of impacts on prime agricultural lands when reviewing applications for federal grants, loans, and other financial assistance, or when approving activities that require federal permits, licenses, or other approvals. This approach is not without precedent. The National Flood Insurance Program, for example, prohibits the issuance of Veterans Administration and Federal Home Administration mortgage loans in flood-prone areas of communities that are not participating in the flood insurance program. Not surprisingly, however, the program has provoked considerable antagonism in some local communities, and the Congress in 1977 toned down even more draconian sanctions that applied to nonparticipating communities.

While few would find such a strong assertion of federal policy desirable or politically feasible in the case of prime agricultural land, it may well be that a more flexible approach toward federally assisted projects would be acceptable. For example, EPA currently is attempting to factor prime land considerations into state and local planning associated with federal grants for sewage treatment facilities.

In any event, the impact of federal programs on farmland has become an important consideration in both the Executive Branch and Congress. Finding an appropriate balance between national concerns about agricultural land and federally assisted activities will be a major challenge.

Federal Assistance for State and Local Planning. The question here is whether the federal government should provide planning and implementation grants to states and localities for their own farmland protection programs and, if so, at what cost and under what conditions?

There is ample precedent for federal planning assistance. The Coastal Zone Management Act, as noted, provides coastal states with planning and implementation grants for coastal area land use planning and regulation. This program, which is voluntary, also has a provision for consistency of federal activities affecting the coastal zone in states with an approved coastal program. While the act identifies a number of components that a state coastal plan must include to receive approval, actual decisions are made by the state or local governments.

Other federal programs, including EPA's 208 areawide water quality management planning program, also provide planning assistance for land use planning.

While the precedents are there, such planning assistance has been controversial. So-called land use planning assistance legislation, which would have provided statewide planning assistance grants similar to those in the coastal zone program, was passed by the Senate in 1972 and again in 1974, but the proposal never received House approval. Also, as mentioned, agricultural land retention legislation, which would have provided grants for state and local demonstration projects, did not pass the 95th Congress, and the outcome of similar proposals in the 96th Congress is far from certain.

There are other planning assistance options, of course. One possibility is an effort to modify existing federal planning assistance programs to encourage state and local farmland retention planning.

Regardless of the approach, however, controversy is likely to arise. Those who advocate such assistance are not likely to succeed unless an approach is devised that is sensitive to the concerns of landowners and to this nation's preference for locally oriented control over the use of land.

REFERENCES

1. Council on Environmental Quality. 1976. *Memorandum for heads of agencies: Analysis of impacts of prime and unique farmland in environmental impact statements.* Washington, D.C.
2. Council on Environmental Quality. 1977. *Environmental quality, the eighth annual report of the Council on Environmental Quality.* Washington, D.C.
3. Environmental Protection Agency. 1978. *Memorandum on environmentally significant agricultural lands.* Washington, D.C.
4. Lee, Linda K. 1978. *A perspective on cropland availability.* Agricultural Economics Report No. 406. Economics, Statistics and Cooperatives Service, U.S. Department of Agriculture, Washington, D.C.
5. Regional Science Research Institute. 1976. *Untaxing open space.* Council on Environmental Quality, Washington, D.C.
6. Soil Conservation Service. 1977. *Potential cropland study.* Statistical Bulletin 578. U.S. Department of Agriculture, Washington, D.C.
7. Soil Conservation Service. 1977. *Resource inventories, 1977: Final estimates.* U.S. Department of Agriculture, Washington, D.C.
8. U.S. Department of Agriculture. 1978. *Secretary's memorandum no. 1827, revised.* Washington, D.C.
9. U.S. General Accounting Office. 1978. *Effects of tax policies on land use.* CED 78-97. Washington, D.C.

13

Evolution of Land Use
Policy in USDA

Norman A. Berg

In June 1972, having just returned from two months of training at the Federal Executive Institute, I found a brief note from the secretary of agriculture that would test everything I had learned in those training sessions. That memorandum asked that I chair a small departmental committee of one representative each from the U.S. Forest Service, Economic Research Service, Agricultural Stabilization and Conservation Service, and Extension Service. The charge was to look into the land use issue and recommend how the U.S. Department of Agriculture (USDA) should deal with national land use policy.

The committee did not start with a clean slate. USDA had extensive experience in soil, water, and resource conservation and land use. A review of that history can help set the stage for understanding much of what has followed.

Making and Coordinating Land Use Policy: Some Early Activities

USDA convened the first National Conference of Land Utilization in 1931.

The 1938 USDA yearbook, *Soils and Man*, discussed the nation and the soil (*1*). Articles on policies for public and private lands dealt with rural zoning and land use regulation.

The 1940 USDA yearbook, *Farmers in a Changing World*, included a section by Milton S. Eisenhower, who was land use coordinator in USDA's Office of Land Use Coordination (*2*). That office, established in July 1937, followed the appointment in 1935 of a Land Policy Committee and, later, a Coordinating Committee.

The need for this action stemmed from difficulties arising when the

147

several new services of USDA set up to deal with depression and drought led to actions that produced land use conflicts. Questions were raised about how far planning should go in a democracy. How much territory should the planning take in, and what is the proper balance between central authority and decisions by the mass of our citizens?

It was obvious that many of the problems of farmers were expressed in terms of land use and that land use was one of the common denominators of the federal and state programs for farm readjustment. For example, the program for income stability and conservation called for individual farm changes in land use, such as shifts from soil-depleting crops to soil-conserving crops; the heart of the rehabilitation program was the farm and home management plan on which loans were based; erosion control and flood control programs were essentially land use programs, based on the physical and economic requirements of the land and the people who used the land. Therefore, if consistency could be attained in the land use phases of all public agricultural efforts, a major step would have been taken in overall program coordination.

The Office of Land Use Coordination brought together for the first time all USDA agencies dealing with land use problems. These agencies agreed upon a nationwide program for systematic coordination, with a view to achieving agreement on needs, aims, methods, and results. This systematic effort included these steps:

● All basic fact-finding work essential to the action program, such as soil conservation and land use surveys, would be coordinated by the appropriate agencies so as to avoid duplication and, more important, to achieve agreement upon the relevant facts.

● Both general planning, involving farmer-cooperation, and detailed planning by experts would be coordinated by the agencies so as to get agreements on general and specific objectives.

● Current policies and programs would be scrutinized regularly so as to iron out conflicts.

● Shortcomings in organization, which hampered unification of programs, would be studied, and appropriate changes would be instituted, such as a gradual shift to common regional headquarters to encourage regional coordination.

● Uniform methods and policies in decentralization and in working with state and local agencies would be developed.

● All existing and proposed legislation would be carefully studied so the secretary could advise Congress of any inconsistencies in basic policy.

● The work of USDA would be coordinated with that of other federal agencies and, especially, USDA would participate actively in the work of the National Resources Planning Board.

The land use coordinator became a liaison officer with other departments of the government concerned about land use, for example, the Department of the Interior, which managed the public domain; the Army Corps of Engineers, which improved rivers and harbors, an activity that dovetails with the work of USDA in retarding water flow and preventing soil erosion in the watersheds above the rivers; and the National Resources Planning Board, whose committees dealt in a broad way with the nation's land and water resources. The need for agreement on facts, aims, and methods among these agencies was both obvious and urgent.

Concurrent with these early steps toward coordination within and among federal agencies, progress was made toward decentralizing some major land use activities of USDA. This was a response to the feeling that local communities were having plans and programs thrust upon them, rather than initiating and carrying out what they themselves wanted to do.

The formation of soil conservation districts began in 1937, operating under state laws and state and local auspices. Under these laws, the planning and action required to solve major conservation problems in many areas were, and still are, squarely up to the local farmers. They could act or not act as they saw fit, and they worked out programs to satisfy their local needs. Federal and state agencies served an advisory capacity, furnishing technical information on request.

In the meantime, for a period of about three years, committees of USDA and the land-grant colleges were meeting and trying to iron out their conflicts and difficulties. The USDA committee, headed by the under secretary, worked constantly with the state committees for a solution to what had come to be called the federal-state relations problem. Finally, in July 1938, at a remote, unused Weather Bureau station called Mount Weather, in Virginia, the groups gathered to address the problem. After two days of intensive discussion, they emerged with a far-reaching agreement.

This agreement declared that the traditional federal-state relationship in research and extension was satisfactory and should continue. But it recognized that the action programs for agriculture, if they were to be correlated and localized effectively, required a new function that should parallel the functions of research and education. This new function was planning, planning that pooled the experience and judgment of farmers, specialists, and administrators.

It was agreed that planning, with first emphasis on land use planning, was to begin in local communities with local committees. Local plans were then to be coordinated for an entire county by a county committee. County plans were to be coordinated statewide by a state committee, of which the state agricultural extension director was to be chairman. State programs were to be integrated for the entire United States by USDA.

Community committees were to consist of farm men and women only. County committees, however, were not only to be composed of farmer members but also the county representatives of state and federal land use programs. The county agent usually served as the executive officer. State committees also were to have farmer members, but the number of federal and state representatives was to increase at this level.

Not all community plans, of course, would need to be considered by the county, nor all county plans by the state, nor all state plans by the federal government. Many phases of county plans could be carried out by farmers, or by the county commissioners, or by a local soil conservation district, or by a state agreement. There was considerable latitude for decentralized action in federal programs.

As a result of the Mount Weather agreement, committees worked in a large number of communities and counties, classifying land and developing plans to meet their own needs. A unified program, based on detailed study, was begun in 1940 in at least one county in each state. Forty-five states appointed state land use planning committees.

The net result of this early venture into national land use planning, especially the agricultural phases of land use, were mixed. It became apparent that water and land use were inseparable. The attitude of heedless and unplanned land exploitation was partially reversed. The point of view emerged that public policy should aim at effecting such ownership and use of land that would best subserve general welfare rather than private advantage only. Knowlege of good land use practices was the key.

However, when the idea that land use policy and public decisions resulting from a careful planning process were viewed as a threat to private property rights, the whole scheme was terminated during World War II throughout rural America.

Renewed Interest in the Land Use Issue

The secretary of agriculture wrote in the foreword of *Land—the 1958 Yearbook of Agriculture*, "This book will stimulate thought about our land and its use. This is as it should be, for discussion often strikes the spark to ignite inspired thoughts that guide us into a better future" (*3*).

The preface by the editor said, "We present no ready program, no easy solution, and no definite policy. This is not our intention or our province; policies and programs are made by the people and their elected representatives."

In January 1962, the secretary of agriculture called a National Conference on Land and People to obtain assistance in shaping USDA's land and water policies and programs. A preliminary report, "A Land and Water Policy for the United States Department of Agriculture," prepared by USDA's Land and Water Policy Committee, was distributed to members of the conference. The report's findings and recommendations were summarized in a series of statements by the secretary of agriculture and members of his staff. The secretary of the interior outlined that department's interest in land and water resources; and the governor of Wisconsin reviewed the state's 10-year program for resource development and outdoor recreation. A panel representing various nonfederal agencies and groups concerned with resource policies and programs expressed their views and led a conference discussion on better use of land and water in the public interest.

The secretary of agriculture urged members of the conference to consider the ideas discussed at the conference or presented in the preliminary report and to send him their comments and suggestions.

The conference summary was given by John F. Timmons, professor of economics at Iowa State University, who said in part:

"State and local governments are important if not senior partners with the federal agencies in designing and putting into effect the kinds of land-use institutions needed for guiding land uses toward long-run objectives.

"As we proceed with the task of ascertaining and implementing solutions to land- and water-use problems, we seek a balance of the following: (1) Research to provide ideas and facts, interpretations of facts, and creative means for achieving peoples' wants; (2) education to disseminate these ideas and facts and to encourage discussion and decision by the nation's citizens and their representatives in the legislative and executive branches of government; (3) institutional change to encourage and guide land-use adjustments towards desired objectives; and (4) money payments to help facilitate land-use changes toward objectives in the public interest.

"Inasmuch as the science and art of predicting needs for lands well into the future are imperfect, the probabilities of uncertainty warrant the concept of a 'contingency reservoir' of cropland which does not get committed irrevocably to other uses.

"Upon this concept, the objective would not be just idling land from the farm plant but instead the objective would be a positive one in terms of prudent provision for an uncertain future. Thus, the objective would possess value to our nation in serving a positive purpose of insuring the nation's future food and fiber needs. Public investments in this purpose would constitute insurance premiums paid for insuring the nation's food and fiber into the future. Under this concept, other uses which might not conflict with the 'contingency reservoir' objective such as certain recreational, forestry, and grazing uses could be tolerated.

"No doubt the secretary will continue and expand the role of the Land and Water Policy Committee as a continuing central core of integration and vision within that department. The committee might well become interdepartmental in light of the joint responsibilities mentioned by both USDA and USDI secretaries.''

In 1966, the secretaries of housing and urban development (HUD) and agriculture asked Norman Beckman and myself to serve as cochairmen of a conference to explore the opportunities of providing improved services to people when land is in transit from rural to suburban and other nonfarm uses. In mid-June 1967, this first National Conference on Soil, Water, and Suburbia was held in Washington, D.C. Taking part were planners, engineers, architects, investors, conservationists, and public officials representing all levels of government. Most represented organizations and agencies directly involved in the transition of land in the nation's growth process.

The secretary of agriculture pointed to the unending tragedy of developing and building on land unsuited to the selected use and added that the problem calls for ''broad comprehensive planning on an area or regional basis...and for public understanding.'' ''I cannot emphasize this enough,'' he declared. ''The individual citizen and his community have everything to gain if soil and water resources are managed properly. They have a great deal to lose if they aren't.''

In light of this extensive history, it was unbelievable that as land use legislation was debated in Congress in the late 1960s and early 1970s USDA was not involved. This long history of land use experience within USDA and the land grant universities was simply ignored.

Even more crucial was that under the early Nixon Reorganization Plan USDA was to be eliminated and the Department of the Interior was to be the nucleus for a proposed Department of Natural Resources. Interior thus became the focal point for land use legislation.

Interior saw the issue of land use as one of inadequate federal, state, and local regulation. Misuse of land could be cured by better regulation, often meaning regulation by a *larger unit* of government. Local government, historically the only level involved in land use controls, would be replaced or supplemented by state controls, operating under federal guidelines.

USDA's constituency, the owners and users of most of America's land, found this to be the wrong conception of the issue and the wrong prescription for curing the nation's land use problems. This constituency mounted heavy opposition to land use bills.

USDA's Concept of the Land Use Issue

Land use problems and issues did not go away. The nation needed to improve the use of its land base to meet ever-pressing demands. The question was how to accomplish this.

USDA had been active in developing a concept of the land use issue and establishing a way to actually improve land use decision-making. The concept is essentially one of informed citizen input into decisions. These decisions involve conflicting social goals. They also require complex tradeoffs among values. Land use questions are seldom absolute. It is not a matter of whether or not you *can* build the subdivision on prime farmland, or whether or not you *can* fill in the swamp for an airport, but whether or not you *should* do these things. Such issues become the battleground where citizens determine the direction of growth and change in our society. Land use decisions are not so much rational designs as *social* and *political* expressions of what people perceive as good or bad for the future.

USDA saw the proper federal role in this process as a *limited* but vital one. Federal investments in such things as roads, schools, airports, or power plants are often the "growth shapers" that overpower all local determinations. Federal lands make up one-third of the nation. Federal guidelines and regulations on everything from air and water pollution control to airport safety either limit or demand local actions. The federal programs, functional in nature, often produce unintended side effects that pave over prime lands, limit productive land uses, or encourage destructive growth patterns. A key federal responsibility is to improve this process and reduce the harmful effects of major federal actions. USDA, particularly in regard to prime farmlands, had been working to see that this was done.

Development of a Secretary's Memorandum on Land Use

With this background, the small committee set up by the secretary in 1972 determined that USDA needed a secretary's policy memorandum on land use. The drafting process began. It also became apparent that a central focal point on land use was needed. Therefore, a draft supplement to the policy memorandum establishing a USDA Land Use Policy Committee was prepared.

To formalize a secretary's numbered memorandum is a formidable task, unless the secretary or one of his top staff initiates the process. Policy takes many shapes and sizes, depending on the issue. At the same time the committee was working to establish the need for a policy on land use, the secretary issued numbered memorandums on subjects as diverse as equal employment opportunity coordinators, rural development, food and nutrition research, remote sensing user requirement task force, and earth resources survey committee.

Land use policy was viewed, of course, as having many facets ranging

across many interests. It attracted people who wanted something in it for
public lands as well as private lands; for extension as well as research; for
technical assistance as well as financial assistance; for the role of each
level of government; and for special land uses, such as cropland, woodland, grassland, wetland, rural land, or urban land.

Finally, many constituents of USDA programs viewed land use issues
with concern. Some even questioned why the topic was discussed in
Washington.

With the cooperation of key agency representatives and guidance from
the assistant secretary for conservation, research and education, the
policy draft reached the desk of the secretary for his consideration in November 1972. In February 1973, the committee had the proposed policy
back on its agenda with a memo from the secretary. That memo suggested that the draft be used as a basis for further study and development of
a broader land use policy statement. In addition, the secretary proposed
a broadening of the representation on the committee that prepared the
draft statement.

Encouraged by the secretary's interest in the proposed policy, the committee took immediate steps to respond by separating the proposed supplement to the policy statement. It rewrote that document and sent it to
the secretary as a memo creating a "Committee on Planning and Policy
for Land Use and Land Conservation." This was quickly signed by the
secretary, becoming Secretary's Memorandum No. 1807, dated March
26, 1973 (4).

This breakthrough led to an eight-agency USDA committee chaired by
an assistant secretary named by the secretary. The committee functions
included policy and legislative strategies, program coordination, surveil-
lance, education and information, and program review. This committee
was to advise the secretary and his staff on land use issues related to
policy, programs, and needed executive and legislative action.

A priority task was to rewrite the policy document, obtain committee
support, and to again ask for the secretary's signature. On October 26,
1973, Secretary's Memorandum No. 1827 was approved by the secretary
and became USDA's statement on land use policy (5). In a note to the
assistant secretary, the secretary commented, "Sorry this took so long
for me to get to it. It's fine."

It was a strong position for USDA to take in 1973 while land use legislation was being debated in Congress. The statement recognized that major responsibility for land use policy (planning and regulation) rests with
local and state governments. USDA also recognized the rights and responsibilities of landowners and users in making decisions within this
framework. It dramatized that through its agencies USDA administers
some 80 programs that influence private as well as governmental land

holders' decisions, urban as well as rural.

The policy statement attempted to define land use policy for the first time as:

"A facet of our general decision-making process on the use of our resources. It is a tool to carry out governmental development policies evolving from decisions on interrelated policies arising from economic, social, or environmental problems. Land use policy and its consequences provide a focal point to identify and resolve conflicts growing out of competing land uses. Land use policy is the expression of society's determination of how its resource, land, is used. Land use policy refers to the total of all those national, state, and local laws, ordinances, and attitudes affecting the short-term or long-term uses of land, private or public, through such mechanisms as ownership, inheritance, taxation, condemnation, zoning, redevelopment, building regulation, master planning and legislative fiat."

Policy guidance itself was quite specific, stating that USDA would:

● Adapt present pertinent programs to help enhance and preserve prime agricultural, range, and forest lands for those uses.

● Promote and help influence the management of rural lands to assure adequate sources of high quality water.

● Intensify establishment of permanent soil and water conservation on the erosion-vulnerable lands returned to cultivation to help increase production of crops and livestock.

● Further coordinate the work of USDA agencies at the state level to make all its land use efforts relevant and harmonious.

● Provide timely information and assistance, including nonfarm interpretations of soil surveys, small watershed hydrologic data, and economic information to local, county, and state land use decision-makers.

● Strengthen and expand USDA's capabilities in harmony with others for surveying and monitoring land and related natural resources and to provide resource condition evaluations to local, county, state, and federal governmental land use decision-makers.

● Help protect rare and endangered plant and animal species and their ecological systems as well as historic, cultural, scientific, and natural systems.

● Help conserve and develop significant waterfowl habitat lands.

● Assist in the reclamation of land surfaces used for the extraction of nonrenewable resources, such as coal, minerals, oil, and gas.

● Expand USDA's efforts to assure wider understanding of how its programs and responsibilities contribute to improved land uses.

● Cooperate fully with other departments in terms of responsibility for policy and leadership.

USDA agencies were directed to emphasize, to the extent possible, including redefinition or modification of their policies, that their programs:

- Increase production of detailed soil surveys.
- Establish land capability criteria to help direct the flow of urbanization to land areas least suited to crops and forests.
- Help guide urban growth to preserve prime farmlands, minimize fragmentation of land holdings, provide adequate water supplies, equalize taxes, dispose waste properly, and provide adequate public health, recreation, and safety services.
- Plan and guide effectively land use in the rural-urban fringe areas and in recreation or second-home subdivisions.
- Control erosion and reduce sedimentation.
- Minimize the impact of surface mining on rural land uses.
- Locate sites for solid waste disposal as an increasingly important land use.
- Give attention to the need for small watershed, floodplain, wetlands, and coastal zone management programs, based on comprehensive land use planning incorporating ecological considerations.

An early result of the committee and policy memoranda was improved communication. In 1974, USDA held regional workshops for its state-level officials. There followed a request that each state establish a land use committee to help state and local officials deal with land use questions. Committees have since been established in every state, with varying organizational structures and ties to existing USDA mechanisms, such as rural development committees. In most states, the USDA state land use committee quickly established itself as the best source of technical assistance available to state and local officials concerned with land use questions or programs.

Seeking a USDA Focus on Land Use

But the land use issue, by itself, was not a particularly attractive one for USDA's focus. There were several reasons for this. If the problem was land use, then what was to be the solution? The Jackson-Udall land use bill was under active consideration, and most of USDA's clientele felt that was not the way to go. If USDA, with its expertise and field delivery system, was to do something constructive, it would have to be on a more clearly focused issue.

There were problems with turf also. USDA did not simply want to replace the Department of the Interior as the federal agency with the lead role in a Jackson-Udall-type land use program. But if attention were stirred up in USDA about the land use issue, that would be seen by many observers as the real motive.

Politically, the term "land use" was becoming inextricably tied to land use regulation and federal regulation at that. The longer the Jackson-Udall bill debate continued, the more politically damaging it became to be associated with anything that could be labelled "land use." (That problem exists to this day, prompting at least one observer to suggest that the Interior bill set back the cause of proper land management and conservation by 10 years or more.)

Finally, there were too many issues in land use that were outside USDA's main focus of interest. Urban growth problems, inner-city decay, facility siting, and similar issues concerned USDA because they affected agricultural land, but they were not issues primarily within USDA's scope. The one issue that clearly was, and that showed promise of becoming an issue of national concern, was agricultural land.

Reconciling Two Schools of Thought on Agricultural Land

Even the agricultural land issue was not without its problems in USDA. The major agricultural policy problem for two decades had been crop surpluses, and the major farm program efforts had been land retirement. To suggest that farmland was a valuable resource that should be protected or even preserved was to fly in the face of the experience of some USDA scientists and policy-makers.

Two schools of thought existed within USDA, and they caused conflicting signals to emerge about the agriculture land situation. The conservation point of view held that farmland, particularly prime farmland, was a national asset that should be protected. On this basis, concern was expressed about the continued loss of agricultural land. The economic point of view looked at the land as a factor in production, evaluated the productive capability of U.S. agriculture, estimated probable supply and demand, and came forth with assurances that America had an abundance of good land for the foreseeable future.

So in late 1974, when the attention of the USDA committee shifted to the issue of retaining agricultural land, these points of view remained to be reconciled. A task force of the committee planned and conducted a national seminar on the Retention of Prime Lands in July 1975. Both the background papers for that seminar and the findings and recommendations of the seminar were published (6, 7).

The seminar brought together representatives of the many points of view. The 80 participants, experts from across the nation in many professional disciplines, were to settle on some conclusions and recommendations. A consensus emerged after two days of work: "The continued conversion of prime production lands to other land uses is a matter of growing concern that will require a great deal of attention in the future."

Although carefully couched in bureaucratic language, the summary of findings and conclusions from the seminar contained the following statement that represented a sharp turn in USDA policy thinking: "The demand for food, fiber, and timber from United States production lands is expected to increase to the point where the production capability of the nation will be tested, although it is not certain when or with what degree of urgency this will occur."

To implement what they suggested was a national policy issue, the participants recommended: "Public interest will be served by maintaining a maximum flexibility of options with respect to future land use needs in a changing and uncertain world. Extreme caution should be exercised in approving actions that result in irreversible conversions of prime farmland to other uses. In some states, problems must be faced now, or significant options for the future will be closed. USDA should be concerned with any actions that will diminish the nation's ability to produce food, fiber, and timber."

The recommendations from the seminar were not USDA policy, but the die was cast. Agricultural land was a national policy issue in a new sense, and USDA had embarked on a new venture in national land use policy leadership.

Actions in Response to the Prime Lands Seminar

USDA's Land Use Committee undertook several actions in response to the seminar. A specific policy statement on prime lands was published on June 21, 1976, as Supplement No. 1 to the Secretary's Memorandum No. 1827 (8). The policy statement called for USDA agencies to make special provisions in their programs and services for the recognition and retention of prime lands.

Meetings between USDA and the Council on Environmental Quality (CEQ) resulted in an August 30, 1976, memorandum to the heads of federal agencies from the chairman of CEQ. That memorandum called for the heads of all federal agencies to include an analysis of the impact of their action on prime lands in the preparation of environmental impact statements.

The CEQ memorandum directed federal agencies to seek assistance from USDA in the definition and delineation of prime agricultural lands. USDA had development of a nationally consistent definition underway at the time and, following substantial local, state, and interest-group input, published its final definition on January 1, 1978, in the *Federal Register*.

To date, little attention has been given the CEQ memorandum. Recent studies show that few environmental impact statements contain any recognition of the effects of a proposed action on agricultural lands, and still fewer actions are modified in deference to their impacts on agricultural lands.

USDA also began an intensive effort to complete workable definitions of prime and unique farmland and to initiate a mapping program so that local, state, and federal decision-makers could better understand the facts. Participants in the Prime Lands Seminar had complained that "a frustrating lack of data prevents a clear picture of either the current situation or the probable future amount of land available or needed for agricultural production."

As a result, SCS issued Land Inventory and Monitoring (LIM) Memorandum-3 on October 15, 1975. This memorandum not only defined prime and unique farmlands, but also established additional categories of important farmlands that could be defined at the state and local levels. It inaugurated a program of mapping these lands on a county-by-county basis that will result in the production of about 400 county maps by the end of fiscal year 1979. Most importantly, it provided a working definition of prime farmland that could be used in conjunction with other monitoring efforts in order to begin the process of inventorying the national supply of good farmland, identifyng some of the trends in its use, and beginning to fill that frustrating lack of information.

One of the payoffs in this effort occurred during legislative consideration of the Surface Mining Control and Reclamation Act of 1977. Concern about the impact of surface mining on prime farmlands in Illinois and surrounding states led Secretary of the Interior Cecil Andrus to tell Congress that he did not "want to replace an energy crisis with a food crisis." SCS advocated special soil reconstruction standards for prime farmlands, and the Carter Administration supported that position. Ultimately, the new act set forth special standards for soil reconstruction after mining on prime farmlands, to the end that agricultural productivity would be restored to the extent technically possible. That focus could not have occurred without the definition of prime farmlands and the newly acquired information about their amount and use.

An Updating of USDA Policy on Land Use

After the Carter-Bergland leadership was in place in 1977, it became apparent that USDA needed an updated policy. The new assistant secretary convened the USDA Committee on Planning and Policy for Land Use and Conservation to solicit agency views on organizational arrangements for defining and implementing land use policy in the new administration. There was concurrence on the continued need for a land use committee within USDA.

On December 17, 1977, Secretary Bob Bergland signed a revision of Secretary's Memorandum No. 1807, creating the current USDA Committee on Land Use (9). This memorandum named as members of the committee the seven agencies of USDA having programs that affect land use in any significant way. The memorandum assigned the committee responsibilities for making recommendations and assisting in actions to help USDA establish and implement departmental and federal land use policies.

The committee then developed a revised departmental policy statement. From January through April 1978, a series of five multistate workshops were conducted on land use, rural development, and energy. Nearly 40 Washington-based departmental officials, agency administrators, and their top staff met and interacted with more than 600 state-level USDA agency heads, regional office administrators, and other top staff members in USDA state and regional offices and land grant universities.

The draft land use policy statement, a major agenda item for the regional workshops, was thoroughly discussed. The statement was revised to reflect the recommendations of these workshop participants, who interact daily with local and state governing officials; with environmental conservation, commodity, wildlife, sportsmen's, energy, and other land user groups at the state and local levels; and with individual farmers, businessmen, industrialists, homeowners, and other landholders.

The secretary signed Secretary's Memorandum No. 1827 (Revised) on October 30, 1978 (10). In response to the Executive Orders of May 24, 1977, on the protection of wetlands and the regulation of floodplains, the secretary signed, on the same day, Supplement No. 1 to Secretary's Memorandum No. 1827 establishing USDA's policy for implementing those Executive Orders (11).

The statement is essentially a codification of USDA's responsibilities that have evolved since 1972. For example, with respect to prime farmlands, it deals explicitly with USDA policy in fulfilling requirements under the CEQ letter of August 30, 1976, on this issue.

The statement used by the secretary with the news media said:

"The policy established by this statement is a reflection of my concern and this administration's concern with the land use issue.

"The document is designed to *emphasize* and *clarify* the department's role in encouraging the retention of important agricultural lands. It will assist agency personnel in responding to policy priorities emerging at the state and local levels.

"This policy reinforces efforts by the department to advocate the retention of important agricultural lands and work with local and state governmental and other federal agencies through establishing procedures for environmental and administrative review. There is no additional *authority* to intervene in decisions of other governmental entities.

"This policy requires that USDA agencies adjust their technical and financial programs to minimize the adverse effects of their actions on important agricultural lands, wetlands, and floodplains.

"With Supplement 1, the revised memorandum constitutes departmental response to the Executive Orders on Floodplain Management and Wetlands Protection. The statement provides the opportunity for the department and *this administration* to demonstrate leadership and concern on these issues.

"The statement continues the department's recognition of the rights and responsibilities of state and local governments for developing public policies and for planning and regulating private land use.

"This department has recently acquired authority under the Surface Mine Reclamation Act (P.L. 95-87) with respect to planning for the surface mining of coal and other minerals. This act requires the federal government to assist in planning for the extraction of coal and other nonrenewable resources to facilitate restoration of the land's productive capacity. In addition, the department has responsibility under the same legislation for reclamation of abandoned surface mined lands. The department's role in this area is also incorporated in this statement.

"This statement contains no major new authority or responsibility for the department. There is added emphasis to actions listed in the 1973 and 1976 land use policy memoranda.

"This statement does not:

"Permit, facilitate or imply federal control of land use decisions of state and local governments, beyond actions required already under NEPA. The department will, however, provide information and assistance useful in generating decisions sensitive to impacts on agricultural lands, and will encourage attention to these matters.

"Stop or discourage development. It simply seeks to help guide the *pattern* of development consistent with important agricultural lands.

"Deprive any individual of property rights.

"My office and the Land Use Committee have worked hard over a period of nearly 18 months to formulate the statement I am signing today. In the process we have involved more than 600 members of the department's field staff leadership from ten agencies in face-to-face discussions. These professionals operate and stand accountable for programs delivering direct assistance to more than 50 million local citizens in over 3,000 counties of the United States.

"By establishing this policy, I am pledging this department philosophically and substantively on this important issue."

In retrospect, USDA has again evolved a policy and established an internal coordinating group for land use matters. This effort has had several benefits. First, a few other federal departments, the Environmental Protection Agency (EPA), HUD, and CEQ, and several state agencies now have developed strong policy positions on land use. Second, the prime land issue has now become a topic on the agenda of many organizations. Third, alternative efforts to retain important farmlands for agriculture have accelerated through legislative action by several states and local jurisdictions. Funding for testing some activities, such as the purchase of development rights, is underway in a few states.

Congress increasingly has considered legislation to establish federal policy on the protection of certain agricultural land, to establish a study committee on the protection of agricultural land, and to establish demonstration programs relating to methods of protecting certain agricultural land from being used for nonagricultural purposes.

Fourth, the secretary of agriculture and the chairman of CEQ, on June 14, 1979, signed an agreement to provide joint leadership in conducting a national study on the retention of agricultural lands. The study will determine the nature, rate, extent, and causes of these losses; evaluate the economic, environmental, and social impacts of these losses in both rural and urban areas; and recommend administrative and legislative initiatives necessary to minimize these losses. A report on the findings is to be made to the president by January 1, 1981.

Eight other federal departments or agencies, including the secretaries of interior, HUD, transportation, energy, commerce, and defense; the administrator of EPA; and the director of the Office of Management and Budget, are being asked to assist this effort through their cooperation in staffing and funding this activity.

Whether all of this activity has saved any farmland from conversion to other uses is not yet clear. Losses of agricultural land go on. Of the rural land converted to urban and water uses between 1967 and 1975, SCS estimated that about one-third was prime farmland. The addition of 29 million acres of land in urban, built-up, and transportation uses between 1967 and 1977 meant that about 1 million acres of prime farmland was converted to nonagricultural uses each year.

USDA defines prime farmland as that land having the best combination of physical and chemical characteristics for producing food, feed, forage, fiber, and oilseed crops. To be classified as prime, the land must meet technical criteria and also be available for agriculture (not already committed to a nonagricultural use). Two-thirds of the land meeting the USDA criteria for prime farmland was being cropped in 1977.

Of the 116 million acres of prime farmland not currently being cropped, SCS estimates that about 45 percent (52 million acres) could feasibly be shifted into cropland production under certain conditions. This acreage is our national reserve.

At the press conference announcing the agricultural land availability study, the secretary of agriculture said, "We need to examine very carefully the fundamental question—private rights versus public interest—how do we join the two?"

This, of course, brings us back full circle to the frustrations of actions in USDA over 40 years ago. Now, as then, the challenge remains—to determine if states and local governments, in conjunction with the federal government, can put into place a program to slow down, if not stop, the rate at which the nation is converting its best agricultural land, short of enacting some type of a national land use law.

REFERENCES

1. U.S. Department of Agriculture. 1938. *Soils and man, yearbook of agriculture*. Washington, D.C.
2. U.S. Department of Agriculture. 1940. *Farmers in a changing world, yearbook of agriculture*. Washington, D.C.
3. U.S. Department of Agriculture. 1958. *Land, yearbook of agriculture*. Washington, D.C.
4. U.S. Department of Agriculture. March 26, 1973. *Secretary's memorandum 1807*. Washington, D.C.
5. U.S. Department of Agriculture. October 26, 1973. *Secretary's memorandum 1827*. Washington, D.C.
6. U.S. Department of Agriculture. 1975. *Perspectives on prime lands*. Washington, D.C.
7. U.S. Department of Agriculture. 1975. *Recommendations on prime lands*. Washington, D.C.
8. U.S. Department of Agriculture. 1976 *Secretary's memorandum 1827, supplement no. 1*. Washington, D.C.
9. U.S. Department of Agriculture. December 17, 1977. *Secretary's memorandum 1807, revised*. Washington, D.C.
10. U.S. Department of Agriculture. October 30, 1978. *Secretary's memorandum 1827, revised*. Washington, D.C.
11. U.S. Department of Agriculture. October 30, 1978. *Secretary's memorandum 1827, revised, supplement no. 1*. Washington, D.C.

14

States' Role in Farmland Retention

Richard C. Collins

Senator Aiken's was a lonely voice when he said some years ago that "every farm program from now on will be a major piece of foreign policy legislation with our family food budget seriously involved" (*11*). The connection between land, food, foreign policy, and prices is not well understood by anyone, but many have not even established the relevance of the connection.

As a result, the only widespread state program aimed at saving farmland in the United States has been the differential assessment of farmland. An understanding of the characteristics of differential assessment will also suggest why any innovations, if they are to be made, will be extremely difficult politically, economically, and legally.

From Hawaii to North Dakota to New Jersey, some 44 states have adopted various forms of differential assessment for farmland. To be sure, one might say that the adoption of these programs flowed as much from urban values as from rural needs. In spite of the powerful impetus given to the food issue through the prime land efforts of the Soil Conservation Service (*13*), the greatest base of political support for reducing farmland conversion has come from those concerned with maintaining urban amenities and open space and reducing the environmental and fiscal effects of sprawling, rapid growth.

Elements of the Farmland Conversion Problem

The farmland conversion issue can be divided into three parts. One deals with the land as a producer of food and fiber. A second emphasizes the land use aspects, mainly open space, environmental quality, and growth control in urban and suburban settings. The third is the property rights issue.

Differential assessment programs have managed to avoid the third issue. It is crucial, therefore, to determine just how effective these programs are in reducing conversions of farmland to other uses.

An Evaluation of Differential Assessment Programs

A study sponsored by the Council on Environmental Quality (CEQ), *Untaxing Open Space* (4), provided a thorough analysis of these laws, comparing them, evaluating their effectiveness, and pointing in the direction that must be followed if these programs are to succeed in preserving farmland and open space. The land use issues that led to the adoption of these laws are summarized in the report:

"Farmers are producers of two entirely different classes of goods for two different markets: agricultural commodities and development sites. The common factor joining these two markets is the farmer's land. When treated as an input to the production of commodities, land has a value which is related to its capitalized economic rent as a factor of production. Its economic rent is determined by such factors as soil quality, topography, distance from the market, access to transportation facilities....

"When land is used for residential, commercial or industrial facilities, its value is determined by its proximity to urban development, transportation facilities, areas of special scenic or recreation interest, etc....

"In many farming areas, especially those on the rural-urban fringe, there are large differentials between the value of land as an input to the production of agricultural commodities and its value as an input to development. These differentials have produced the crisis which has led most states to adopt some form of differential assessment...which permits agricultural land...to be assessed at values approximating its value as an input to agricultural production rather than as a site for development."

Apart from the fiscal, tax, and equity issues that the report so adequately details, the major issue remains: Do these laws keep land in agriculture? CEQ concludes that they do not.

Before accepting this conclusion, however, it is useful to consider the major categories of differential assessment because they suggest some useful directions for the future. Table 1 shows the various features of these laws.

Preferential Assessment. This category provides tax benefits to the owners of eligible land without imposing any restrictions on the conversion of the land. There is no attempt to recapture the difference between the use assessment and the development value at the time of conversion. Although there may be considerable differences among states in eligibility criteria and the tax benefits conferred, the aim of preferential assessment is to provide relief to farmers. Such objectives as excluding speculators or tying in preferential treatment to planning and zoning policies are clearly secondary (4).

Deferred Taxation. This category of differential assessment laws is distinguished from pure preferential assessment by efforts to recapture the taxes that would have been borne by the landowner if the land had been assessed at its development value. This is usually achieved by a rollback tax for a specified number of years or by some form of retroactive application of taxes on the development value. For the farmer who continues to use his land for agricultural purposes, the tax continues to be deferred. For those who eventually convert the land to urban uses, the difference between the use tax and the development value is deferred until the time of conversion.

Restrictive Agreement. In this form of differential assessment, the use tax is accompanied by a legally enforceable agreement that assures that the land is maintained in agriculture for a specified period or that the landowner pays a penalty for conversion before the contract period expires. The distinguishing feature of a restrictive agreement is that the owner is reasonably certain that he will not be able to develop his land until the end of the run-out period (4).

Although not classified in table 1, two states, Michigan and Wisconsin, have developed programs that link the tax relief to the state income tax. When agricultural land is included in a local jurisdiction's agricultural land program, the owner is allowed a state income tax deduction if his local property tax exceeds a certain percentage of his income. This is an interesting feature because it unties the program from local property tax considerations and relates the tax benefit not to land value alone but to the ratio of income to tax liabilities.

The popularity of various differential assessment laws rests in no small part on the fact that they rely on the voluntary nature of the farmer's participation. This has led to some distortions and disappointments from a land use perspective, however. Under a voluntary program, the more restrictive the agreement, the more reluctant farmers are to join. By the same token, the greater the pressure from urbanizing influences, the greater the reluctance of farmers to commmit their land to agriculture over a long term. This pattern has been observed in California and elsewhere.

As the authors of the CEQ study (4) assert:

"With respect to the goal of retarding the conversion of farm and other open land, differential assessment is marginally effective and its cost in terms of tax expenditures is high, in most cases, so high as to render it an undesirable tool for achieving this goal. It has its principal effect on the supply of land which is put on the market by reducing the farmer's costs of production and thus increasing the profitability of far-

Table 1. Provisions of state differential assessment laws 1977.

Program Characteristics	Arizona	Arkansas	Colorado	Delaware	Florida 1	Idaho	Indiana	Iowa	Missouri	New Mexico	North Dakota	Oklahoma	South Dakota	Wyoming	Alaska	Connecticut
Pure Preferential Assessment																
Year of enactment	67	69	67	68	59	71	61	67	75	67	73	74	67	73	67	6:
Eligible uses																
Agriculture	•	•	•	•	•	•	•	•	•	•	•	•	•	•	•	•
Open space, environmental protection	•											•				•
Timber or forest	•	•		•	•		•	•	•	•		•				•
Recreation	•											•				
Additional eligibility requirements																
Minimum farm income required			•						•						•	
History of eligible use required		•	•						•				•	•		
Minimum length of tenure within family									•							
Land must be planned for eligible use																
Land must be zoned for eligible use														•		
Sanctions on conversion																
Rollback taxes collected (no. of years)															7	
Interest on deferred taxes															•	
Penalty based on market value in year of conversion																
Other penalty																•
Restrictive agreements																
Minimum length of term (no. of years)																
Scope of program																
Statewide	•	•	•	•	•	•	•	•	•	•	•	•	•	•	•	•
Local option																
Voluntary, requires application		•		•	•				•	•					•	•
Automatic for eligible lands	•	•			•	•	•				•	•	•	•		
State subvention payments provided to offset revenue loss															•	

Source: Updated from (4).
*Total rollback of deferred taxes.

ming. It has no effect on the decision to sell for non-economic reasons, such as retirement or death. It also has no effect on the major component of the demand for conversion of land—accessibility to growing urban centers. It may even cause effective demand to increase since developers will be willing to bid more for land, realizing that as long as they deep [sic] it in approved uses, their carrying costs will be lower.''

The report was written before Proposition 13 passed in California,

														Deferred Taxation														Restrictive Agreements				
illinois	Kentucky	Louisiana	Maine	Maryland	Massachusetts	Minnesota 1	Minnesota 2	Montana	Nebraska	Nevada	New Hampshire 1	New Jersey	New York 1	New York 2	North Carolina	Ohio	Oregon	Pennsylvania 1	Pennsylvania 2	Rhode Island	South Carolina	Tennessee	Texas	Utah	Virginia	Washington	California	Florida 2	Michigan	New Hampshire 2	Vermont
70	76	71	56	73	67	69	73	74	75	72	64	71	71	73	74	63	66	74	68	75	76	66	69	71	70		65	67	74	73	69
2	4	10/15	2	4	3	7	4	5	7		2	5			5	4	10	5	7	2	5	3/5	3	5	5	7			*	7	
																											10	10	10	10	

which adds even greater support to the analysis. Especially noteworthy is the fact that differential assessment laws do not deal with the demand side of the equation in the conversion of rural land, nor do they deal with those aspects of the conversion decisions that are unrelated to property tax issues.

One could summarize the CEQ report findings, then, by saying that economic issues are not the only factors causing farmland conversion. Where economics are important, the property tax break may not be decisive, and the uses to which differential assessment is put may actually increase the conversion of land.

The report makes a number of significant recommendations on the fiscal and informational aspects of differential assessment, but more importantly, the report concludes (4):

"...differential assessment is an inadequate tool for achieving the goal of maintaining current use. It is however a useful component of a broader approach which should have the following characteristics:

"a. Eligible land should be designated specifically following studies of its capability for agriculture, the need for farmland and land in other open uses, and the projected demand for land for urban development, vacation houses, strip-mining, etc. It is especially important that the agricultural districts designated be large enough to be functionally and economically viable and located so that they will be relatively free from intrusion of urban and suburban activity...Therefore, designation should be made by *state, regional, or possibly by county government, rather than by local government.*

"b. Strict controls should be placed on the development of designated land. If these controls exceed the limits of police power regulation, compensation should be paid to the owners, by such techniques as public purchase of development rights or the transfer of development rights. Funds for the public purchase of rights should be raised by the level of government which designates the eligible land, the major part of the funding coming from *special levies on other land when it is developed.* A capital gains tax covering at least a 15-year period would be one such levy" (emphasis added).

After reviewing the CEQ study, it is difficult not to accept its suggestions for future directions:

"...differential assessment programs which are not part of a comprehensive land development regulation system are counterproductive in terms of the broader goals of urban development. The benefits which they provide for individual farmers...are more than counterbalanced by the disadvantages they entail in creating special tax shelters in which owners of developable land may thrive until their personal economic plans coincide with those of the market generally. Such programs should either be amended or made a part of a larger system of resource management and development regulation. Such a system would entail the designation of agricultural and development districts, staging of capital facilities and development, compensation, and differential assessment."

States' Role in Agricultural Land Retention: Some Propositions

The CEQ report and its conclusions seemingly are a necessary base for a series of propositions concerning the role of the states in agricultural land retention.

● The most widely adopted state programs aimed at retaining agricultural land have been the differential property tax programs now in force in nearly all states. Unfortunately, if these programs are not incorporated into a more inclusive land use planning context, they may hurt agricultural land retention more than they help. The cost of the programs and their acknowledged ineffectiveness will bring them under increasing scrutiny. If coupled with an effective land use planning program, however, they could be important factors in state programs for agricultural land retention.

● Although an issue of growing importance, agricultural land retention still has not become a heavyweight compared with certain other land use issues in the states. Differences among states are considerable, but there remains widespread disagreement among experts and the general public on the issue's validity. Some see the retention of farmland as an emotional, doomsday appeal designed to support the exclusionary, no-growth programs of upper middle-class suburbanites.

● States must be the keystone of any successful effort to retain agricultural land. The states are legally, politically, and institutionally best situated in terms of controlling policies that affect the use and conversion of farmland to other uses. But their actual use of these powers is by no means a certainty. This is so because state legislatures are probably not the best forum for a debate on the property rights issue that must be addressed.

● The states' role, though crucial to the effectiveness of agricultural land retention, will not move evenly or successfully without federal initiatives. The federal effort need not be farmland legislation specifically, nor take the form of general land use legislation, although that would be desirable. The more likely short-term federal initiatives will be in encouraging state coordination of planning activities required in air and water pollution programs, transportation, housing, drinking water, solid waste and coastal zone planning, and the requirement for environmental impact statements.

● Perhaps the most hopeful initiative beyond more effective state implementation of federal planning requirements and regulations that affect agricultural land would be state executive and legislative programs aimed at the control of urban growth. Urban growth control strategies reduce the demand for agricultural land. To the extent that a state plan or state legislation requires local and regional plans to manage urban growth, the pressure on agricultural land will become an explicit factor in local and state policy. Conceptually, however, such plans will be aimed at maintaining urban values as much as preserving agribusiness or farmland.

● Of the three branches of government at the state level, the executive branch offers the most immediate opportunities for preserving agricultural land. The courts have generally supported state legislation on land use, but the legal uncertainty in many states and the reluctance of state legislatures to enter the fray mean that executive control over public investment, combined with influence over the various state agencies whose programs affect agricultural land, offer the best prospect for immediate action. Ultimately, of course, state legislatures and the courts will have to address the property rights issue.

● Agricultural land issues raise directly and dramatically the perennial conflicts over the respective balance between public and private rights in land, the appropriate reach of the regulatory power, and the constraints of the "takings clause." The need to resolve these issues and to reach an agreement on what is politically acceptable and fair may lead to significant changes in public attitudes toward property and development rights as well as to experimentation with transferrable development rights, compensable regulations, negotiated damages rather than "just compensation," and perhaps more remotely, some linking of federal agricultural subsidy programs and state land use restrictions.

States' Role in Land Use Planning

In examining these propositions, it must be remembered that one treads on thin ice in making any generalization about the states. Although constitutionally equal, the states are distinct political, social, and economic entities. Differences in political party structure, degree of urbanization, type of agriculture, and relations with neighboring states all produce significant variations. In agricultural terms alone, wheat farming in Kansas can hardly be compared to dairying in Florida or to vegetable farming of California.

Growth Management. Assuming the CEQ report conclusions are accepted, the most important proposition is that states are both the keystone to agricultural land policy and a bellwether of trends in land use policy. Most informed observers accept the fact that the states are constitutionally and legally in a pre-eminent position on land use regulation. It is also generally acknowledged that these powers traditionally have not been employed directly by the states, but have been granted to local governments in the form of planning and zoning enabling acts. At the same time, in rural areas, where local planning and zoning of the type that has characterized urban land development have been absent, there has been little direct state involvement. In fact, the federal government's influence on rural land has probably been more important than either state or local regulation.

It is not surprising, therefore, to find that much of the innovative land use planning over the last decade has come from the exercise of powers conferred upon local governments by the states. Gradually, a strategy and congruence among these innovations has emerged. It is called growth management, and it may be described ideally as:

"...a process that attempts to influence the characteristics of growth—its rate, amount, type, location, and quality—in order to enhance the positive impacts and to limit the negative ones. Broadened impact growth management simply extends the scope of impacts considered beyond the traditional concerns for protection of private property, the neighbor, and the local resident, to include the rights of the regional resident and the potential resident. It weighs distributive outcomes, civil rights, and environmental quality in an attempt to balance fairly the impacts of the government's action among all affected parties. Finally, it explicitly describes the relationships between its objectives and techniques and the public health, safety, and welfare, so that it can hold up under strict scrutiny by the courts" (7).

Although growth control measures have been generated principally in suburban and exurban areas attempting to control urban growth, such local measures exercise an influence toward greater state and regional planning that will consider farmland retention in its fuller context.

One of the most troubling issues that has arisen in local growth management programs is exclusionary zoning. The term "exclusionary" could, of course, include zoning itself, but programs that have been especially criticized include large-lot zoning, minimum square footage requirements in buildings, and expensive planned-unit requirements. Generally speaking, any program that restricts the development of land or reduces the amount of land available for housing is potentially vulnerable to exclusionary charges, particularly in the face of higher housing costs and some evidence of population growth in a particular region.

Exclusionary charges could also include any program aimed at reducing the demand for agricultural land. There is a widely shared suspicion among planners, legislators, and the courts as well, that the agricultural land arguments may be covers for no-growth or exclusionary policies. Disagreement among farm and agricultural experts about the seriousness of cropland loss, or the lack of definitive information about the importance of any particular land in terms of the national total, gives some credence to this suspicion. In the absence of specific and compelling testimony, farmland retention can be seen as implausible or of insignificant value. There is no difficulty in getting expert testimony to support the view that the land's value in agriculture is lower than its value in an anticipated use, that there is a need for housing somewhere, and that "those Cassandras who keep running around waving their arms, wringing their hands, and crying that urban growth is taking over all our good farmland" (9) are talking nonsense.

Concerns about exclusionary effects, however, need not run counter to preservation objectives. In fact, a major effect of litigation against exclusionary zoning has been that state courts have begun to call for an evaluation of regional needs for housing (7). This, in turn, generates pressure for a regional or state planning program to bring about equal housing opportunity. These plans, when developed, consider where housing development is favored, but also where it is not favored. This requires explicit consideration of open space, rural character in the exurban perimeter, and agricultural needs, including the importance of agriculture to the diversity and health of the local economy.

The other side of exclusionary zoning is the competition among governments for high tax-producing but low service-demanding uses. These include regional shopping centers, industrial facilities, or other capital intensive uses of land. These uses often produce the greatest impacts of regional concern. These impacts may be explicitly environmental, air pollution, for example, or they may relate to the growth-inducing impacts of the development, which can increase land speculation and induce a feeling of uncertainty about the future among nearby farmers.

Concern about these growth impacts at the regional level impels a logical response identical to that related to the exclusionary issue: a greater concern for planning the region's growth. A regional perspective normally provides the impetus for state planning, or at least state legislation that explicitly calls for regional planning under state guidelines.

The state role necessarily grows when local or regional conflict exists. No other entity has the appropriate power to authorize the conditions of local accommodation or to impose a solution. This is not to suggest that state land use planning will be achieved easily. Local governments still guard their powers jealously; landowners remain skeptical of power exercised far from home; and federal state, and local agencies will be suspicious of any power that might subordinate their goals to a more general growth plan.

The celebrated "quiet revolution in land use control" is really only a colorful phrase to describe the emerging state role in land use planning. In one sense, this phrase dramatizes the expectations about the distribution of power between the states and their local governments: It is "revolutionary" that the states would begin to assert a more positive direction.

Table 2 shows some of the forms this state involvement has taken. Compare the frequency of differential assessment programs with other forms of state intervention in land use issues.

It appears likely, then, that the inadequacy of local planning and zoning, whether found in the form of competition for tax base or in efforts to shift the need for low- and moderate-income housing to another jurisdiction, will only intensify the revolution in land use control.

In addition, it should be remembered that the attitude of state courts toward state land use regulation has been almost uniformly positive. As one student of state court reaction to land use regulation concluded, the courts "have uniformly upheld state land use programs as legitimate attempts to control environmental and growth-related problems" (10). Although the litigation reviewed did not specifically address farmland retention measures, it is indicative of a broader situation. State courts are less likely to see "exclusion" or "takings" or "due process" issues when they evaluate state actions rather than actions by local governments. The degree of judicial deference apparently grows because the courts are interpreting the actions of a coordinate and equal branch of government. One might also surmise that they have greater respect for state professionalism and legislative processes than they do for local government actions.

States are aware of the costs and problems that accrue because of their failure to have a state land use policy. A Council of State Governments (COSGO) task force investigated the state of land use planning in 1975 and reported serious problems. Among the costs noted was the "conversion of productive agricultural land and forests to other uses" (5). This same report concluded that the extensive "failure of existing land use planning and regulatory measures" could be traced to "the shortcomings of a concept of land ownership and the public interest in the private use of land which is not consistent with current realities."

In one sense, the nation's most prominent land use issue is the appropriate distribution of land use power among the levels of government. The COSGO report suggested redefining the powers, noting that this redefinition need not involve a radical departure from either past practice or current concepts. Land use planning and regulation of development to some extent have always been an intergovernmental activity. While virtually all preparation and administration of land use plans has been by local governments, authorization to exercise these powers has always

Table 2. State land use programs (6).

State	Comprehensive Permit System*	Coordinated Incremental†	Mandatory Local Planning‡	Coastal Zone Management§	Wetlands Management
Alabama				X	
Alaska		X		X	
Arizona		X			
Arkansas					
California		X		X	
Colorado					
Connecticut		X		X	X
Delaware		X		X	X
Florida	X	X	X	X	X
Georgia		X		X	X
Hawaii	X	X		X	
Idaho			X		
Illinois				X	
Indiana		X		X	
Iowa					
Kansas					
Kentucky					
Louisiana				X	X
Maine	X	X	X (LTD)	X	X
Maryland		X		X	X
Massachusetts				X	X
Michigan				X	
Minnesota		X		X	X
Mississippi				X	X
Missouri					X
Montana		X	X		
Nebraska			X		
Nevada		X	X		
New Hampshire				X	X
New Jersey				X	X
New Mexico		X			
New York	X	X		X	X
North Carolina		X		X	X
North Dakota					
Ohio				X	
Oklahoma					
Oregon		X	X	X	
Pennsylvania				X	X
Rhode Island		X		X	X
South Carolina				X	
South Dakota					
Tennessee					
Texas				X	X
Utah		X			
Vermont	X	X			X
Virginia			X	X	X
Washington		X		X	X
West Virginia					
Wisconsin		X		X	X
Wyoming		X	X		

Source: Prepared by the Council of State Governments, based on information collected by the Council of State Governmen Land Use Planning Reports 1974 and 1975 and the U.S. Department of the Interior Office of Land Use and Water Plannin and the Resource Land Investigations Program Data compiled October 1975.

*State has authority to require permits for certain types of development.
†State established mechanism to coordinate state land use-related problems.
‡State requires local governments to establish a mechanism for land use planning (e.g., zoning comprehensive plan plannin commission).
§State is participating in the federally funded coastal zone management program authorized by the Coastal Zone Manageme Act of 1972.
||State has authority to plan or review local plans or the ability to control land use in the wetlands.
#State has authority to determine the siting of power plants and related facilities.

Power Plant Siting#	Surface Mining**	Designation of Critical Areas††	Differential Assessment Laws‡‡	Floodplain Management§§	Statewide Shorelands Act|| ||
X	A			X	
X			B		
X			A	X	
X	A, B		A	X	
X	X		C	X	
X	X	X	A	X	
X			B	X	
			A		X
X	A	X	A, C		
	A, B				
X	X	X	B	X	
	X		A		
X	A, B		B	X	
	A, B		A	X	
	A, B		A	X	
	A, B				
X	A, B		B		
X	A	X	B	X	
X	A, B	X	B	X	
X			B		
	X		C	X	X
X	X	X	B	X	X
				X	
X	X		A	X	
X	A, B	X	B	X	X
X			B	X	
X		X	B		
X			B, C		
X			B	X	
X	A		A		
X	X	X	B	X	
	X		B	X	
X	A		A		
X	A		B		
	X		A	X	
X	A	X	B		
X	A	X	B		
X			B		
X	A		B		
	A	X	A		
X	A, B		B		
	X		B		
	A		B		
X	X		C	X	
	A, B		B		
X	A		B	X	X
	A, B			X	
X	X	X		X	
X	A		A		

*State has statutory authority to regulate surface mines. (A) State has adopted rules and regulations, (B) State has issued technical guidelines.

†State has established rules or is in the process of establishing rules, regulations, and guidelines for the identification and designation of areas of critical state concern (e.g., environmentally fragile areas, areas of historical significance.

‡State has adopted tax measure which is designed to give property tax relief to owners of agricultural or open space lands. (A) Preferential Assessment Program—Assessment of eligible land is based upon a selected formula, which is usually use-value. (B) Deferred Taxation—Assessments of eligible land is based upon a selected formula, which is usually use-value and provides for a sanction, usually the payment of back taxes, if the land is converted to a noneligible use. (C) Restrictive Agreements—Eligible land is assessed at its use-value, a requirement that the owner sign a contract, and a sanction, usually the payment of back taxes if the owner violates the terms of the agreement.

§State has legislation authorizing the regulation of floodplains.

\|\|State has legislation authorizing the regulation of shorelands of significant bodies of water.

been required. Finally, the report indicated that efforts to redefine the roles of various governments "stemmed not so much from a failure of local government as they did from the increasing complexity of an urbanizing society and its broadening and increasingly destructive impacts on land use."

Another study of the condition of state planning, however, indicates the tremendous political sensitivity of state land use planning proposals (*14*). Too often, the study concluded, "state planning" is equated with "state land use planning," and that association is enough to kill relatively noncontroversial reorganizations of state activity. This reaction is the result of people's association of "land use planning" with potential encroachment upon property rights.

Nevertheless, a state can employ a number of strategies or approaches that would allay the fear of those who are concerned about local powers or private property rights. The appropriate approach must depend upon state political realities as well as the nature of the land use problem. Consider some of these possibilities:

First, a state can, by using its taxing and spending powers, encourage local action to preserve farmland by offering payments or tax subventions that reduce the local impact of differential assessment. Michigan and Wisconsin already provide for a sort of "circuit-breaker" system, where property taxes above a certain proportion of income can be used as a credit against state income taxes. California authorizes payment to local governments of a percentage of taxes lost through use of differential assessment. Obviously, a state can provide data and standards for preservation of agricultural land and it can require planning as a condition of state tax support.

Second, a state could adopt statewide standards for agricultural land retention and require that local government plans be consistent with that state plan. Oregon provides an example of this type of effort. In effect, Oregon requires each local government to draw up a plan that confines urban service districts to specified boundaries. The plan must also include exclusive farm use zones. If the local plan does not conform, it can be invalidated.

Third, a state could plan for and regulate farmland directly under its general powers. California attempted to do just this in the proposal to create a State Agricultural Resources Council, which would have identified and mapped prime agricultural land and restricted the subdivision of that land to situations where the state determined that urban needs demanded it (*3*).

Decentralized Coordination of Planning. One obvious way to make palatable the extension of state influence is to combine greater regulatory control with an opportunity for local participation in the planning process and to provide financial support for any mandated program that would affect local revenues or expenditures.

Beyond this, the states' role will be advanced as a result of increasing federal standards in air and water quality management and in federal requirements for planning in other functional programs. States also are seen as an alternative to increased federal intervention. Proposed federal action represents a powerful stimulus to state and local interests who fear a shift in power to the "feds." The intense controversy over the various federal land use bills has persuaded many federal officials concerned with land use that direct involvement by the federal government in land use planning is too controversial to pass the Congress. Many Executive Branch officials, aware of the political sensitivity of direct federal involvement, favor a stronger state role, but with federal support. These officials are inclined to accept the view that coordination of federal functional programs can best be achieved at the state and regional levels rather than in Washington.

The argument for decentralized coordination is augmented by the fact that state governors would be the beneficiaries of state reorganization to streamline administrative processes. There already are some 137 federal programs that have a direct impact on land use (*1*). Among these are the U.S. Department of Housing and Urban Development's comprehensive planning program, the Coastal Zone Management Act, the Clean Air Act, the Federal Water Pollution Control Act, and the Rural Development Act. These programs beg for some form of effective integration. The governor's office and executive branch of state government are perhaps the most likely places for this to take place. In fact, those national land use bills proposed previously attempted to provide for direct federal grants that would have encouraged the states to develop plans for programs they were already operating but which lacked a coherent policy framework.

State and federal governments require no new legislation to capitalize on the opportunities for coordination of existing programs, only more effective exercise of powers that already exist. The states, through their ability to comment on federal programs, to develop plans for the implementation of other federal programs, and their undoubted impact upon the pattern of growth throughout the state as a function of state expenditures for highways, utilities, etc., possess great opportunities to reduce pressures on agricultural land and to establish more desirable urban growth patterns as well.

Coordination is the process by which those not directly responsible for making a decision have an opportunity to influence the decision. The need to coordinate, therefore, offers an opportunity for competing values, including agricultural and environmental values, to meet and struggle for priority. Agricultural land has not received the policy visibility, nor has it achieved the organizational representation at the state level which would make it a more significant factor in the consideration of programs which affect it. This is partly a result of the low profile U.S. Department of Agriculture (USDA) officials have taken in these matters. It is also a result of differences among farming interests at the state level. In examples throughout the country, we have already seen how a policy confined to "incentives" is feasible, but more intensive regulatory approaches which might affect the development value of farmland create significant opposition.

An Environmental Perspective. While increasing awareness and sophistication about the growth-shaping effects of public investments has been beneficial, agricultural land retention is only slowly establishing itself as a major environmental problem. Steps to organize capital improvements and the timing and location of public facilities in an effort to control development have been taken primarily at the local level. State policy and plans remain a rarity. If intergovernmental cooperation and coordinated state planning are largely matters of estabishing a balance among competing, conflicting, and overlapping but legitimate objectives, agricultural land retention needs a firmer base of support from both the food supply and environmental points of view.

Farmland does not enjoy the same environmentally critical status afforded to steep slopes, floodplains, wetlands, marshes, shorelands or other land where the supply is obviously limited and the environmental consequences are more direct and better understood. Understandably, people find it difficult to believe there is a shortage of land for food production when our recent history portrays the agriculture problem as one of surpluses and expensive governmental subsidies to reduce production. Amid this confusion, agricultural land retention needs a more visible, effective spokesman.

It is significant that the Environmental Protection Agency (EPA) has begun to consider draft regulations on its own programs that affect farmland. Rather than confine itself to the USDA classification of "prime farmlands," EPA has adopted the broader designation of "environmentally significant farmlands." In its draft regulations, the agency notes that many of its programs affect farmland and that it has no policy respecting the impact of its programs on farmland. Emphasis in the EPA policy, while acknowledging the primacy of food production on agricultural land, is on the broader environmental values of farmland as a buffer, an assimilator of wastes, and a protector of more sensitive resources, such as water supplies and marshlands. The policy also discusses secondary impacts of agricultural land conversion on ecological systems and demands for public investment if conversion perpetuates sprawl development.

In effect, EPA's draft regulations broaden the farmland issue beyond food production and, like USDA's categories of farmland of "statewide" or "local significance" provide a scope and validity to the farmland issue that goes beyond merely productive soil quality on the one hand or the aesthetic and psychic benefits it provides as "open space" for Sunday drives on the other hand. Successfully combining these values with concerns about food production and agriculture as an industry considerably enhances the base of ecological support for farmland as a "critical area."

Also, unlike USDA, which keeps a rather low profile on land use issues in spite of its state and local offices, EPA programs for water supply, solid waste management, drinking water safety, water quality protection, and air quality planning put the agency in a highly visible and often controversial role in affecting state and local growth plans.

Accompanying a greater effort on the part of federal agencies to determine the environmental impacts of their own programs in farmland, states must assume a greater role in performing their own evaluation of federal programs. The so-called A-95 project review and notification system, named after the circular that authorized the process, already has been identified as the "single most pervasive coordinating technique" and the only one used by all 50 states (14). However, the same study that established this fact also noted that effective use of the power to comment on federal progams and their impacts on state policies varies from state to state.

The A-95 process encourages state and local governments to review and comment upon the impacts of federal grants or programs being considered within the state. It permits a coordinated state or regional effort that assesses federal programs in terms of state or local plans. The key issue at the state level, therefore, is leadership by the governor in coordinating state plans. The potential for agricultural land retention through coordination of programs and vigorous leadership from the governor's office is perhaps the best short- to medium-range strategy for farmland policy. For the most part, federal programs can be subordinated to state policies, *if there are state policies.*

The land use plan is probably the closest thing to a comprehensive plan that can be achieved practically at the state level. One recent evaluation (15) concluded:

"...land use planning at the state level is encompassing social and economic concerns as well as physical, and is addressing elements as diverse as settlement patterns, transportation, housing, natural resource conservation, location of state facilities, recreation, and industrial development. The objective of land use planning appears to be changing from directly controlling growth to coordinating development consistent with environmental and land use concerns. State initiatives are directed to power plant siting, environmental regulations, capital improvements planning, floodplain regulations, and mandated guidelines for local land use planning and control."

The evaluation goes on to say that economic planning, a traditional state role, is being modified by new legislation into a form of growth policy or growth management planning.

Examples of State Planning Initiatives. Farmland objectives will normally arise as part of a coordinated effort to manage growth. In Massachusetts, for example, former Governor Dukakis articulated a state growth plan that provided a basis for review of federal, state, and local programs. It also provided a set of objectives that would guide state programs (*15*).

Perhaps the most widely known use of the growth policy under Dukakis's leadership was his use of executive powers to discourage development of a regional shopping center in a rural area. He maintained that the shopping center would drain off desirable investment from a neighboring town and also take good farmland, even as it induced further undesirable growth and real estate speculation. This, Dukakis held, conflicted with the state growth plan he had articulated, and he threatened to deny access from state highways to the shopping center if it were approved.

Perhaps the most comprehensive articulation of a state growth plan is that of California's Governor Jerry Brown (*2*). This plan has a clear "compact growth" orientation. Its influence on rural and agricultural land can be seen by evaluating its demand-reducing features. The Brown program is a product of a U.S. Department of Housing and Urban Development comprehensive planning grant and a state legislative requirement to articulate "state policies, recommend state, local and private actions and steps to carry out these policies and to coordinate state functional plans." It has three major urban development priorities. The first is to renew and maintain existing urban areas, both cities and suburbs. The second is to develop vacant and under-utilized land within existing urban and suburban areas and areas presently served by streets, water, sewer, and other public services. Open space, historic buildings, recreational opportunities, and the distinct identities of neighborhoods should also be preserved.

The third priority involves the use of immediately adjacent land when urban development is necessary outside existing urban and suburban boundaries. Noncontiguous development would be appropriate when needed to accommodate planned open space, greenbelts, agricultural preservation, or new town community development.

A variety of programs are directed to achieving these priorities. Incentives and initiatives that encourage revitalization of existing areas and encourage the provision of services and benefits to built-up areas are accompanied by, or consistent with, discouraging development in areas used for agriculture or open space. Where substantial noncontiguous development would be permitted, it would be balanced against open space and agricultural land objectives.

Among the particular programs worth noting are the following:

● The state would give preference in the allocation of funding for water supply sources and safe drinking water supply to the already built-up areas.

● Public transit would be encouraged to provide a more attractive basis for in-filling and redevelopment in urban areas.

● Special tax investment credits would be given to those locating within the built-up areas.

● Legislation is proposed that would place a tax on land that has been held only a short time in order to discourage speculation in land. Although the professed reason for this legislation is to reduce the inflationary impact of speculation, it directly reduces the incentive to purchase agricultural land for short-term gain.

● Local governments would be required to adopt urban service district boundaries and capital improvements programs. These boundaries and public expenditure plans would be consistent with the comprehensive plans of local governments and would also meet regional needs. This would serve as a basis for staging, locating, and servicing what new urban development would occur.

The Brown program depends upon state legislative action as well as use of the governor's administrative power. However, this planning document is probably the best single illustration of the artificial distinction made between urban policy and rural policy. Although still useful for some purposes, this distinction must not obscure the essential continuity between reducing urban sprawl, public expenditures, the timing and staging of urban growth, and protecting rural land, agricultural production, and open space.

Incentives to urban investment and coordination of local and state investments are clearly disincentives to conversion of undeveloped land into urban uses. Incentives that work to induce investment in already built-up areas wherever possible necessarily reduce pressure on undeveloped land—in many instances, land which is currently in agricultural production. An urban policy that aims at compact growth and has strong executive leadership can be a decisive factor in reducing demand both in the sense of acreage and in discouraging speculative behavior. Obviously, an urban policy, by itself, is not a sufficient step for retaining agricultural land, but it is an emphatic prerequisite.

Overcoming Pessimism on Land Use Planning

Despite the growing interest in agricultural land retention throughout the country and the search for mechanisms to accomplish this objective, a sort of political impasse, however temporary, has been reached. Notwithstanding national publicity about the purchase of development rights in Suffolk County, New York, authorizations for transferrable development rights in Bucks County, Pennsylvania, and voluntary and mandatory agricultural zoning, there exists little hope in any of these efforts, on the basis of their records, for encouraging a national direction.

There are five reasons for this pessimism. First, differential assessment remains the great hope, though, by itself it cannot keep land in agriculture. When coupled with more stringent land use restrictions, differential assessment tends to lose its appeal among those who stand to profit most from land conversions.

Second, any proposal to regulate agricultural land by public action, whether at the state or local level, confronts major political opposition from some segments of the agricultural community and from real estate and construction interests.

Third, efforts to purchase development rights or easements that would keep land permanently in agriculture fail on the cost issue. New Jersey's experience with the Green Acres Program is the most recent example of a program stymied by cost and related factors. It is unlikely that there will be the necessary political support for the taxes required to purchase development values. In fact, there may even be a movement in some parts of the country, including Virginia, to back off from differential assessment because this form of assessment shifts a portion of the tax burden to urban dwellers.

Fourth, land use innovations that seemingly offer the best possibility for compromising the regulatory and compensaton issues run into difficulties because of doubts about their legality or the complexity of implementation. Most promising is the use of transferrable development rights. However, despite considerable discussion of the concept and an increasing familiarity with the idea because of the adoption of clustering and planned unit development programs, it still is not operational in terms of agricultural land retention.

Fifth, constitutional and legal issues are considerable no matter what type of program is suggested to reduce the conflict between compensation and regulation. States often lack enabling legislation that would allow experimentation at the local level. By the same token, states do not often have legislation that permits direct action.

Additional problems arise because of judicial decisions in some states about the appropriate reach of the regulatory power, requirements for compensation if the government takes an interest in land, and so forth. However, constitutional limitations are much less formidable than the calculated political exaggeration of individual "property rights" made by opponents of agricultural zoning. The United States constitution, state constitutions, and judicial interpretations are much more supportive of regulation that would keep land in agriculture than is commonly believed.

The current policy impasse is largely the result of the conflict between traditional notions of private property rights and the steps required to create a successful land retention program. Some reconciliation of the compensation versus regulation issue is essential to further progress.

As one observer of our land use system from the United Kingdom noted, there are two major hurdles that must be overcome before the United States can create an acceptable, realistic, and effective land use planning system (12). First, there must be "much greater regional, state and federal involvement in the determination of land use policy and in securing its implementation, together with the public acceptance of the need to do so." Second, "a solution must be found for dealing with the financial windfalls and wipeouts which are respectively bestowed or inflicted on landowners as a result of land use regulation."

Aside from problems of accurate information and data, which are formidable in themselves and which call for new studies and information systems, it is the two issues above that are being cautiously addressed. At this moment, however, there appears to be no concept or program that has obtained sufficient professional, political, or popular support to meet the windfall-wipeout question.

The basic idea of—and also a major factor in its political appeal—is that it takes a conservative view of private property rights, allows for compensation of those whose land will not be extensively developed, and does it without calling for direct expenditures from the public treasury. The regulation versus compensation is finessed by a transfer of value through the sale of development rights from one group of owners to another. This is the most frequently suggested windfall-wipeout mitigation technique (8).

A recent study (8) dealing with the windfall-wipeout question concluded, somewhat pessimistically, one hopes, that whether "...any windfall for wipeout scheme will be adopted in America is problematical. The authors initially had hoped that logic would carry the day. Planners, environmentalists, do-gooders, socialists, and the like are relatively easily persuaded that windfall recapture is desirable, but not if wipeout mitigation also is provided. On the other hand, landowners, developers, private entrepreneurs, and the like all favor wipeout mitigation, but not if it is funded by windfall recapture.''

Although the search for mitigation measures is admittedly difficult, farmland retention is probably the most promising area for creating a workable windfall-wipeout scheme. Farmland has a current use that provides some reasonable return. Land has intrinsic value for agricultural use. The basis for protecting that value is not much different than the justifications for zoning in urban areas to avoid conflicting uses among different types and intensities of land use. More than that, many people actually sympathize for the "urgent" situation of bona fide farmers. These same people have less favorable attitudes toward developers, land speculators, and construction industry interests with regard to compensation for restrictive regulations.

Perhaps more than any other group in our society, farmers evoke a favorable response when they express concern about the impact of land regulation on the value of private property. There is widespread, if unsophisticated, support for the farmer because, many believe, farmers have not received the same benefits as have other sectors of the economy. If there is some concern about agribusiness, there is nevertheless a reservoir of support for farmers. It is understood that, in terms of return on capital invested, labor, and productivity, the farmer has lagged behind his industrial suppliers and competitors. It is understood that the value of the farmer's land is the capital value that would compensate for a relative lack of cash income during many years of work and production.

There is also an appreciation for the costs and individual injustices that develop when land use rules are changed. Those who have made their money are allowed to keep it; those who planned on making money have their hopes dashed. From the perspective of those concerned with windfalls and wipeouts, the issue could thus be stated: Is there a way to retain the most suitable land in agriculture without extraordinary public expense that is fair to all and generally acceptable to farmers?

The search for such a solution will be difficult. It cannot be achieved without new ideas and political creativity. If a way is found, it must somehow disengage farmers from other groups that capitalize on the more popular appeal of farmers to realize their own less politically appealing and less legally defensible pursuit of capital gains and quick profits.

Clearly, we have only begun to think about the issue. A flurry of ideas and concepts will likely emerge in coming years. Meanwhile, effective use of state powers to combine urban policies, to coordinate state expenditures effectively, and to apply federal programs creatively to reduce the impacts on the demand side of the conversion equation are the best immediate hope to slow down land conversions until a fuller resolution is possible.

REFERENCES

1. Advisory Commission on Intergovernmental Relations. 1977. *Regionalism revisited: Recent areawide and local responses.* Washington, D.C.
2. California Office of Planning and Research. 1978. *An urban strategy for California.* Sacramento.
3. Collins, Richard. 1976. *Agricultural land preservation in a land use planning perspective.* Journal of Soil and Water Conservation 31(5): 182-189.
4. Council on Environmental Quality. 1976. *Untaxing open space.* Washington, D.C.
5. Council of State Governments. 1975. *Land: State alternatives for planning and management.* Lexington, Kentucky.
6. Council of State Governments. 1976. *State growth management.* Lexington, Kentucky.
7. Godschalk, David, et al. 1978. *Responsible growth management: Cases and materials.* Center for Urban and Regional Studies, University of North Carolina, Chapel Hill.
8. Hagman, Donald, and Dean Misczynski. 1978. *Windfalls for wipeouts: Land value capture and compensation.* American Society of Planning Officials, Chicago, Illinois.
9. Hart, John Fraser. 1977. *Comments on the conversion of agricultural land to urban uses.* International Regional Science Review: 157.
10. Hess, David E. 1977. *Institutionalizing the revolution: Judicial reaction to state land use laws.* The Urban Lawyer 9: 183.
11. Holden, Constance. 1975. *Is America due for a national food policy?* In Lerga and Johnson [eds.] *Food for People Not for Profit.* Ballantine Books,
12. Moore, Victor. 1977. *Land for the public good.* The Center Magazine (December): 26.
13. U.S. Department of Agriculture. 1975. *Perspectives on prime lands.* Washington, D.C.
14. U.S. Department of Housing and Urban Development. 1976. *State planning: Intergovernmental policy coordination.* Washington, D.C.
15. U.S. Department of Housing and Urban Development. 1977. *Coordinating state functional planning programs: Strategies for balancing conflicting objectives.* Washington, D.C.

15

Local Programs to Save Farms and Farmlands

William Toner

If one is alarmed at the paucity of state and federal programs to save farms and farmlands, there is reassurance and hope in the actions of dozens of communities across the country. While state legislatures and the Congress ponder various schemes, many cities, counties, and townships have quietly developed their own solutions. The result is an abundance of unique local efforts to save farms and farmlands.

It is difficult to categorize local programs. There are no national or state models that have been widely copied. Communities have worked mainly with existing enabling legislation and with other existing support programs. But what is different is that communities have shaped these traditional tools to their own ends, altering conventional approaches; putting the tools in new, untested combinations; and emerging with imaginative new arrangements of police and fiscal powers that work.

To understand what these communities have done, it is essential to understand why they have done it. To understand why they have done it, it is essential to understand the values these communities are trying to protect.

The Values Involved

Perhaps the most important feature of the agricultural community is that it is a community, much the same as exists in small towns or neighborhoods. As an agricultural community, it supports a host of social, economic, cultural, and environmental networks (4). These networks provide the values that communities try to protect in their effort to save farms and farmlands.

189

Consider, for example, the economic network. At its center are the farms and farmers. But the network also includes feed suppliers, machinery suppliers, mechanics, agricultural workers, farm organizations, and cooperatives as well as the businesses in the rural service centers that provide general support for agricultural activity. This mix of economic institutions makes up the agricultural economic base of a community. In saving farms and farmlands, therefore, many communities are saving their economic base.

Similar values can be seen in examining local environmental resources. For example, farmlands provide habitat for flora and fauna. They also protect, sometimes consciously and sometimes not, wooded areas, steep slopes, recharge areas, wetlands, and small watercourses. Of course, not all these resources are protected by agriculture. Some are deliberately destroyed. But overall, the agricultural community preserves environmental values that would otherwise be lost.

Other values are visible in the preservation of historical and archeological artifacts, the maintenance of a healthy local public treasury, the provision of a vast land resource to meet future food or energy needs, open space or flood control values, and on and on (8, 9).

Each of these networks, which collectively comprise the agricultural community, provides a series of values. Taken together, these are the values that a community attempts to protect in saving farms and farmland.

Threats to Agricultural Values

The prevailing pattern of urban development threatens virtually all the critical agricultural values—social, economic, cultural, and environmental. Yet it is the individual farmer that is affected in the most direct and immediate ways.

Consider the farmer who farms next to a major new subdivision. To begin, property taxes on the farm take a sharp jump as the land is assessed at its highest and best suburban use. The tax increase, in turn, is used to pay for the cost of servicing the subdivision, the farmers's new neighbor.

On the farmland, there is a new laced pattern of snowmobile ruts, the legacy of the previous winter and subdivision sport. More recently, four-wheel-drive vehicles have cut a jagged swath of their own over some of the steep slopes and through a cash crop, damaging the land, increasing runoff, and taking income from the farmer's pocket.

At the same time, the farmer discovers suburban dogs chasing fowl and animals, city children harassing the cattle or breaking fences, or adult neighbors who steal or ruin produce. Suddenly, too, country roads are no longer safe for big farm machinery at 20 miles per hour because suburban traffic whips along at 55 miles per hour.

If the damage, harassment, and hazards were not enough, the farmer is also faced with nuisance action from the new neighbors. Odors from hog pens and feedlots eventually drift into the subdivision. So do pesticide residues, which, in some cases, pose direct health hazards to residents. Similarly, suburbanites resent farm production schedules that may call for noisy late night or early morning operations, operations that are essential to the agricultural industry.

Taken together, the nuisance and health threats cause the suburbanites to act. Suits may be filed, or local governments may be asked to impose various constraints on farm operations. The net result for the farmer is an increase in the cost of operation, if there can be any operation at all.

Given the pressures exerted on individual farmers, the agricultural community slowly begins to unwind. Some farmers sell, getting out of the business or moving to new, distant farms. As more farmers leave, social, economic, cultural, and environmental networks begin to unravel. Farm businesses close, suppliers leave, distributors cut operations, farm workers disappear, and the agricultural community loses its dominant political influence. The values that were once central to the agricultural community are no longer to be found.

The rise of local programs to maintain farms and farmland is a direct result of this traditional development process. At one time, the agricultural and urban communities both acted under the assumption that it was not only natural but inevitable for the agricultural-to-urban transition to take place. And both communities acted accordingly.

But in the last 10 years, this attitude was first challenged and then changed. Agricultural land uses are now, in some places, being considered permanent land uses, as valued and as important as urban land uses. Communities are preparing plans and adopting regulations and taxing and spending tax dollars with the express purpose of saving their farms and farmland.

Common Characteristics of Local Actions

Although most local programs to save farms and farmland are unique, they share a common set of characteristics. A review of the most effective local programs shows eight common features.

The first characteristic is that the programs are simple and neat. They rely upon the most traditional regulatory devices—zoning and capital improvements planning—applied in the conventional fashion. Typically, however, the force of the regulatory device is directed toward the maintenance of farms and farmland, not as a transitional use, but as a permanent use.

A second feature is that local programs combine traditional tools and techniques to maintain farms and farmland. Previously, local programs relied upon one tool or one approach. Currently, communities are applying all the tools at their command—general plans, zoning, capital improvements, annexation agreements—and they are putting the tools together in unique combinations.

Third, local programs are flexible to meet the needs of the individual farmer. For example, most farmers want to be able to add at least one housing unit to the farm for sons, daughters, or relatives who work in the operation. Generally, most programs are designed to meet this need. Similarly, most programs recognize that each farm exhibits varying degrees of agricultural productivity. Some of the land is excellent, some of it just isn't suited to production. As a result, local programs often incorporate performance standards governing the land, standards that enable unproductive acreage to be put to a more intensive use, perhaps as a small residential development.

Fourth, local programs are tailored to local conditions. Obviously, agriculture is a vast industry, composed of many parts and built upon a widely varying resource base. Because of this, communities build their preservation programs around local needs, local resources, and local values. Local programs are thus unique, not machine copies of one another.

Fifth, the most effective local programs are designed by the people most affected by them—the farmers. These programs are built from the ground up, with the agricultural community setting goals and objectives, identifying issues, establishing alternatives, selecting a program, then carrying it out. These grassroots efforts have produced the most interesting, innovative, and effective local programs.

Sixth, local programs are characterized by trial and error. In many cases, communities have been attempting to maintain farms and farmland for years, but they have seen their attempts fail for a variety of reasons. With each failure, the programs are re-designed and applied, until something finally works. The communities have not been afraid to experiment to identify the minimum regulatory framework necessary to do the job.

Seventh, communities often rely heavily upon regional and state agencies for basic information, interpretative reports, and the identification of alternative management arrangements. Regional agencies often supply critical information in the way of aerial photographs, data summaries on agricultural and other lands, land use projections, and the like. Similarly, local soil conservation districts as well as Soil Conservation Service (SCS) offices provide key resource people and information on the location, quality, and condition of soils and water management. This information is critical for local decision-makers.

Finally, local programs are also careful to identify land needed for future urban and suburban development. Communities recognize that the other half of farmland preservation is urban development. And in their analysis, communities almost always discover that there are more than sufficient lands within and adjacent to established communities to accommodate foreseeable development. The community plan for the maintenance of farms and farmland is nearly always joined by an equal commitment to the maintenance of appropriate land for future urban use.

Of course, not all local programs share all eight characteristics. But most programs share a majority of them, and it is essential to keep them in mind when designing programs.

Classes of Local Programs

The most effective local programs can be separated into three major classes that are distinguished by their zoning approach: (1) large-lot, (2) quarter/quarter, and (3) sliding-scale. Obviously, the programs are distinguished by more than the zoning technique, but the zoning technique permits a convenient distinction (*9*).

Large-Lot Zoning. This is the largest category of effective local approaches. But the current application is quite unlike the historical application that generally included large-lot requirements in agricultural areas and limitations on nonagricultural uses.

In the past, large-lot exclusive agricultural zones suffered two major flaws. First, the minimum lot size was generally too small to support a working farm, but it was not large enough to deter rural subdivisions. Lot size thus offered little protection for farmers while attracting rural subdividers. As a result, the agricultural area was easy prey to nonagricultural uses.

Second, although the term "exclusive agricultural zone" was tossed about, most planning commissions did not see fit to interpret it quite so literally. As a result, zoning changes were given as a matter of course, regardless of the effect of the change on agricultural uses. Thus, the exclusive agricultural zone was neither exclusive nor necessarily agricultural.

In the newer preservation programs based upon large-lot size, these flaws are overcome. First, communities are taking a performance approach to the identification of an effective minimum lot size. The definition of the minimum lot size is anchored in the minimum size necessary to establish a working farm. Lot-size minimums are tied to the local economics of farming, reflecting local soil resources, historical farming practices, and local crop or animal production averages.

Because of this new approach, there is no uniformly accepted minimum lot size. Instead, it varies from place to place.

● In San Luis Obispo County, California, the minimum lot size in the agricultural area is 360 acres. This reflects the arid climate and historical ranching practice.

● In Weld County, Colorado, the agricultural area features two minimum lot sizes, 80 acres in irrigated areas and 160 acres in nonirrigated areas. Obviously, irrigated areas are much more productive per acre than nonirrigated areas.

● In Kendall County, Illinois, the agricultural area requires a 60-acre minimum, up from 20 acres in 1977.

The historic difficulty of granting zoning changes in the exclusive agricultural zone has also been overcome. The principal change in the newer programs has been with the decision-makers themselves. But this change in attitudes has also been supplemented by two changes in the zoning approach.

On the attitudinal side, decision-makers are treating agricultural land as a permanent, not a transitional, land use. As a consequence, it is much more difficult to get a zoning change in agricultural areas, particularly those areas that are not adjacent to urban areas.

The zoning ordinance reflects this attitudinal change. Most ordinances in these programs now set forth specific criteria that must be met in order to get a zoning change from an agricultural to a nonagricultural use. The criteria generally are based upon factors that would make a specific parcel unsuited for agricultural use and suited for nonagricultural use. Moreover, even if a zoning change is granted, the resulting development is a low-density use, which is generally compatible with surrounding agricultural uses.

The zoning change criteria include both planning factors and agricultural considerations. For example, ordinances often specify that distance to urban areas be considered along with service availability and the types of adjacent land uses. On the agricultural side, decision-makers examine the quality of soils, shape of the parcel, access to the parcel, current use, historical use, and surrounding land use. By examining this list of criteria against the parcel, decision-makers are able to grant or deny zoning changes on the basis of strict planning and agricultural factors. As a result, zoning changes that are granted are consistent, reasonable, and supportive of the broader agricultural and urban policies.

The application of these criteria for zoning changes also moves the ordinance in a performance direction. Proponents of change must demonstrate that their parcels do not perform well as an agricultural use or perform better as a nonagricultural use. In so doing, these ordinances get much closer to the purpose of agricultural and nonagricultural zones than was the case previously.

Two counties in Illinois, DeKalb and Boone, have taken this performance approach a step further. Ronald Darden, planning director of De-Kalb County, developed a performance definition of a farm. By using this performance definition, the counties have been able to de-emphasize minimum lot sizes while insuring that only agricultural uses are permitted in the agricultural areas. This, of course, solves the problem of the hobby farm.

The performance definition works as follows. First, a farm is defined as any agricultural operation that produces a minimum of $10,000 (1976 dollars) in agricultural production. Thus, if a person wants to build a residential unit in the agricultural zone, the individual must demonstrate that the associated farm will generate at least $10,000 worth of agricultural production.

In order to make the production estimate, DeKalb and Boone Counties rely upon the production averages in an agricultural statistical bulletin for a variety of cash crops and animal units. The proposal is evaluated against the production averages to determine projected production income. If the income is $10,000 or more, the permit is granted. If it is less, the permit is not granted.

With this performance definition, DeKalb and Boone Counties insure that the agricultural district will be used for agricultural purposes. At the same time, the definition is flexible enough to account for advances in technology that might otherwise fall victim to a limiting minimum lot size or to an out-of-date list of permitted agricultural uses. Moreover, it brings the actual operation of the ordinance much closer to the real purpose of the regulation—to maintain farms and farmland.

To illustrate varied approaches, let's examine five local programs that share a large-lot approach.

● DeKalb County, Illinois. The county's program began in 1972 with a comprehensive plan that identified farmland preservation as one of its cornerstones. As in many communities, however, the county implemented the agricultural element through a 5-acre minimum lot size that soon fell victim to a host of rural subdivisions. After much experimentation, the county settled on a performance definition of a farm or a 40-acre minimum. The ordinance also set forth criteria to evaluate proposed zoning changes that insure that zoning changes are only granted to parcels that are best suited to nonagricultural uses.

Evidence indicates that the approach has worked. Between 1972 and 1975, for example, the county lost well over 600 acres of agricultural land to nonagricultural uses annually. By 1978, this figure had dropped to roughly 150 acres per year.

● Tulare County, California. Tulare County is a good example of a community that used nearly every resource at its disposal to prepare and maintain its farmland preservation program. From the state level, the county has made good use of the Williamson Act to lower the tax burden on farmers. Second, the county has taken advantage of California's unique Local Agency Formation Commission to insure that city annexation policies conform with and support the preservation plan. Third, all elements of the county's general plan are mutually supportive and, by law, are reflected in the county's zoning ordinance. The zoning ordinance must conform to the general plan. The plan thus shapes the ordinance. Fourth, the plan itself was partially prepared through the efforts of a Farm Council, which was principally responsible for the preservation element of the plan and for the character of the agricultural ordinance.

The ordinance includes minimum lot sizes ranging from 10 to 80 acres, depending upon soil qualities. It also includes a sophisticated but simple evaluation system for examining proposed zoning changes in the agricultural area. Finally, the county was able to shape capital improvements to reinforce the plan, both to maintain farms and farmland and to provide quality service for urbanizing areas. The result of this careful, grassroots planning effort is a preservation program that works.

● Walworth County, Wisconsin. Walworth County provides spectacular relief for the 9 million people in Chicago and Milwaukee who live only hours away. With 37 lakes, thousands of acres of prime farmland, and a pleasing kettle moraine landscape, the county is everything that Chicago and Milwaukee are not. It was not surprising, therefore, that Walworth citizens were dismayed to learn that during the 1960s over 70 percent of the new subdivisions were going on prime lands (7).

In response to the threats, the county embarked on a long and productive planning program that was centered around four main goals: (1) preservation of prime agricultural land, (2) preservation of environmental corridors, (3) concentration of urban development in established growth centers, and (4) maintenance of agriculture and recreation as strong components of the local economy. It took seven years, from 1967 until 1974, to develop and to adopt a comprehensive zoning ordinance that met the four key goals.

The ordinance features six major land use classifications and 26 separate zoning classifications. The key zoning classification for the preservation of prime farmland, A-1, is based on a minimum lot size of 35 acres. This zone includes about 50 percent of the County.

But the Walworth County story is not to be found in the highly sophisticated zoning ordinance as much as in the process and the people and institutions that led them to it. The Southeastern Wisconsin Regional Planning Commission is a good example. In 1967, this commission produced a regional plan that was in large part based upon environmental data.

Walworth County adopted this plan as its own, and, later, used much of the data in developing and applying its own land use regulations.

SCS produced a soil survey of the county that was incorporated into the land use regulations and other plans prepared for the county. The survey was an essential tool in identifying prime soils. Similarly, technical guides produced by SCS were also incorporated into the county's ordinance.

The Farm Council, a county-wide advisory group, played a central role in the definition of key issues, in the identification and development of regulatory standards, and in explaining and promoting the proposed county ordinance at a host of public hearings. This council, composed of members of the agricultural community, was the most important citizens group behind the program. The council worked with the program from the beginning.

Similar supportive roles were played by the University of Wisconsin Extension Service, the County Park and Planning Commission, the county's soil conservation district and the County Agricultural Committee. By seeking the support, participation, and hard work from all of these groups, the county was able to develop a program that met county needs and enjoyed (after 550 public meetings) wide public support.

The degree of public support was evidenced by the actions of the 17 townships within the county, which, if the program was to work, had to adopt the ordinance. Sixteen of the 17 townships adopted the ordinance, and the seventeenth adopted a similar ordinance. Nine years elapsed from the time the county embarked on its initial planning effort until the time when the last township ratified the resulting ordinance.

An important postscript to this case stems from Wisconsin's (1977) Farmland Preservation Act (3). This act provides planning and zoning incentives for farmland preservation at the local level while, at the same time, offering (income) tax relief to farmers who participate in local planning and zoning programs.

Initially farmers can receive income tax credits by signing contracts in which they agree not to develop their land. The amount of this tax credit depends upon the ratio between net household income and property tax. Basically, those farmers with the highest ratio of property tax to household income receive the greatest tax credit.

In the permanent phase of the program, which begins in 1982, the income tax credit depends upon action by the local government. For farmers to remain eligible for the minimum tax credit, urban counties must adopt exclusive agricultural zoning and rural counties must adopt an agricultural preservation plan or exclusive agricultural zoning. If counties adopt both an agricultural preservation plan and exclusive agricultural zoning, farmers become eligible for the maximum tax credit.

By June 30, 1979, the Wisconsin farmland preservation program had shown remarkable results (5). Nearly 2 million acres of farmland had been protected through zoning or through contracts with farmers. Forty-six counties were preparing agricultural preservation plans, while seven counties had exclusive agricultural zoning in effect and another 22 counties were preparing zoning ordinances to qualify for the plan.

According to state officials, the program's success thus far is due to the planning/zoning/tax credit approach, which has a unique appeal in both urban and rural areas. In urban areas the appeal is primarily that of farmland preservation, while in rural areas the appeal is based primarily on tax credit. With these goals tied to planning and fiscal methods, the result is a state program that seems to be working well at the local level. And one should not be surprised to note which county came through first with both a certified preservation plan and a certified preservation ordinance—Walworth County.

● Black Hawk County, Iowa. Taking a county with over 70 percent of its soils in Class I or II and coupling it with an urban population of 110,000 is certain to produce rural/urban conflicts. In Black Hawk County, this conflict resulted in leap-frog subdivision on prime agricultural soils.

The county's ordinance at that time allowed subdivisions in agricultural areas, provided the subdivisions met a 3-acre minimum lot size. Worse, along hard-surfaced roads, the minimum lot size was one-half acre, hardly a detriment to premature rural subdivisions.

To correct the problem, the county adopted a simple but effective ordinance. The ordinance set a 35-acre minimum in the agricultural area. To deal with the large blocks of Class I, II, and III soils, the county began working with a "corn suitability rating."

The corn suitability rating is merely an index of productivity for various soil types. But this index is much more specific than the broader system of land classification. With the rating, for example, it is possible to distinguish several types of soils in any of the classes in terms of productivity.

With the rating, the county was able to set a minimum level of productivity that would receive the most stringent regulatory attention. For example, in the agricultural area, all soils with a corn suitability rating of 85 or more might require a 35-acre minimum lot size. Depending upon its effectiveness, the level could easily be changed to include more or less land, and the county would be assured that the land so included would be the most productive.

The rating is also helpful in dealing with specific cases. For example, if a farmer wants to change the minimum lot size, it would be important to know the various corn suitability ratings for the soil types on the property. If the ratings are below the minimum, a change might be granted. But the important point is that the rating gives the county a sensible evaluation tool, one that can be applied and understood by the farmers themselves.

About 70 percent of Black Hawk County is now governed by the 35-acre minimum. As testimony to the success of the program, four nearby counties, Bremer, Buchanan, Butler, and Grundy, have adopted similar ordinances.

● Pitkin County, Colorado. Pitkin County, which includes the Aspen area, is known more for its skiing than for its agricultural production. And while the dominant economic force is recreation, the county enjoys a sizeable agricultural base. To protect its recreational, residential, and agricultural resources, Pitkin County has embarked on an ambitious growth management plan (2).

The plan is centered in a growth management quota system (adopted 1978) and an elaborate land use code (adopted 1976). The quota system is used to control the new residential development each year, and the land use code controls the location and character of this development.

The code is heavily performance oriented. Although it contains the usual districts—20-acre to 30-acre minimum lot sizes in agricultural areas—and specifications governing uses in the districts, it also sets forth a series of performance standards that must be met before building permits, zone changes, conditional uses, subdivisions, or planned unit developments are approved.

The general policies and detailed performance standards govern the entire county and all zoning districts within it. Therefore, all development, regardless of district, must conform with general policies and the detailed performance standards that are used to implement general policies. This is in addition to the usual zoning requirements.

The performance standards and general policies on which they are based cover a range of economic, energy, equity, environment, and public service factors that are affected by new development. Among these policies and performance standards are a series related to agriculture.

Four main general policies govern agriculture: (1) to insure that development surrounding agricultural land, or near such land, does not make continued agricultural operations impractical, (2) to encourage the exclusion of primarily agricultural areas from taxing districts that may be formed (for nonagricultural purposes), (3) to avoid development patterns that will require water to be taken out of agricultural uses, and (4) to protect agricultural operations from disruptions associated with neighboring nonagricultural development (1).

The detailed performance standards go on to require that "the development proposal would insure the preservation of at least ninety-five percent of the acreage of land available or potentially available for the production of food crops, and would not impair productivity..." (*1*). Similar performance standards are then set governing hay, grains, or feed production, as well as standards for irrigated and pasture land.

The Pitkin County approach is a rigorous one in terms of both the minimum lot size in agricultural zones and the detailed set of performance standards. When this is matched with the residential quota system, one would presume that the agricultural base is well protected. But since the entire program has only been in operation since 1978, it is difficult to make assumptions about its success or failure. However, the approach is considerably different from most other communities and merits careful scrutiny.

Quarter/Quarter Zoning. Quarter/quarter zoning is a new and intriguing device that has been adopted by a number of Minnesota counties—Dakota, Rice, Carver, Blue Earth, Scott—and townships. Under quarter/quarter zoning, each land owner is permitted one dwelling unit per quarter/quarter section of land. A farmer owning one-quarter section is thus permitted four units—a quarter/quarter section (40 acres) of one-quarter section (160 acres), with one dwelling unit per quarter/quarter section equals a total of four dwelling units.

The distinguishing feature of quarter/quarter zoning is that it permits farmers to sell small parcels while retaining the bulk of the land in farming. This is in contrast to zoning ordinances that, by virtue of 10-, 20-, 30-, or 40-acre minimum lots, force the farmer to sell large chunks of the farm to develop a single lot. Under quarter/quarter zoning, overall density is kept at the one unit per 40-acre level, while the actual lot sold is generally less than 2 acres.

Quarter/quarter zoning is also attractive to farmers who want to sell off small, unproductive farm acreages, but who do not want to turn their farms into giant subdivisions. Most communities encourage farmers who want to take advantage of quarter/quarter to sell those parcels that are among the least productive agricultural areas. Nevertheless, the parcels must demonstrate acceptable levels of performance as residential sites.

There are several interesting features to the quarter/quarter programs in Minnesota. For example, programs in Dakota and Carver Counties receive considerable support from the Twin Cities (St. Paul/Minneapolis) Metropolitan Council (*6*). The council has prepared and adopted a regional development policy and plan that is implemented through the council's authority over capital improvements, such as roads, parks, sewers, and airports. As constructed, the regional plan and implementation strategies work in direct support of local preservation plans. Similarly, the local plans work to reinforce the regional development policy.

There are also a series of adaptations to the basic ordinance. In Blue Earth County, for example, owners of contiguous parcels may transfer permitted lots from one parcel to the other. The ordinance also provides for bonus lots that may be granted for land that has not been used in the previous five years for agricultural purposes.

In Dakota County, Douglas Township has adopted quarter/quarter zoning, but the township has increased the permitted lots per quarter/quarter section. In one area of the township, two lots per quarter/quarter section are permitted. In another area, six lots per quarter/quarter section are permitted.

Communities using this new tool report good success and solid public support. Many local planners feel the technique is a particularly strong, adaptable, and effective one.

Sliding-Scale Zoning. Sliding-scale ordinances are another innovative effort to maintain farms and farmland. Under the sliding-scale approach, permitted density in the agricultural area varies inversely with the size of parcel ownership. For example, if a farmer owns a 20-acre parcel, the sliding-scale might grant two lots, an average of one per 10 acres. However, if the farmer owns 100 acres, the sliding scale might permit only 4 lots, or an average of one per 25 acres.

Sliding-scale ordinances have been adopted in several townships of York County, Pennsylvania, and Baltimore County, Maryland; and in the Dakota County, Minnesota, Townships of Ravenna and Eureka. In each of these communities, the number of lots permitted on the sliding scale varies. This is a reflection of differing patterns of land ownership, varying pressure from urban development, and local histories in land use regulation.

An attractive feature of many of these ordinances is that they pay particular concern to the type of land that may be used for residential development. In Peach Bottom Township (York County), for example, the ordinance specifies that residential lots must be placed on less productive soils or on lands that are not suited to agricultural production due to size, shape, groundcover, topography, etc. In the event that a farm contains *only* high quality soils, the unit will be permitted on prime land.

The Peach Bottom ordinance takes this concept a step further in providing for additional lots (more than permitted under the scale) if the land under consideration is not suited for agricultural production. To this extent, the Peach Bottom ordinance is performance oriented. Similar provisions are contained in the Baltimore County ordinance and the Dakota County ordinance.

As with the quarter/quarter approach, the sliding-scale approach permits farmers to sell small parcels of land for residential use without danger to the farm itself. Since the sliding scale varies inversely with farm size, the overall permitted density in the agricultural area will be small if the average farm size is large.

Communities report that the sliding-scale approach is working. Local officials generally apply the criteria rigorously and do not freely change the zone. The inclusion of performance criteria to identify the location of permitted lots and to guide future residential development is also meeting with success. Since the criteria are well defined, officials report little difficulty in interpreting them. The net result for most communities is a sizeable reduction in the number of premature rural subdivisions and a sizeable increase in the farms and farmland maintained.

A Lesson Learned

If there is any single lesson to be learned from successful local programs, it is that no one way or method will work for all communities. Instead, communities must examine a variety of approaches in light of their own needs and adapt or invent accordingly. What the innovative communities have shown is that it is possible to save farms and farmland by relying upon existing programs, enabling legislation, and institutions. This is their central, important, and reassuring contribution.

REFERENCES

1. Aspen/Pitkin County Planning Office. 1976. *Pitkin County land use plan.* Aspen, Colorado.
2. Aspen/Pitkin County Planning Office. 1976. *The Aspen/Pitkin County growth management policy plan.* Aspen, Colorado.
3. Barrows, Richard L. 1977. *Wisconsin's new Farmland Preservation Act: A comparison with other states.* In *Economic Issues.* University of Wisconsin—Extension, Madison.
4. Berry, Wendell. 1977. *The unsettling of America, culture and agriculture.* Sierra, Totowa, New Jersey.
5. Farmland Preservation Program Staff. 1979. *Participation in the Wisconsin farmland preservation program.* Madison, Wisconsin.
6. Godschalk, David R., et al. 1978. *Metropolitan Council, Minnesota.* In *Responsible Growth Management: Cases and Materials.* Center for Urban and Regional Studies, University of North Carolina, Chapel Hill.
7. Kolb, Harold, and James Johnson. 1978. *Walworth County: Can we save Marlboro County?* In Peter W. Amato [editor] *Farmland Preservation Planning: State of the Art.* University of Wisconsin—Extension, Madison.
8. Miner, Dallas D. 1976. *Farmland retention in the Washington metropolitan area.* Metropolitan Washington Council of Governments, Washington, D.C.
9. Toner, William. 1978. *Saving farms and farmlands: A community guide.* American Planning Association, Chicago, Illinois.

16

The European Experience With Farmland Protection: Some Inferences

Dallas Miner and Martin Chorich

Agricultural land in Europe faces most of the same development pressures felt in the United States. Many European nations undergoing the sort of urban sprawl common in America have taken measures to preserve agricultural land. This sprawl owes to a number of factors, most important of which is the fact that many European countries continue to urbanize. In 1946, 55 percent of the French population resided in cities. By 1968 the figure had risen to 70 percent.

Not only has the number of urban residents increased, but their per capita living space has grown as well. Higher living standards have led to construction of more single-family homes in American-style suburbs.

Many countries also have adopted regional development schemes in order to shift new industrial development to outlying and depressed regions. British attempts to locate new industry in North England and Wales, French moves to develop the Midiregion, and continuing Italian efforts to reduce the economic disparities between the industrial North and less-developed South all fall into this category.

Urban growth adversely affects agriculture in several ways. The flight of people to the cities results in lower rural populations. Urban growth both consumes land and drives up the price of farmland adjacent to the urban area, rendering many continuing agricultural land uses economically untenable. In West Germany, for example, agricultural land in outlying areas sold for an average price of $15,000 per hectare ($6,075 per acre) in 1975, while farmland adjacent to major metropolitan regions averaged $26,000 per hectare ($10,525 per acre).

The traditional advantage of farmland close to urban areas in supplying city markets with high-value specialty crops also has eroded because of lower tariff barriers and improved transportation. Israeli oranges compete with Spanish oranges in Madrid in the same way that California tomatoes compete with New Jersey tomatoes in New York City. Further complicating all of this is the tendency for urban areas to expand on the most fertile lands.

No Common Approach

Despite the similar problems faced by agriculture in the industrial West, policies and approaches in managing urban growth vary considerably from nation to nation. The great geographic, sociologic, and economic differences among countries in Europe preclude all but the most rudimentary generalizations concerning any common "European approach" to land use management.

While some European nations have population densities far greater than the United States, others remain more sparsely populated than America. Norway, Finland, and Sweden all have small populations and abundant open space, although much of this open space is in forests and mountains. Other countries, such as West Germany, Great Britain, and the Benelux nations, have population densities comparable to the most highly urbanized regions of the United States. Despite extremely dense populations, some countries, such as Great Britain, France, and West Germany, have high proportions of arable land in comparison with their total land areas.

Much European farmland lies close to urban areas. In Belgium, for example, all of the country's farmland lies within so-called peri-urban areas. West German officials have classified 27 percent of their country's land area as peri-urban.

Not surprisingly, attitudes and policies on preserving farmland from urban encroachment vary considerably from nation to nation. Generally speaking, countries with low overall population densities, one or two large urban areas, and abundant open space do not place a high priority on controlling rural land use. They restrict planning activities to urban regions. Other nations have adopted specific policies to preserve agricultural land. Still others view urban encroachment as a natural consequence of industrialization and rely on foreign sources for agricultural products.

Even where the problems of peri-urban agriculture receive official recognition, approaches to solving these problems differ. Some countries take regulatory approaches to control rural land use, while others attempt to maintain agriculture as a land use competitive with industrial and urban uses. Policies that fall into the latter category include measures to increase the size of individual holdings, the provision of urban-style cultural and social services in rural areas, and special tax benefits designed to keep farms in a family after the retirement or death of a generation of proprietors.

France, for example, places little emphasis on regulatory approaches. Instead, government-sponsored private corporations (SAFER's) buy and resell farmland to farmers interested in increasing the size and economic viability of their holdings. SAFER's have the right of first refusal in all land sales within this jurisdiction. They operate as revolving funds, buying and selling land, and paying nominal dividends to their investors. Because SAFER's historically have attempted to conserve their funds by purchasing lower cost rural land, their influence in peri-urban areas has been somewhat spotty due to higher land prices in these areas.

On the whole, European officials have somewhat less regard for the sanctity of property rights than is common in North America. European planners often make decisions affecting owners' property rights without compensating for the financial consequences of those decisions.

A relationship apparently also exists between population density and stringency of land use controls. The Netherlands, Great Britain, and West Germany all feature comprehensive land management schemes, while the less densely populated Scandanavian countries, despite their reputation for imposing bureaucratic solutions to social problems, follow almost *laissez faire* policies for rural land use.

Some Pertinent Examples

The following examples of agricultural land use policy in selected countries represent major tendencies found throughout Europe. While some of these countries are not large or densely populated, the examples illustrate variations in land use policy through observation of some archetypes.

Finland. Finland presents a fairly typical example of a sparsely populated country with few urban areas and little agricultural land. Not surprisingly, the lion's share of planning activities occur in and near urban areas, most notably the Helsinki region. Helsinki has experienced rapid growth in recent years. Although most of Finland's open space is mountainous and remains in forest, the amount of agricultural land has declined because of reductions in rural population and urban growth.

The Country's Building Act and Statute of 1958 establishes a system of regional, master, general, municipal, town, rural, and shoreline plans. The first three present general goals and policies to be followed in individual land use decisions. The latter, more localized plans, resemble American-style zoning maps in their specification of permissible uses.

Overall, these plans emphasize economic development. They do not address the urban encroachment issue specifically. However, the Helsinki regional plan attempts to steer new growth to areas with existing infrastructures (roads, sewage, utilities and so on) to minimize the cost of development. If anything, the plans place greater emphasis on preserving forests, which are almost all privately owned.

With limited agricultural production, Finland relies on foreign trade to provide much of its food. But this may change soon. Pending changes in the Building Act before parliament may place new emphasis upon agriculture.

West Germany. West Germany has accomplished the feat of rebuilding a war-shattered economy and accommodating a population of 60 million people in a land area the size of Oregon, while maintaining 29 percent of its land in forests and 55 percent in agriculture.

Since German basic law, akin to our common law, takes special note of "the social obligations of private property," it is not surprising that the West German system relies on an array of planning objectives backed by economic incentives. The most significant aspect of this system is urban limit lines within which developers have unlimited right to build, while tracts outside these lines are almost permanently devoted to low density land uses. Inside the development zones, property owners may subdivide and improve their lands. In turn, the government cannot downzone these lands without paying compensation for development rights cost. Owners outside the development zone receive no compensation for adverse changes in their land zoning status.

Additional features of the German system that work to preserve agriculture include low property taxes on farmland and regulations that restrict farmland purchases to farmers or other agricultural interests.

The Netherlands. The Netherlands' strong tradition of land use planning, which began with the country's first attempts to reclaim land from the North Sea in the thirteenth century, has resulted in one of the most comprehensive land planning programs in the industralized West. Holland enacted its first municipal planning laws in 1901 and adopted its first national planning legislation in the 1950s.

Despite its status as a small country with the world's highest population density, the Netherlands planning system is relatively decentralized. Most planning activities occur at the municipal level. The National Council for Physical Planning issues general policy guidance and reviews local planning efforts.

The planning laws require compensation of landowners adversely affected by planning decisions. As an ultimate sanction, the government may expropriate land developed in defiance of regulations. But even then the owner must be compensated for the expropriation.

To preserve farmland against urban encroachment, the Dutch have adopted a long-term rural redevelopment effort. This undertaking emphasizes improving the ability of agricultural land uses to compete with urban-industrial uses. A major element of the program is to increase farm size as a means of improving productivity and efficiency. Overall, the Dutch allow agriculture the complete freedom to develop, in this way harnessing market forces in the interest of preserving agriculture and open space.

As the Dutch government continues its program of diking and landfilling along the coast, new land generally is devoted first to agriculture. The seacoast of Holland is a matrix of canals and blocks of farmland growing not only the flowers the country is famous for but consumable crops as well. In time, as the new land stabilizes, plans will provide for new cities and some industrial expansion. However, agriculture will remain an important use of the expanding land mass.

Great Britain. The United Kingdom enacted its first land development controls in the Town and Country Planning Act of 1947. The Act established a land planning system that includes two types of plans: *structure plans*, with goals and policies followed by a jurisdiction in individual land use decisions; and *local plans*, which specify permissible uses on a property by property basis.

All new developments must receive approval by local government. The British system does not compensate landowners adversely affected by planning decisions. In contrast to the United States, the British consider land use decisions a political function of local government rather than an administrative function. Policies applied on both the local and national levels vary according to which political party controls the relevant decision-making body. Indeed, the story of land planning in Great Britain since World War II corresponds closely to the ebb and flow of Conservative and Labour party control of government.

The courts play a minor role in the British planning system. They have no right to overturn a decision reached by a governmental body. Also, parliamentary legislation usually includes clear policy guidance to local officials, further reducing the opportunity for judicial interpretation.

A continuing controversy in British land planning is the degree to which the public holds land development rights. The Community Land Act of 1975, passed by the most recent Labour government, nationalizes the right to develop land. Under the Act, local governments buy up undeveloped land and sell it to developers at its development value. In this way the public realizes the capital gains inherent in land development.

The Conservative opposition attacked the system as unduly socialistic, and some analysts suspect that landowners have trimmed back plans to improve or update their land until the new Conservative government honors the party's pledge to repeal the Act. Other observers criticize the law because it does not specifically require local governments to conduct their development activities in accordance with their local land use plans.

This emphasis upon land use planning as a political process necessarily implies a great deal of public participation in planning decisions. Britain does indeed have a strong public planning constituency. Groups, such as the Council to Protect Rural England, closely monitor land use decisions all over the country for compliance, in CPRE's case, with goals of protecting open space.

In practice, British planners have shown great care for preserving open space and agricultural land. London's greenbelt is world famous as an example of open space preservation and control of urban sprawl. Where urban development does occur, most notably in the nation's new towns program, British planners take pains to steer it to areas of marginal agricultural promise, close to existing service infrastructures.

Despite England's extensive planning efforts, a great deal of controversy exists as to their efficacy. Some analysts argue that planning has failed, noting a sharp rise in urbanization of agricultural land in recent years. Others point to figures that show while an average of 62,000 acres of agricultural land were converted to urban uses each year in the 1930s, the urbanization rate declined to 29,000 acres annually in the 1950s, and rose only to 40,000 to 43,000 acres a year during the boom years of the 1960s.

Conclusion

It is difficult to draw general conclusions from the variety of experiences with agricultural land issues in Europe. As in the United States, where counties and states are adopting different programs, there is no single approach to farmland preservation in Europe.

As mentioned, two key differences between European countries and the United States are the role of the national government and the relationship between government and landowners. At this time there is no clear national policy in the United States on farmland preservation. In contrast, a few European governments have adopted strong policies, which they are implementing through direct land use controls.

On the second point, land in the United States is regarded more as a market commodity than as a national resource. The rights of individual property owners are a dominant concern in any retention program. In several European nations property owners have much less discretion in changing from agriculture to another land use. In fact, it simply cannot be done in some instances. Agriculture is *the* established land use.

The likelihood of such a strong, national approach to agricultural land retention in this country is uncertain. Open to serious question is the desirability of this deep an intervention into the traditional relationship between government and the landowner. But this relationship is certainly changing, and many would argue that government already has intruded deeply into the domain of private property rights.

In time a national posture or policy probably will emerge in this country on the maintenance of our most productive agricultural lands. It is not likely to be patterned in any purposeful way after any particular European experience, however. Rather, it will undoubtedly be general in scope, place the burden of emphasis on state and local governments, and, most importantly, acknowledge the need for equity in dealing with the private landowner.

REFERENCES

1. Chassagne, E. 1977. *Community of land use: Historical development and limitations corrective mechanisms—the French system as an example.* Organization for Economic Cooperation and Development, Paris, France.
2. Coughlin, Robert E. 1977. *Saving the garden: The preservation of farmland and other environmentally sensitive land.* Regional Science Research Institute, Philadelphia, Pa.
3. Duerksen, Christopher J. 1976. *England's Community Land Act: A Yankee's view.* Urban Law Annual 12: 49-76.
4. Ikaheimo, Esa. 1977. *Peri-urban agriculture of the Helsinki region.* Organization for Economic Cooperation and Development, Paris, France.
5. Lassey, William R. 1977. *Planning in rural environments.* McGraw-Hill, New York, N.Y.
6. Mrohs, Edmund. 1977. *Peri-urban agriculture in the Rhein-Ruhr region.* Organization for Economic Cooperation and Development, Paris, France.
7. Organization for Economic Cooperation and Development. 1978. *Agriculture in the planning of peri-urban areas—synthesis report.* Paris, France.
8. Organization for Economic Cooperation and Development. 1976. *Land use policies and agriculture.* Paris, France.
9. Reilly, William K. 1976. *Thoughts on the second German miracle.* In *CF Letter.* The Conservation Foundation, Washington, D.C.
10. Shroad, Marion. 1976. *Does planning check the rate of farmed land loss—arguments for and against.* Council for the Protection of Rural England, London.

Index

211